Perfect
800

Perfect 800

Advanced Strategies
for Top Students **SAT Verbal**

R. Brigham Lampert

Routledge
Taylor & Francis Group

NEW YORK AND LONDON

First published 2011 by Prufrock Press Inc.

Published 2021 by Routledge
605 Third Avenue, New York, NY 10017
2 Park Square, Milton Park, Abingdon, Oxon OX14 4RN

Routledge is an imprint of the Taylor & Francis Group, an informa business

Copyright © 2011 by Taylor & Francis.

Edited by Lacy Compton
Cover and Layout Design by Marjorie Parker

Library of Congress Cataloging-in-Publication Data

Lampert, R. Brigham.
Perfect 800 : SAT verbal : advanced strategies for top students / R. Brigham Lampert.
    p. cm.
Includes bibliographical references.
ISBN 978-1-59363-434-6 (pbk.)
1. SAT (Educational test) 2. American College Testing Program. 3. Universities and colleges--United States--Entrance examinations. I. Title.

LB2353.57.L36 2011
378.1'662--dc22

                      2010037797

ISBN 13: 978-1-59363-434-6 (pbk)

Dedication
Dedicated to my wife Jennifer, the best teacher I know.

Contents

Contents

Acknowledgments

I owe thanks to many individuals for their influence and aid prior to and during the composition of this particular work, but chiefly to two parties: Dr. Joyce VanTassel-Baska, without whose encouragement and aid I simply would not have the professional opportunities that I have today; and Ms. Lacy Compton and the staff at Prufrock Press, whose patience, professionalism, and trust I absolutely appreciate and value. Thank you.

"To grammar, even kings bow."
—Molière, *The Learned Ladies* (1672)

Chapter 1

Introduction to Students

Welcome, and congratulations on making a very smart decision—to take the pursuit of improved intellectual aptitude and academic excellence into your own able hands. You may be holding this book for any number of reasons: You probably want to perform as highly as possible on the SAT test, you might want to expand your vocabulary by learning about the origins and parts of complicated words, or perhaps you really want to understand just why and where to put those confusing commas (the "put it where there's a pause" rule of thumb is just insufficient, after all). Regardless of why you have decided to use this book, you have made a very good choice.

To my knowledge, the approach to instruction and growth that I took in crafting this book is unique among SAT preparatory texts, most of which simply contain an explanation of the test itself, a few simple tips for success, and a whole bunch of practice tests and answer keys. Many teachers call the type of preparation that such a book offers "drill and kill," an ominous name for something that is supposed to help you grow!

This book does include the same kind of practice assessments, as well as access to two online multiple choice tests that provide you with individualized question-by-question results and strategies, but its major content is a precisely organized daily curriculum for improving your facility with vocabulary, grammar, punctuation, and comparative thinking. As a career classroom teacher, I believe that major intellectual growth and the accumulation of scholarly knowledge take time. Just as a bodybuilder cannot develop powerful muscles overnight, as a gymnast does not reach the Olympics in 1 or 2 months, so too can students not truly achieve their mental potentials in a short amount of time. Contrary to what all of those test prep books and tutoring services apparently want you to believe, there is no magic bullet that can quickly slay the SAT.

Real growth takes time, and patience is a critical ingredient of any kind of success, but time by itself is not enough. To conquer the SAT and expand your linguistic understanding, you also need to undertake smartly the right regimen, which is where the curriculum that you are holding comes into play. To get out of this book your full intellectual benefit and test preparation, you will need half a year—6 months of completing a one-page worksheet or multiple choice quiz every day. You can think of them all as academic vitamins; the SAT is looming, and it's time to get healthy!

What to Expect on the SAT

Recently, the national media has spotlighted a growing minority of colleges that have chosen not to require students' completion of the SAT, but instead to accept it as an optional part of applications (Bruno, 2006; Landau, 2008). Relieved young adults nationwide might rejoice at this perhaps overstated news, but the fact remains that the vast majority of American undergraduate institutions still require their applicants to complete—and to excel on—the SAT. Therefore, the test should really be considered not only an important part of your college planning process, but also an experience for which you really must be prepared, knowing ahead of time what you will face.

Parts of the SAT

The SAT, as you surely already know, is one really long test: 3 hours and 45 minutes, not including stretch breaks. It is comprised of 10 sections of tasks administered one after another. Your performance on these 10 sections is then apportioned out over three different numerical scores: Math, Critical Reading, and Writing. Each of these three scores can range from 200 to 800, so the entire SAT is designed to serve as a measurement of your intelligence, knowledge, and readiness for college, calculated from 600 to 2400.

This book will not help you to prepare for the mathematical portions of the test. Instead, *Perfect 800: SAT Math*, also available from Prufrock Press, is an excellent resource that I recommend. The curriculum included here *will* prepare you fully for the test's Critical Reading tasks: identifying and using vocabulary correctly, comprehending both long and short passages of prose, and making inferences and judgments based on authors' points of view.

The Writing portion of the SAT includes a larger variety of tasks. This book's course of study will prepare you to spot and diagnose grammatical errors, edit sentences successfully, utilize punctuation correctly, and fix issues with diction and syntax. This text does not specifically address two additional tasks of the Writing test, improving large paragraphs and composing a timed argumentative essay, although the learning imbibed from your daily regimen will indirectly help you with both of them.

Timing

On average, you have about 1 minute to answer each multiple choice question on the SAT. The actual breakdown is not legitimately that simple, however, because more time is required to complete the reading comprehension portions of the test than the error identification sections, for example. All told, time management is critical to SAT success, for students who take much more than 1 minute on a given question or two usually have to rush through other questions at the end, rarely performing well overall as a result.

Field-Testing

A little-known fact about the SAT is that one of those 10 sections completed by students actually does not count toward their scores. The College Board, which produces this test, among others, always includes one "practice" section on every SAT, the purpose of which is to field-test newly written questions for their utility and validity (i.e., whether they are actually well-written questions that can be used legitimately on a later SAT). Students never know which section of the 10 is the field-test section (although it will not be the essay assignment), so you should try your best on every one. Nevertheless, if you walk out of the SAT worrying that you did just terribly on one section that you did not understand, then cheer up . . . perhaps it won't count.

What This Book Contains

According to study results published by the College Board itself, students can improve their results on the SAT through coaching, preparation, and practice (Powers & Rock, 1998). Obviously, not all types or styles of coaching and preparation offer equivalent amounts of impact. In using this book and its particular approach to SAT preparation, you of course want the greatest improvement possible. To that end, contained in these pages is a complete, classroom-tested curriculum for not only growing as a student and thinker, but also earning a high score on the SAT. You will absolutely learn more from it than from a couple of sessions of "drill and kill."

Daily Worksheets

The heart of this text is a series of 162 worksheets, to be completed one day at a time. All of the worksheets are formatted in the same manner, and they each require of you the same skills and mental processes. Please examine the following sample, which is identical in layout to the 162 that you shall complete.

Grammar and punctuation. The top of each worksheet requires you to analyze one sentence containing some sort of grammatical error. This sentence could be incorrect because of punctuation, word choice/diction, incorrect sequencing of words and phrases/syntax, or structure, but it definitely contains only one error. Explanations of how and why all worksheets' sentences must be rewritten can be found on pages 191–236, but you should never look there first. Instead, try to find the error yourself, then correct it on the worksheet. Next, you should explain why that particular correction was necessary, and then name the type of error; this final task will probably prove difficult at first, but over the course of your preparation, you will slowly begin to recognize the commonness of many errors and more easily name them all.

Vocabulary and morphology. The middle of each worksheet holds the vocabulary word of the day. Its central oval is connected to five other shapes that must be filled. Prefixes, suffixes, and roots are linguistic building blocks, small parts of *our* language that we have taken from others, such as ancient Greek and Latin. These small parts are called "morphemes," and the process of identifying, defining, and studying them, which is what you do as you complete each worksheet, is called "morphology." For a more detailed explanation of morphology, as well as of its close cousin, etymology, please read the section on Vocabulary, Etymology, and Morphology on pages 23–25 in Chapter 2 of this book.

On the other side of the central oval, you are required to put the morphemes' individual meanings together to determine the overall definition of the vocabulary word; you should feel free to write the definition both with precision (i.e., using the morphemes' particular meanings) and in your own words. The final shape, "What It Looks Like," can be filled in one of two ways: You can either describe with words an example of that vocabulary word in reality, or you can draw an example. Both of these approaches will help you to remember a word's definition by providing you with something realistic to which you can mentally affix your vocabulary.

Analogical exercise. The SAT did not always require students to write essays. When I took the test in the early 1990s, it instead included a section

Ungrammatical Sentence:

When I arrived at my new school, I underwent the infamous process of "newcomer induction;" it was not as trying as I worried that it would be.

Explanation of Error:

Type of Error:

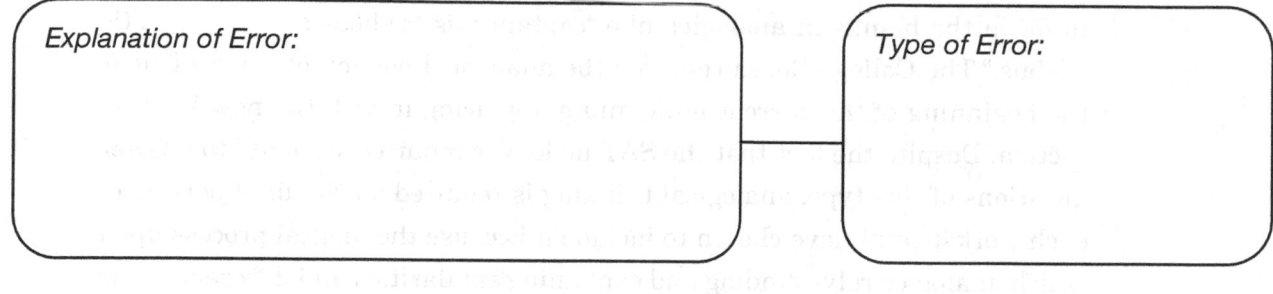

Prefix:

Definition:

Root:

induction

(Sample #1)

Suffix:

What it Looks Like:

Analogous Exercise:

induction : naturalized citizens   _____ : police officers

Why? Nature of the Relationship:

Original Analogy Using the Vocabulary Word:

of analogical reasoning; probably some of your teachers recall the same experience. An analogy is a comparison of things based on their relationships to one another, and this portion of the test required students to choose how best to fill in the blanks in analogies like "captain : (is to) boat as _____ : (is to) bus." The College Board removed the analogical portion of the SAT near the beginning of the current millennium, replacing it with the new Writing section. Despite the fact that the SAT no longer requires students to answer questions of this type, analogical thinking is required on the final portion of each worksheet; I have chosen to include it because the mental process upon which analogies rely—finding and explaining similarities and differences—is simply the most effective way to learn and remember new academic information (Marzano, Pickering, & Pollock, 2001). To complete the bottom portion of each worksheet, you need not only to fill in the blank to complete the analogy, but also to explain why your choice completes the comparison correctly and to come up with an original analogy using the day's vocabulary word.

As you can see from the completed example of the sample worksheet, the entire daily process is straightforward, despite requiring some advanced intellectual reasoning. Keep in mind that if you ever get stuck, explanations as to how worksheets should be completed are found in the answer key on pages 191–236 of this book. Use those daily explanations to double-check your own thinking and work.

Each daily worksheet should take no more than 10 or 15 minutes to complete, which is not a huge investment of time to achieve the big results of improved vocabulary, grammatical understanding, and SAT performance. At the end of 6 months, however, your thinking skills, cache of linguistic knowledge, and familiarity with the SAT will have developed strongly.

Practice Quizzes

Beginning on page 237 of this book, you will find nine quizzes that assess your understanding of information used to complete the worksheets. Each multiple choice quiz is designed to follow a series of 18 consecutive worksheets, so the first quiz tests your understanding of worksheets 1–18, the second quiz assesses your knowledge of worksheets 19–36, and so on. The quizzes are formatted to resemble actual portions of the SAT, and they thereby make up the part of this curriculum where you get to practice those test-taking strategies that I list in this chapter. The sections on each quiz include:

- *Section 1: Fill in the blank.* The first section of each multiple-choice quiz assesses your ability to choose and use vocabulary. Many such questions appear on the SAT itself, formatted in a similar way, so building your familiarity and comfort with fill-in-the-blank vocabulary questions will

Ungrammatical Sentence:

When I arrived at my new school, I underwent the infamous process of "newcomer induction;" it was not as trying as I worried that it would be.

Explanation of Error:
Semicolons are placed outside of quotation marks.

Type of Error:
Punctuation

Prefix:
in = inside

Definition:
the act of leading someone inside of a larger body or group.

Root:
duct = lead

induction
(Sample #1)

Suffix:
ion = the act or state of

What it Looks Like:
a process of education and/or a ceremony.

Analogous Exercise:

induction : naturalized citizens

going through the Police academy : police officers

Why? Nature of the Relationship:
the former is the process by which someone joins the latter group

Original Analogy Using the Vocabulary Word:
Induction = anyone
baptism = religious convert

pay off on the test itself. Some questions require the choice of one vocabulary word and some require two, but in all cases you will only be able to choose words (and variations of them) from the previous 18 worksheets.

- *Section 2: Revision.* On Section 2 of each quiz, you must determine how to write correctly an underlined portion of a sentence. Sometimes the underlined portion will be written correctly already, and sometimes entire sentences will be underlined, but make sure that you pay careful attention to punctuation marks and to the portions of each sentence that are *not* underlined; they might be necessary to find the correct answer. This part of each quiz resembles a portion of the SAT used to calculate your Writing score.

- *Section 3: Error recognition.* Next, you do not need to correct any errors—you just need to spot them. This section of each quiz mimics another part of the Writing test, which is more difficult than sentence revision in one critical way: In this case, a great variety of things could potentially be wrong with a sentence, so you must be on the lookout for many more grammatical "traps." Again, you will ultimately use the same skills and knowledge to succeed on the SAT itself.

- *Section 4: Reading comprehension.* Pound for pound, comprehension and analysis of prose passages constitute more of the SAT than any other task does. Questions based on paragraphs join fill-in-the-blank vocabulary questions to make up the entirety of a student's Critical Reading score, from 200 to 800. Section 4 of each quiz in this book requires you to read and understand a passage of text with which you are probably not already familiar, and then answer multiple-choice questions using your vocabulary words.

Glossaries

At the back of this book, on pages 259–275, are two glossaries that will probably become invaluable to you as you move through this curriculum. You should definitely feel free to use them as a resource while completing the worksheets, and you may even be more successful in the first place if you take some time to read and familiarize yourself with them before starting the curriculum. The two glossaries are described below:

- *Morphemes.* This glossary includes all of the morphemes found in this book, which are thus necessary to complete its curriculum. Each morpheme's entry defines it, offers etymological information, and provides an example of its usage. Keep in mind that the English language contains many morphemes not found in this glossary, so you should not consider this list exhaustive.

- *Grammatical terms and errors.* The second glossary includes many key grammatical terms with which you must be familiar in order to succeed with this program of study. These grammatical terms range from the commonplace (noun) to the particular (demonstrative pronoun), and in some cases even to the whimsical (seesaw conjunction); it includes names of errors (faulty comparison) and explanations of common acronyms (e.g.), as well as parts of sentences and speech. Again, while this list should not be considered exhaustive, it surely will serve you as a very helpful resource.

Extraneous Online Tests

Finally, your use of this book entitles you to access two online tests designed to assess even more fully your learning and readiness for the SAT. The tests can be found by visiting http://www.prufrock.com/perfect800. The first test is based on worksheets 1–81, and the second on worksheets 82–162. They are formatted identically to the 9 multiple choice quizzes found in this book, although the order of sections and the numbers of questions found on the online tests vary, just as they will on the actual SAT. After you complete each test, the online service will provide you with a personalized score and diagnosis, identify which questions you answered correctly and incorrectly, suggest worksheets for you to revisit in order to boost your performance, and assess whether you are ready to achieve to your desired level in taking the actual SAT.

This last component of the results report will quantify your performance as a Verbal score from 200 to 800. It is important to note that although this curriculum's tests and quizzes resemble the SAT, they do not require you to edit longer paragraphs of text, nor to compose a timed essay. Therefore, the numerical scores with which you are provided online should not be considered true reflections of what you will earn on the actual SAT, which differentiates between Writing and Critical Reading performances; instead, you should consider this Verbal score a relative, albeit accurate, combination of these two areas.

How and Why to Use These Materials

Undertaking your own preparation for SAT success is commendable, and it surely will be made easier and less stressful if you follow the course of study provided by this book. Moreover, adhering to the daily regimen outlined below will get you through the curriculum within 6 months. Realistically, it is acceptable and perhaps inevitable that you will have to skip a day or two, or otherwise alter the course of study to fit your schedule; after all, there are college visits to make! As any successful dieter or physical exerciser will tell you, however, daily consistency is the key to achievement, so try your best to stick rigidly to the following program.

Three Steps

No matter what piece of this curriculum you complete on any given day, you should follow this simple rule: Keep your progress to one part per day. Do not try to cram the first 9 worksheets into your brain at once; it assuredly will not work. Give yourself room to breathe, time to absorb information, reflect, and sleep on it. The three steps to finishing this program successfully are:

- **Complete one worksheet per day.** On the first day of your studies, complete Worksheet 1. You may need to use the glossaries and the explanations found on pages 259–275, which is fine. Look over the worksheet again later that day, perhaps several times. Set it aside in a place that you will remember; you are going to come back to all of your worksheets later to study them. On the second day, complete Worksheet 2, and so on.
- **Take a quiz after every 18 worksheets.** Each multiple-choice quiz is based on a series of 18 consecutive worksheets, so once you have completed Worksheets 1–18, gather them up and revisit them, studying their information to whatever degree necessary. On the 19th day of your studies, do not complete a worksheet; instead, take and score the first multiple-choice quiz. You will complete Worksheet 19 on the following day, the 20th, so let the quiz constitute all of what you accomplish in one day. Do the same thing once you have completed Worksheets 19–36, then Worksheets 37–54, and so on.
- **Take an online test in the middle and at the end.** The same direction stands for the two online tests. After you have completed Worksheets 1–81, take the first test online. Do not complete any additional worksheets on that day. Peruse your score report and suggestions, then review the worksheets suggested for you. Worksheet 82 can wait until tomorrow. At the end of the curriculum, complete the second online test, assessing your understanding of worksheets 82–162. Your final steps? Review as necessary . . . then, take the SAT.

Benefits of Following the Curriculum

Undertaking the learning processes provided by this book will help you in several important ways. This entire curriculum requires patience, persistence, and careful attention, but at the end of it, the growth that you experience should be clear and will include the following:

- **Academic and intellectual growth.** An intelligent young person already, you should finish this curriculum having gained an enhanced vocabulary, improved editing skills, an understanding of punctuation devices and rules, a thorough grasp of common English syntax, experience with diagnostic morphology, stronger reading abilities, and improved facility with analogical thinking. A pretty good outcome for 10 minutes a day!

- **Improved SAT performance.** Especially in utilizing this book's multiple choice quizzes and online tests, your familiarity with SAT sections, questions, and skills will grow. You will enter the testing area when it really counts, already knowing what to expect and having practiced how to succeed. The next step? College acceptance!

- **Preparation for college-level thinking.** Once you get there, hopefully having matriculated to the college of your choice, you should find greater success than you perhaps would have otherwise. This curriculum is designed to strengthen your writing and editing skills, which will be necessary regardless of your chosen field of undergraduate study. Your vocabulary and reading comprehension will be stronger, which is important because so much learning is accomplished in college through independent reading materials. Moreover, your problem-solving abilities and study habits should be enhanced, so guiding your own chosen course in college will be both easier and more rewarding.

Strategies for Success

Going through this book's learning program will help you to succeed on the SAT, but this book by itself is not the only testing advantage that you may need. It is also helpful to go into the experience knowing what to expect and having several strategies—insiders' tricks—for each section that you will be asked to complete.

To Guess or Not to Guess: How the Test is Scored

The first thing that you should know is how the College Board is going to score your results. As previously noted, each SAT contains more than 150 questions of various kinds, plus one essay to be written. The essay is graded from 2 to 12 points. All multiple-choice questions are scored according to this formula: Correct answers add 1 point to your score, incorrect answers subtract 1/4 point from your score, and omitted questions (yes, you *can* leave some blank) neither add to nor subtract from your score. This scoring system suggests a very simple tip for making educated guesses on questions to which you do not know the answers—after eliminating obviously incorrect answers, or if you can whittle down the possibly correct answers to three choices, then you should guess, as the odds will then be in your favor. If you cannot eliminate one or two choices, then do not guess, lest you be more likely to lose points than gain them.

Tips and Strategies for Error Recognition Questions

The following strategies should be helpful in guiding you to pick the correct answers to those questions that ask you to find the errors in sentences:

1. *Read each sentence, not just each underlined choice, carefully.* You are going to select only the section of each sentence that contains an error, but sometimes those errors are only visible in relation to something elsewhere in the sentence. For example, if you need to diagnose a "neither/nor" error, then you must be sure to spot both the "neither" and the "nor," even if they do not appear in the same answer choice. In other words, *do not* just read the underlined portions.

2. *Think about how an underlined choice should be corrected before you choose it.* Yes, you should probably guess if you can use a process of elimination to whittle the possible answers down to three, but you are even more likely to pick the correct answer to a question if you can identify just how it should be corrected. In other words, if you identify a misused comma in an underlined section of text, knowing exactly why it is wrong and how it should be written correctly, then feel confident in choosing that answer—you know your stuff!

3. *Keep in mind that some sentences do not contain errors.* Students sometimes trick themselves into thinking that every sentence contains an error; do not fall into this trap. To analogize, a good doctor knows not only how to diagnosis someone's illness, but also how to identify a healthy patient.

Tips and Strategies for Sentence Revision

The tips listed below should be helpful to you as you undertake the sentence revision section of the SAT test:

1. *This type of question requires almost the opposite skill.* Although error recognition questions ask you to identify whether and where errors exist in sentences that may be correct as written, these questions for the most part assume that there is an error in each sentence, and they even point out to you where it is . . . you just have to know how to fix it. Do not imagine errors existing in places that are not underlined;

assume that those parts of each sentence are correct. If you have completed your worksheets and studied your grammar and punctuation, then these questions might be easier for you—not as many things could potentially be wrong with each one.

2. *Not so fast . . . these sentences also might be correct as written.* Note the third tip above, and do not fall into the trap of thinking that something *must* be wrong. The contents of this book should help you to know—not to suppose—how and why to fix each error, so if you cannot spot what's wrong, then think twice before taking a wild guess.

3. *Make sure to read each possible answer in the context of the entire sentence.* Each of these questions will present a possible revision of only one part of a sentence, so something that may appear correct by itself might actually conflict with another correctly written part of the sentence. It is rare that one of these questions asks you to consider revision of an entire sentence, so make sure that you do not just investigate the stand-alone choices without reading the rest.

Tips and Strategies for Reading Comprehension

If you want to improve your reading comprehension score, then you might consider the following suggestions:

1. *Read engagingly; mark up your test.* As a whole, questions requiring the understanding and interpretation of prose passages constitute more of the SAT than any other type of question does. There are *a lot* of these questions, and adding the time that it takes to answer them to the additional time necessary to read each passage . . . well, it's only human nature to zone out after a while. To prevent yourself from doing so, try to practice engaged reading by interacting with the passages, marking them up when you hit a key character, big idea, important date, new topic, crucial sentence, or anything else worth noting. Additionally, some students find it helpful to scan each series of questions first, then just pencil a mark next to each part of the passage about which a question will be asked (e.g., "On line 7, the word 'horticulture' expresses . . . "). Afterward, having begun to read the passage as a whole, those students know that every time they hit a pencil mark, it's time to perk up. There's a question about *that* part of the text.

2. *The passage must support your answer.* You should recognize that the general SAT is not supposed to test students' knowledge of a particular field of study, but rather aptitude for utilizing basic skills and common knowledge. Therefore, every question of this type is answerable

based strictly on information given in or assumable from its relevant passage. Do not convince yourself that a particular answer is correct because of something that you learned in science class, because it is just like that thing that you heard on the news, or because it kind of, sort of has to do with what the passage is about. If it's not clear in or from the passage, then it's not correct.

3. *Determine the author's intention, audience, and point of view.* Let's say you are asked to read a passage about Ronald Reagan, then answer 10 questions about it. To do so correctly, your knowledge and/or opinion of the former President is totally inconsequential; the SAT is not testing your personal philosophies. Instead, you should determine *the author's* point of view. Is the purpose of the passage to criticize, to applaud, or to inform someone about Reagan? Was it written for a newspaper, a history textbook, or a letter home? Are the people likely to read this passage for, against, indifferent to, or ignorant of the former President's policies and impact? If you can figure out all of the above information, then you will likely be able to answer correctly most of those 10 questions.

Strategies for Vocabulary Usage

The following suggestions will help you improve your scores on the most dreaded part of SAT study for many students—vocabulary:

1. *Know your prefixes, suffixes, and roots.* Many students find these questions difficult because words—potential answers—are written in isolation, totally devoid of context. If one of the answer choices is "interject," but you do not know what that word means . . . well, you must be up a creek, right? Not if you have completed, have studied, and now remember this book's daily worksheets. After all, you recognize the root "ject" from Worksheet 91 and the prefix "inter" from Worksheet 40; by putting the two together, you know that the word's literal meaning is "to throw between." *Voilà*, all of a sudden you know the definition of the word and whether it is the correct choice. Our language is constructed in just this way (piecemeal), so study those morphemes!

2. *Pay attention to negative, transitional, and introductory words and phrases.* This section of the SAT tests both students' vocabularies *and* their ability to comprehend the meanings of sentences. Take, for example, a sentence like "Despite my own hunger, I probably could not be accurately described as -----." Of the five imagined choices, the correct answer is the word "famished," but a student would not understand

the correctness of that word if he or she neglected to read or focus on the words "Despite" and "not"; in other words, take the word "not" out of this sentence, and "famished" does not make sense at all. Questions involving such words are tricky because they obscure straightforward meaning, so pay those little words careful attention.

3. *Use a process of elimination to make two-word questions simpler.* Some questions of this type require you to choose a pair of words that complete a sentence correctly, thereby making your task twice as difficult; after all, it is harder to solve two problems than one. Actually, if you consider the meaning of each word alone, then you might be able to eliminate answer choices not because they are totally incorrect, but because they are at least *partly* incorrect. In other words, even if the first part of choice (d) makes sense, if the second part does not work, then (d) is not the answer, period.

General Test-Taking Strategies

The strategies in the previous sections are great for just the verbal sections of the test, but you have to take the math portion too, right? The advice below will help your performance on the SAT as a whole; after all, you are aiming to raise that composite score and get into the best colleges possible!

1. *Bring your own watch.* Because time management is so important to success on the SAT, a prudent preparation for the test is to ensure that you always know how much time is left on any given section. You cannot guarantee that you will be seated facing the clock while taking this test, and even if you are, then you cannot guarantee that you are going to remember to look up at it as often as you should. Wear a watch to the test, and set it on your desk. As each section begins, mark the time and calculate exactly when your time for that section will end, then write them both down. If you can keep track of time yourself, then you are less likely to run out of it when it matters.

2. *Chew gum.* No kidding! No matter what rules your teachers may have about gum-chewing in their classrooms, science has demonstrated that, both in scholastic classes and when taking standardized tests, students who chew gum actually outperform students who do not chew gum in several measurable ways (Gajilan, 2009; Roan, 2009). For years, I heard this idea and professed its common sense to my students. It only makes sense, after all, that repetitively moving muscles close to the brain helps to keep a person alert, but I was never sure how substantiated the claim was. Now that scientific studies demonstrate the legitimacy of this tactic, you can bank on it. Do not

expect miracles, of course; a stick of gum is no match for good, old-fashioned studying, but you *should* feel confident in knowing that carrying a pack of gum to the SAT is akin to having at least a small secret weapon.

3. *Skip questions, but come back to them.* Every multiple-choice question is worth 1 point if answered correctly. How hard or easy a question is does not change that value, so if you find yourself spending too much time on one particularly difficult question, then circle it and skip to the next one. Leave that answer blank for the time being, but try to leave enough time at the end of the section so that you can return to all of those questions with which you had trouble. One of the worst things that you could do to yourself on a 25-minute section of the SAT is to spend 15 minutes trying to puzzle out the correct answer to question #2, then have to rush through all of the rest. Because easy questions are worth as much as difficult questions, make sure to answer all of the easy ones first.

You have surely heard the old expression that life is a journey. Well, so is education. From beginning to end, your schooling leads and transforms you, ultimately taking you to what we all hope is a beautiful, fulfilling destination. The SAT is a major part of that journey, just as is the transition from high school to college. I hope that this book helps you to take the wheel, accelerate your intellect, and cruise to success. Good luck!

Chapter 2

Introduction to Teachers

As of 2010, there is no national mandate enforcing the aggregate number of days that school divisions in the United States must require students in their communities to attend school each calendar year. All states' Departments of Education, and largely individual school districts themselves, are allowed to dictate how many instructional days constitute one academic year in their respective locales, although the majority of them require 180 days, which is effectively the norm in this country.

This book offers an instructional methodology for grammar, vocabulary, analogical thinking, and SAT Verbal test preparation intended to fill an entire academic year of 180 days. This curriculum includes 162 daily worksheets, each of which should require no more than 10 minutes to complete, alongside 9 quizzes that synthesize the content of those worksheets and are formatted to mimic the SAT Verbal test sections. Additionally, two larger exams are available online, likewise formatted to resemble the SAT, but incorporating and assessing students on a greater amount of material than the quizzes do. All told, then, this book offers 173 days of focused, systematic instruction specifically aimed to raise students' lexical faculties, grammatical awareness and abilities, and SAT Verbal scores. Allowing several days for the inevitable fire drills, assemblies, early releases, and inclement weather delays, that's a full school year of field-tested, pedagogically sound English instruction.

Contents of This Book

The heart of this instructional methodology is surely the cadre of 162 daily instructional worksheets. The reproducible page found here is a sample, with which you can introduce your students to this daily activity.

The completion that this worksheet requires is separable into three distinct portions: the grammatical section at the top of the page, the morphological content in the center, and the analogical activity at the bottom. All of the 162 worksheets are formatted identically to this one, and each one asks of students the same engagement and task completion.

The sentence at the top of the worksheet always requires correction. In some cases the error stems from a misuse of punctuation, in others it is syntactical in nature, while in still other worksheets the error concerns incorrectly used diction. This sample worksheet requires that the semicolon be placed outside of the quotation marks, where semicolons always go. Additionally, students in all cases are asked to explain the grammatical errors, then categorize or name them. The sequence of 162 worksheets has been structured so that every error is presented three times, which will aid students' retention of their learning through reinforced, sequenced instruction.

Next, students are asked to dissect each vocabulary word of the day into its composite prefix(es), root, and suffix(es). The class's morphological cache will grow steadily as the year proceeds and students progress through these daily worksheets, for almost every root morpheme arises at least twice throughout the course of this curriculum, and the prefixes and suffixes recur far more readily. Students will thus not only learn *how* and *why* particular English words actually mean what they do, but also discover linguistic patterns that can effectively grow their lexicons and lexical potential far beyond the scope of just these 162 individual words. Please note that the 162 vocabulary words are not equally complicated, nor perhaps equally new to students. The word "sympathetic" (Worksheet 158), for example, is a much more common word than is "exonerate" (Worksheet 38); students are likelier to know and to use the former than the latter, even before instruction via this curriculum. Nevertheless, I urge you not to skip any of the sequential worksheets, even if a given vocabulary word strikes you as "too easy." After all, the purpose of progressing through this curriculum is not only to garner new words for students' personal lexicons, but also to encounter, recognize, and master the morphemes of which many, many more English words are constructed. In other words, the most important learning to be gained from Worksheet 158 is not the definition of the word "sympathetic" itself, but rather the meanings and usages of the morphemes "sym," "path," and "ic"—themselves the keys to unlocking a vocabulary much larger than 162 words.

Ungrammatical Sentence:

When I arrived at my new school, I underwent the infamous process of "newcomer induction;" it was not as trying as I worried that it would be.

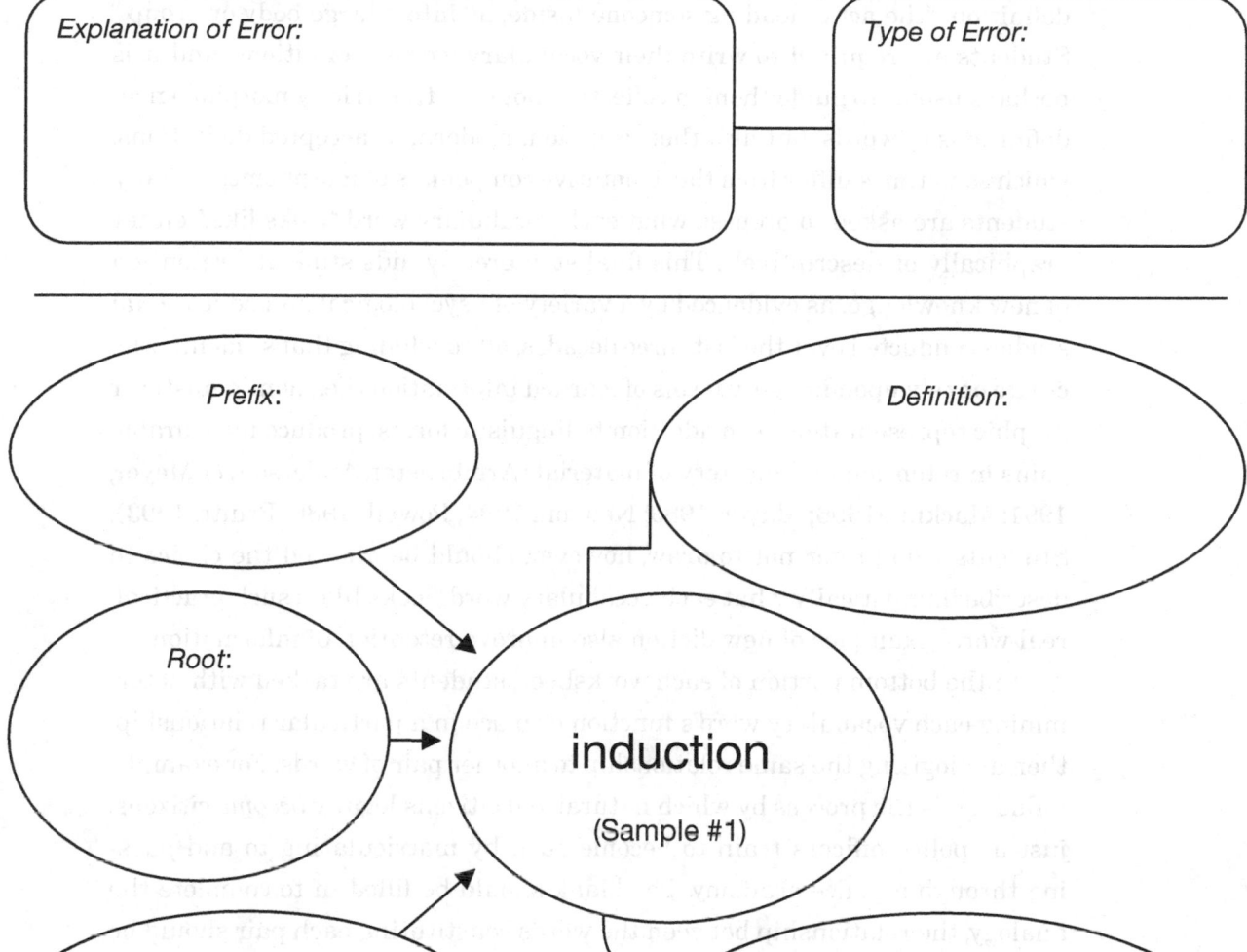

Explanation of Error:	Type of Error:

Prefix:

Definition:

Root:

induction

(Sample #1)

Suffix:

What it Looks Like:

Analogous Exercise:

induction : naturalized citizens   _____ : police officers

Why? Nature of the Relationship:	Original Analogy Using the Vocabulary Word:

On this sample worksheet, the vocabulary word of the day, "induction," is separable into the prefix "in-," the root morpheme "duct," and the suffix "-ion." Compounded, the three morphemes constitute the vocabulary word's definition: "the act of leading someone inside, as into a large body or group." Students are required to write their vocabulary words' definitions, and it is perhaps useful to guide them in collecting not only the strictly morphological definitions of words, but also their common, modern, or accepted definitions, which sometimes differ from the denotative compounds of morphemes. Finally, students are asked to propose what each vocabulary word "looks like," either graphically or descriptively. This final step greatly aids students' retention of new knowledge, as evidenced by a variety of psychological and educational studies conducted over the last three decades, all concluding that students who create or rely upon imagery forms of learned information (i.e., nonlinguistic or graphic representations), in addition to linguistic forms, produce measurable gains in retention and mastery of material (Armbruster, Anderson, & Meyer, 1991; Macklin, 1996; Mayer, 1989; Newton, 1994; Powell, 1980; Pruitt, 1993). Students who prefer not to draw, however, should be allowed the choice to describe linguistically what each vocabulary word "looks like"; such practical, real-world examples of new diction also improve retention of information.

In the bottom portion of each worksheet, students are tasked with determining each vocabulary word's function or place in a particular relationship, then analogizing the same relationship to another pair of words. For example, induction is the process by which naturalized citizens legally *become* citizens, just as police officers train to become such by matriculating to and passing through a police academy. The blank should be filled in to complete the analogy, the relationship between the words constituting each pair should be explained, and the students need to construct an original analogy using the same vocabulary word.

This second reproducible page demonstrates how the sample worksheet should appear when completed properly.

I recommend that you share this sample worksheet, in both its original and completed forms, with your students prior to administering to them Worksheet 1, the first of 162 that they will need to complete. Modeling the procedure for students in this way will help them to envision what they must accomplish each day and will greatly expedite the rate at which they can jump into the assigned task. Moreover, I strongly urge that you not simply tell students how to complete each portion of these worksheets, but rather let them guess and hit upon the "right answers" themselves. It is sometimes difficult for teachers to allow ample wait time after questioning students for verbal responses. After all, we might posit, if students do not know the

Name:_____ Date:_____

Ungrammatical Sentence:

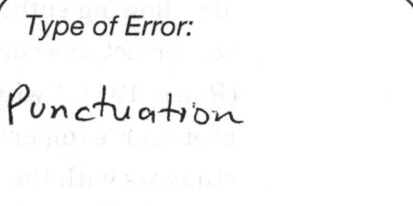

When I arrived at my new school, I underwent the infamous process of "newcomer induction;" it was not as trying as I worried that it would be.

Explanation of Error:
Semicolons are placed outside of quotation marks.

Type of Error:
Punctuation

Prefix:
in = inside

Definition:
the act of leading someone inside of a larger body or group.

Root:
duct = lead

induction
(Sample #1)

Suffix:
ion = the act or state of

What it Looks Like:
a process of education and/or a ceremony.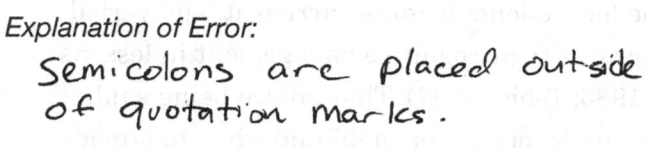

Analogous Exercise:

induction : naturalized citizens

going through the Police academy : police officers

Why? Nature of the Relationship:
the former is the process by which someone joins the latter group

Original Analogy Using the Vocabulary Word:
Induction = anyone
baptism = religious convert

correct answers to our questions, then we must not be doing a fine enough job of teaching them; silence is thus subliminally, if not consciously, associated with instructional failure. Contrary to this very human tendency to fill dead air, allowing sufficient wait time for students to guess, arrive at, and verbalize correct answers actually improves their cognitive engagement in lessons (Rowe, 1974; Swift & Gooding, 1983; Tobin, 1987). That advice being said, it is of course important to know when "enough is enough" and when to provide students with the information, with which they simply might be totally unfamiliar, necessary for success on any part of a task.

As stated previously, in addition to the daily worksheets, there are nine multiple-choice quizzes included in this book, each of which assesses students' mastery of the material delivered via the previous 18 sequential worksheets. These nine quizzes mimic the SAT Verbal test portions in form and requirements, and students' success on the quizzes should not only demonstrate their mastery of this book's morphological and grammatical content, but also raise their level of comfort in fulfilling the cognitive demands of the SAT itself, thereby raising students' SAT scores through familiarity. This outcome would be consistent with the College Board's own published findings that coaching has a positive effect on students' performance on the SAT (Powers & Rock, 1998).

Answer keys are provided for each of the nine quizzes, as well as for the 162 daily worksheets, and two glossaries—one of grammatical errors and terms and the other of morphemes—round out this text's curriculum. I advise you to make both of these glossaries available to students when you first begin using the series of worksheets, as they should prove to be invaluable resources throughout your pupils' studies.

Pedagogical Framework

Grammatical Instruction

As most English teachers in American public high schools can testify, a great number of students at all educational levels are taught simply—and incorrectly—that a comma should be inserted into a sentence "where there's a pause." Even more inaccurately, some instructors amend that rule by informing students to "put a comma where you take a breath." Sadly, but truly, such misinformation guides forever how, where, and why many young people use commas in their writing.

Syntactical misunderstandings are just as common. Sure, many students know the rule that sentences should not end with what many can only identify as "those little words beginning with 'p,'" but those same students are perhaps hard-pressed to identify actual prepositions themselves, and probably more unlikely to explain the underlying reason for this "no concluding preposition" ban. In my experience, rare is the ninth grader who actually identifies a split infinitive as a grammatical error, and as for how one correctly uses a semicolon . . . forget it.

This stereotyped portrait of American education is probably painted unfairly, but I offer it to illustrate why and how I approach grammatical instruction in this book. Students should absolutely be taught where and how to use semicolons correctly, but such instruction is insufficient. They should also be taught terminology relevant to that instruction (e.g., independent vs. dependent clauses), as well as the reasons behind particular grammatical rules and the causes of common grammatical errors. Finally, I believe that students should be able to discuss English grammar using precise diction, thus requiring them to know the common names of terms and errors: split infinitives, misplaced modifiers, introductory phrases, appositives, and so forth. Accomplishing all of the above has been my goal in designing the grammatical lessons found in this book, all of which require identification, correction, explanation, and naming of errors. In fact, these daily grammatical lessons mimic the class-starting activities that I have used throughout my career, and the academic and intellectual gains that my own students have achieved as a result of such concise, precise daily practice have been (perhaps paradoxically) both inspiring and predictable. Year after year in my own experience, the educative utility of my own "daily edits" is as assured as anything can be in the dynamic, uncertain life of a classroom educator. Please note that a glossary of grammatical terms encountered in this book can be found on pages 269–275.

Vocabulary, Etymology, and Morphology

The terms "etymology" and "morphology" are used interchangeably by many people, but the two fields of study are actually concerned with different, albeit related, aspects of word formation. Morphology is concerned with the creation of words via morphemes, or small, wholly indivisible units of linguistic meaning. Etymology is concerned with the cultural origins and transformations of those morphemes, and thus of the larger words that they help to form. Plainly stated, morphology is concerned strictly with structure and word mechanics, while etymology is concerned with history. Both fields are relevant to the pedagogical approach to vocabulary instruction taken by this book.

A brief explanation of the term "morpheme" is here purposeful. The word is derived from the Greek "*morph*," which means "form." Morphemes are the smallest units of linguistic meaning; they cannot be subdivided into smaller units of meaning, but are linguistic versions of chemically pure elements. Prefixes, suffixes, and root words can all be (and often are) morphemes, and they may take any number of syllables, so long as they are not further divisible into even more units of meaning. The English morpheme "bi," for example, consists of one syllable, while "salamander" consists of four; neither morpheme is separable into parts. English words, as those in most languages, are created through the joining together of morphemes. A glossary of morphemes encountered in this book's vocabulary instruction can be found on pages 259–268.

Etymology somewhat expands the linguistic focus of morphology, venturing beyond the meaningful parts of which words are composed and into their historical origins. A case in point is the word "hippopotamus." Many people would perhaps assume that this word, like "salamander," is a large morpheme itself, but etymologists can quickly point out that the word is actually Latin, having been adopted into English. Moreover, it was firstly taken into Latin from ancient Greek, an even earlier language. Knowing this history, one can identify in the word two ancient Greek morphemes: "*hippos*," meaning "horse," and "*potamos*," meaning "river." As such, the word "hippopotamus" is far from an independent English morpheme, but is rather an ancient word meaning "river horse," an aptly descriptive phrase for the large animal that it signifies.

At this point, it is perhaps prudent to issue to the reader a *caveat emptor* concerning this book's dealings with etymology and morphology. I am neither an academic etymologist nor a scholarly morphologist, but a high school English teacher whose particular area of expertise is pedagogical content knowledge; in other words, I can make no claim that the morphological dissections of words presented here are indubitable, simply that they will help students to improve their vocabularies. Consider, for example, the word "defamation" (Worksheet 80). Certainly, the prefix "de-" and the root "fam" mean "lowered fame" or "away from renown," but scholarly etymologists and morphologists debate potential meaning and history of the suffix(es). On one hand, proponents of a particular theory of construction identify the suffix "-tion" as an alternate form of "-ion," indicating "the act or condition of," thereby finding in the infix "-a-" a conjunctive device, devoid of communicative meaning in itself. Another camp, however, argues that the "a" and the "t" actually coincide, being derived from the verbal suffix "-ate," leaving "-ion" as a secondary suffix. The frustrating—at least for me—part of this debate is that there seems to be no conclusive outcome; both arguments are sensible and supportable, and I in this book have chosen to adopt the latter, simply because it seems to me probably *more correct* than the alternative, especially considering additional derivations such as "defamatory." As such, and admitting such, I of course leave myself open to objections from linguists and etymologists who may disagree with my morphological conclusions. To state the case plainly, I am less concerned with "where the 't' comes from" in a given word than I am with growing students' vocabularies through precisely organized, reinforced vocabulary instruction. *This*, after all, is the goal of utilizing morphology and etymology here.

Analogical Thinking

In elementary and secondary schools nationwide this past decade, perhaps no educational text was more widely adopted, circulated, and *taught* to teachers as was *Classroom Instruction That Works: Research-Based Strategies for Increasing Student Achievement* (Marzano, Pickering, & Pollock, 2001). The book presents the findings of a massive meta-analysis conducted by Mid-continent Research for Education and Learning (McREL), whose researchers sorted through great numbers of other meta-analyses and studies concerning all kinds and styles of instructional techniques, essentially trying to determine which of the thousands of pedagogical approaches that teachers can adopt are, simply stated, the best. McREL found via this meta-analysis that, as measured by average effect size, the single most effective instructional strategy impacting student achievement is the guiding of students in identifying similarities and differences between curricular materials (e.g., between a newly learned vocabulary word and a previously mastered word, or between one situation involving particular diction and a parallel situation).

The reason why *Classroom Instruction That Works* was, and continues to be, so widely read and circulated is twofold, I believe: Firstly, its goal to separate the pedagogical wheat from the chaff remains a pragmatic and valuable one; and secondly, the size and scope of its meta-analytical review actually gave it the credence to claim the ultimate accomplishment of that goal. Thus, while it is true that the College Board in 2005 removed analogies entirely from the testing methodology of the SAT, the function of analogical thinking—finding similarities and/or differences between juxtaposed situations and their component parts—was demonstrated by McREL to be the single most impactful teaching strategy utilizable by teachers. Numerous studies and reports from past decades suggest the verity of this conclusion, which is seconded both by common sense and by years of classroom experience (Alexander, 1984; Chen, 1996; Dagher, 1994; Newby, Ertmer, & Stepich, 1995). Thus, despite the College Board's removal of the infamous analogies section from the SAT, the cognitive and instructional value of analogical activity is the reason why these exercises constitute the final portion of every daily worksheet.

Quizzes and Tests

The nine multiple-choice quizzes included in this book are designed to resemble the SAT Verbal test portions. They are not facsimiles of the SAT itself, but are formatted similarly to it and require of students comparable cognitive exercises. Each quiz should be administered following 18 days of sequentially completed worksheets, so the first quiz assesses students' mastery of Worksheets 1–18, the second quiz regards Worksheets 19–36, and so on. Assuming a traditional academic calendar comprised of 5 school days per week, that's effectively one quiz per month.

The first section of each quiz asks students to fill in blanks in sentences using vocabulary words or derivations of them. Half of these sentences contain only one blank, where the correct word to fill must be ascertained from the context of the rest of the sentence, while the other half of the sentences contain two blanks, requiring students to choose pairs of appropriate words. The second section of each quiz asks students to consider underlined portions of sentences, sometimes including minute punctuation marks. The students must recognize if those underlined portions are written correctly or incorrectly—based, of course, on the grammatical errors delivered via the previous 18 worksheets—and how they should be rewritten if they are indeed incorrect. The third section of all quizzes assesses students' ability not to correct, but to identify errors if and where they exist. It always contains several sentences, four portions of each of which are underlined, accompanied by a fifth underlined clause students can select to indicate that there is not a grammatical error present in the passage. Students must select for each sentence one of the five underlined portions, indicating their recognition of grammatical inaccuracy or perfection. Finally, the fourth section of each quiz requires students to read a selection of prose, then answer questions following the selection that assess both their comprehension of the passage and their knowledge of and facility with the previous 18 worksheets' vocabulary words.

All four of these quiz sections mimic portions of the SAT Verbal test. They thus serve both to assess students' learning of the worksheets' materials and to augment their levels of comfort with the form of the actual SAT test itself. The two larger tests available online are formatted in the same way, although the orders and sizes of the sections vary.

Wholly, the curriculum contained in this book, if administered and learned fully, will help students both to succeed on the SAT examination and to understand more fully and fulfillingly our language itself. I sincerely hope that you find its contents and methodology both practical and practicable. Have a good year!

Chapter 3

Daily Worksheets

Name:______________________________ Date:____________

Ungrammatical Sentence:

Heroic railroad engineer Casey Jones' reputation became enormous, though it was literally as <u>amorphous</u> as air.

Explanation of Error:

Type of Error:

Prefix:

Definition:

Root:

amorphous

Worksheet 1

Suffix:

What it Looks Like:

Analogous Exercise:

amorphous : air

______________ : wood

Why? Nature of the Relationship:

Original Analogy Using the Vocabulary Word:

Name:_____ Date:_____

Ungrammatical Sentence:

I implied from my <u>pedagogue</u>'s lecture that although New Zealand was not directly involved in battles during World War II, it was certainly affected.

Explanation of Error:

Type of Error:

Prefix:

Definition:

Root:

pedagogue

Worksheet 2

Suffix:

What it Looks Like:

Analogous Exercise:

books : pedagogue   _____ : painter

Why? Nature of the Relationship:

Original Analogy Using the Vocabulary Word:

Ungrammatical Sentence:

In *Romeo and Juliet*, many different people were <u>culpable</u> for the tragic outcome, including the lovers themselves and their feuding families.

Explanation of Error:

Type of Error:

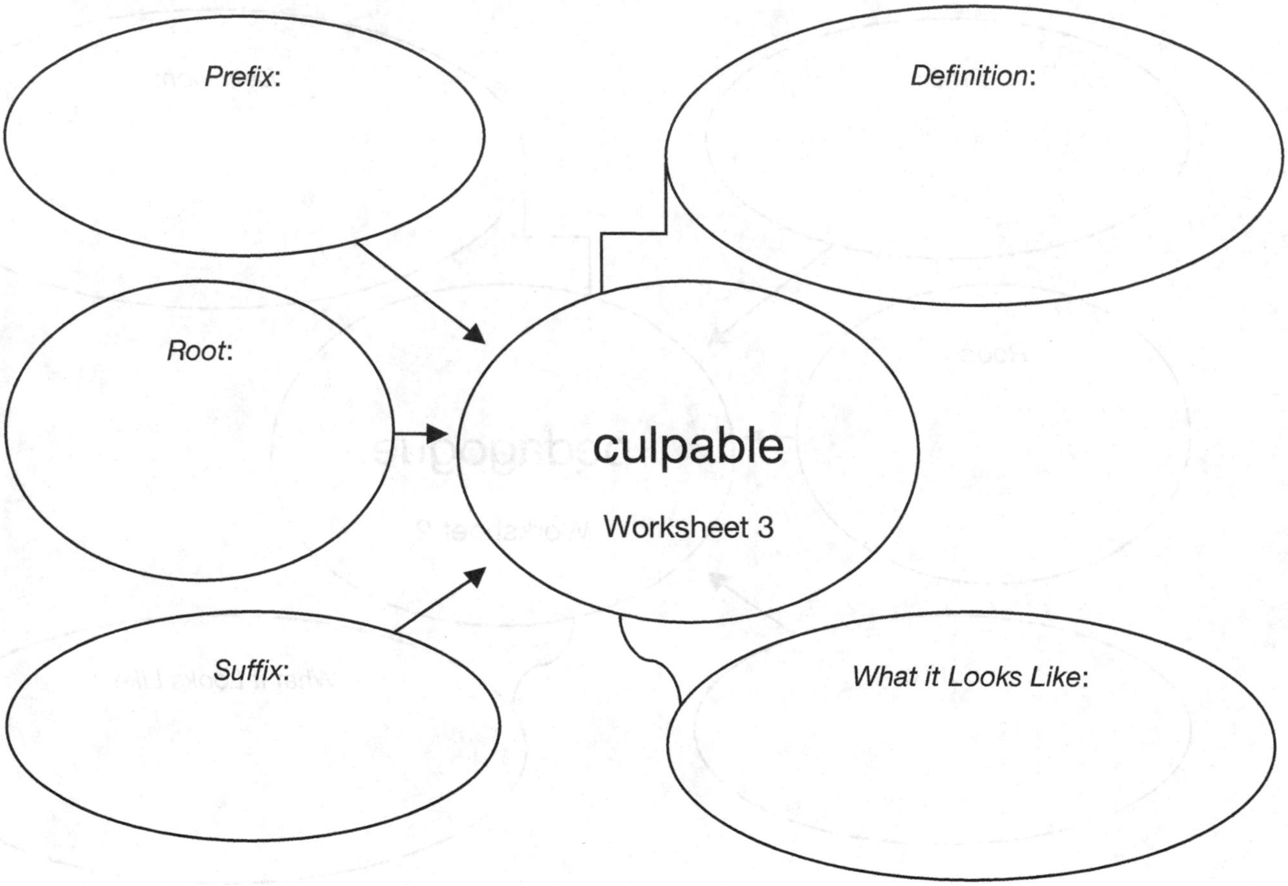

Prefix:

Definition:

Root:

culpable

Worksheet 3

Suffix:

What it Looks Like:

Analogous Exercise:

culpable : mistake   _____ : success

Why? Nature of the Relationship:

Original Analogy Using the Vocabulary Word:

Worksheet 3

Name:______________________________ Date:__________

Ungrammatical Sentence:

Many centuries ago various groups of barbarians were belligerent toward encampments and fortifications on the fringes of the Roman Empire.

Explanation of Error:

Type of Error:

Prefix:

Definition:

Root:

belligerent

Worksheet 4

Suffix:

What it Looks Like:

Analogous Exercise:

pacifist : belligerent ______________ : hopeless

Why? Nature of the Relationship:

Original Analogy Using the Vocabulary Word:

Worksheet 4

Name:____ Date:____________

Ungrammatical Sentence:

Neither my brother or my sister can be described as an individual of great <u>dignity</u>; they are both far too wild and annoying to earn that title.

Explanation of Error:

Type of Error:

Prefix:

Definition:

Root:

dignity

Worksheet 5

Suffix:

What it Looks Like:

Analogous Exercise:

dignity : falling down ____________ : earning an award

Why? Nature of the Relationship:

Original Analogy Using the Vocabulary Word:

Ungrammatical Sentence:

The college professor a man of great knowledge and passion tried to prove with <u>indubitable</u> logic that biology was the most important of sciences.

Explanation of Error:	*Type of Error:*

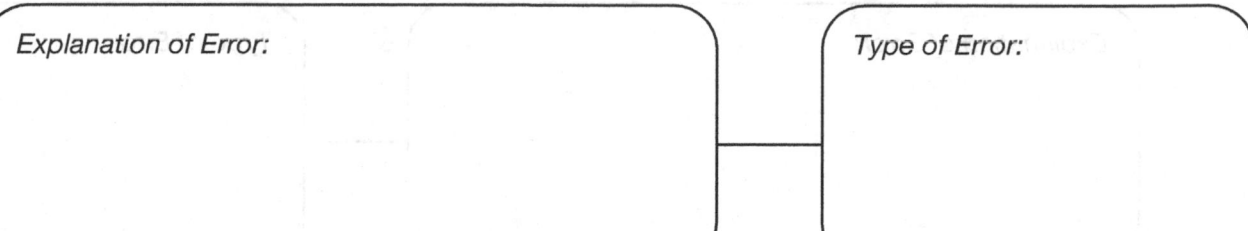

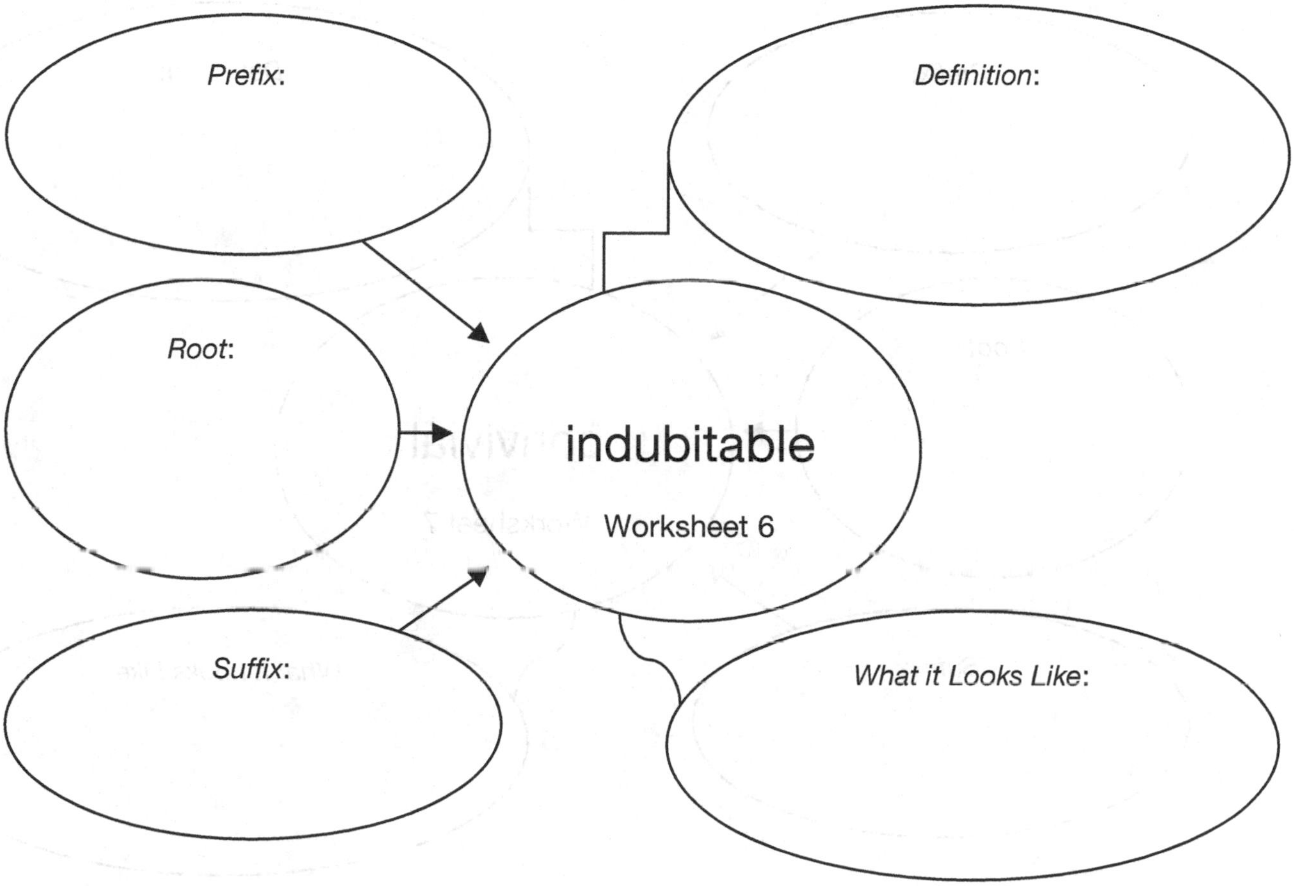

Prefix:

Definition:

Root:

indubitable

Worksheet 6

Suffix:

What it Looks Like:

Analogous Exercise:

indubitable : fact   _____ : hypothesis

Why? Nature of the Relationship:	*Original Analogy Using the Vocabulary Word:*

Worksheet 6

Ungrammatical Sentence:

The <u>convivial</u> student was fond of his friends, his teachers,
and he also enjoyed spending time with his parents.

Explanation of Error:

Type of Error:

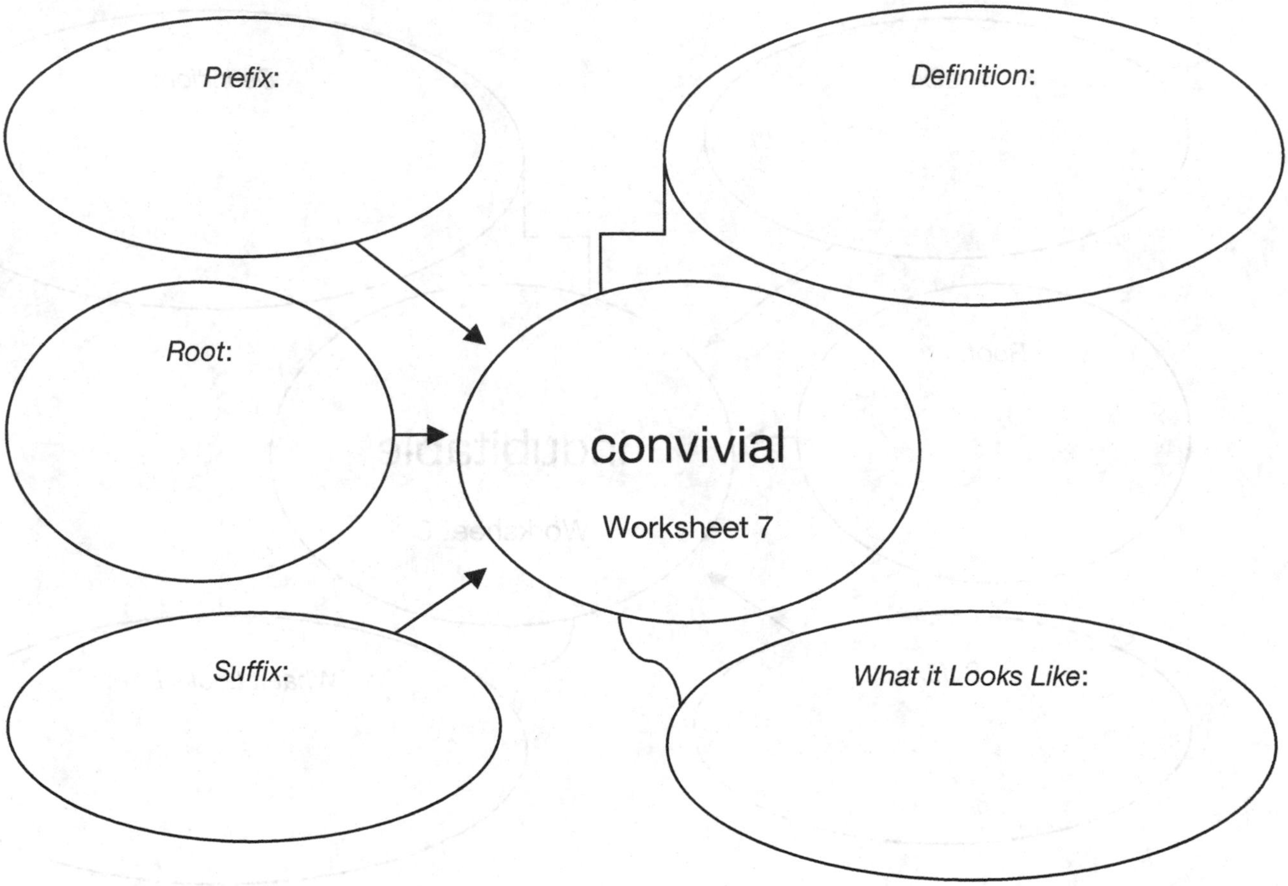

Prefix:

Definition:

Root:

convivial

Worksheet 7

Suffix:

What it Looks Like:

Analogous Exercise:

convivial : hermit _____ : ringmaster

Why? Nature of the Relationship:

*Original Analogy Using the Vocabulary
Word:*

Worksheet 7

Name:____ Date:____________

Ungrammatical Sentence:

The burglar tried to quickly <u>abduct</u> as many valuables as he could fit into his bag; luckily, the police prevented him from doing so.

Explanation of Error:

Type of Error:

Prefix:

Definition:

Root:

abduct

Worksheet 8

Suffix:

What it Looks Like:

Analogous Exercise:

abduct : snatch

______________ : give

Why? Nature of the Relationship:

Original Analogy Using the Vocabulary Word:

Ungrammatical Sentence:

The gray suited politician delivered his address to the audience slowly, as if he were delivering a <u>eulogy</u> instead of a victory speech.

Explanation of Error:

Type of Error:

Prefix:

Definition:

Root:

eulogy

Worksheet 9

Suffix:

What it Looks Like:

Analogous Exercise:

mourner : eulogy   _____ : graduation speech

Why? Nature of the Relationship:

Original Analogy Using the Vocabulary Word:

Worksheet 9

Name:____________________ Date:__________

Ungrammatical Sentence:

Though I was ultimately unable to <u>incarnate</u> my fortune, yet I did earn a modest savings account.

Explanation of Error:

Type of Error:

Prefix:

Root:

Suffix:

Definition:

What it Looks Like:

incarnate

Worksheet 10

Analogous Exercise:

incarnate : solid ____________ : amorphous

Why? Nature of the Relationship:

Original Analogy Using the Vocabulary Word:

Worksheet 10

Name:____ Date:__________

Ungrammatical Sentence:

Do you think that the President of the United States has more or less <u>autonomy</u> then an average citizen has?

Explanation of Error:

Type of Error:

Prefix:

Root:

Suffix:

Definition:

What it Looks Like:

autonomy

Worksheet 11

Analogous Exercise:

toddler : autonomy ______________ : dignity

Why? Nature of the Relationship:

Original Analogy Using the Vocabulary Word:

Name:______________________________ Date:__________

Ungrammatical Sentence:

You could say that John almost idolized Paul Bunyan because he was handy with an axe and he owned a large, relatively docile pet ox.

Explanation of Error:

Type of Error:

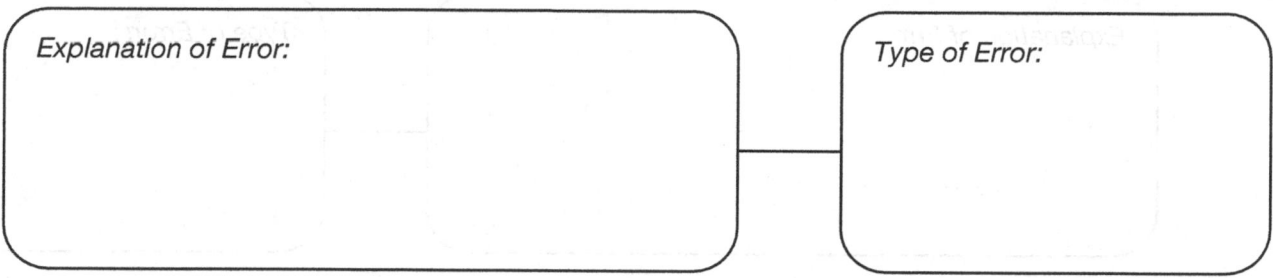

Prefix:

Definition:

Root:

docile

Worksheet 12

Suffix:

What it Looks Like:

Analogous Exercise:

kitten : docile ____________ : belligerent

Why? Nature of the Relationship:

Original Analogy Using the Vocabulary Word:

Worksheet 12

Name:____ Date:__________

Ungrammatical Sentence:

The carpenter tried to fix the creaky staircase, but he was actually the person whom most exacerbated the annoying problem.

Explanation of Error:

Type of Error:

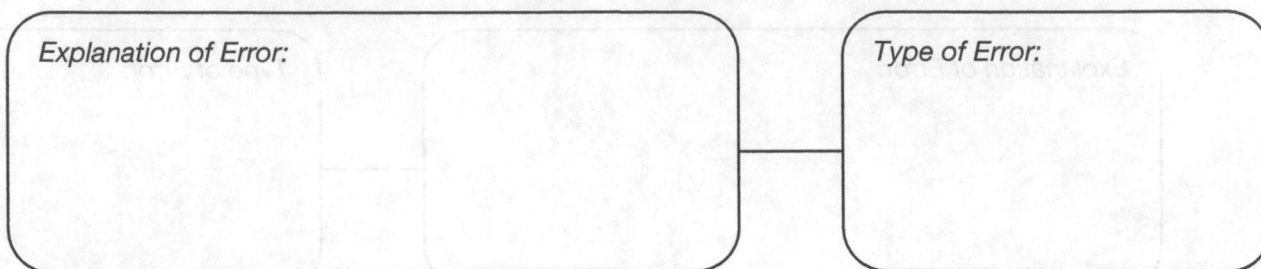

Prefix:

Definition:

Root:

exacerbate

Worksheet 13

Suffix:

What it Looks Like:

Analogous Exercise:

water leak : exacerbate

______________ : abduct

Why? Nature of the Relationship:

Original Analogy Using the Vocabulary Word:

Ungrammatical Sentence:

Its impossible to believe that my grandfather was once not a <u>magnanimous</u> individual, but that conclusion is absolutely implied by my mother's tales.

Explanation of Error:		Type of Error:

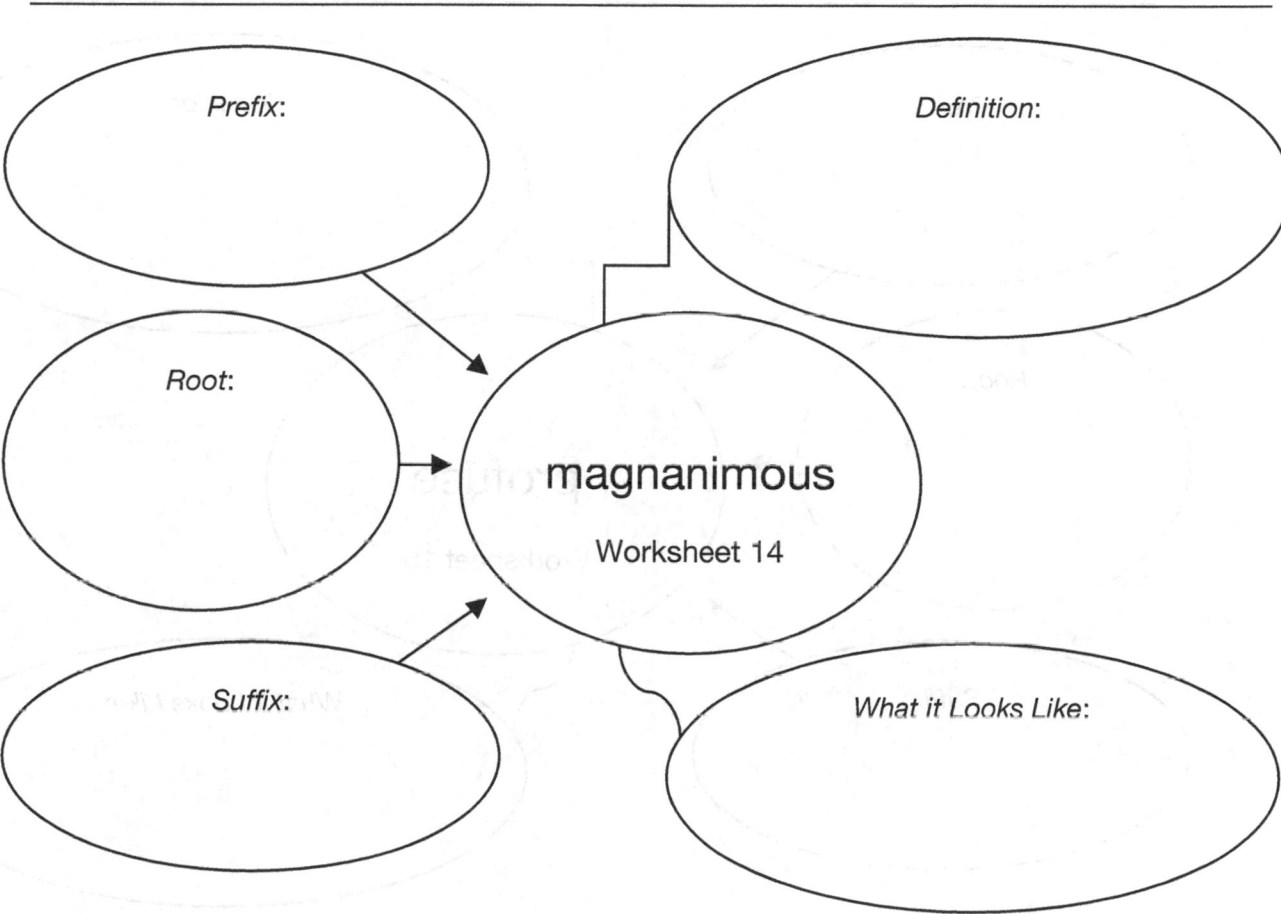

Prefix:

Definition:

Root:

magnanimous

Worksheet 14

Suffix:

What it Looks Like:

Analogous Exercise:

magnanimous : Mother Teresa   _____ : Goldilocks

Why? Nature of the Relationship:	Original Analogy Using the Vocabulary Word:

Ungrammatical Sentence:

My favorite professional hockey goalie allowed a <u>profuse</u> amount of goals during the game, far more than his rival on the other team.

Explanation of Error:

Type of Error:

Prefix:

Definition:

Root:

profuse

Worksheet 15

Suffix:

What it Looks Like:

Analogous Exercise:

dictionary : profuse   _____ : indubitable

Why? Nature of the Relationship:

Original Analogy Using the Vocabulary Word:

Name:____ Date:____________

Ungrammatical Sentence:

Attempting to describe in a letter his hometown's <u>inherent</u> characteristics, the student wrote eloquent and full about both weather and geography.

Explanation of Error:

Type of Error:

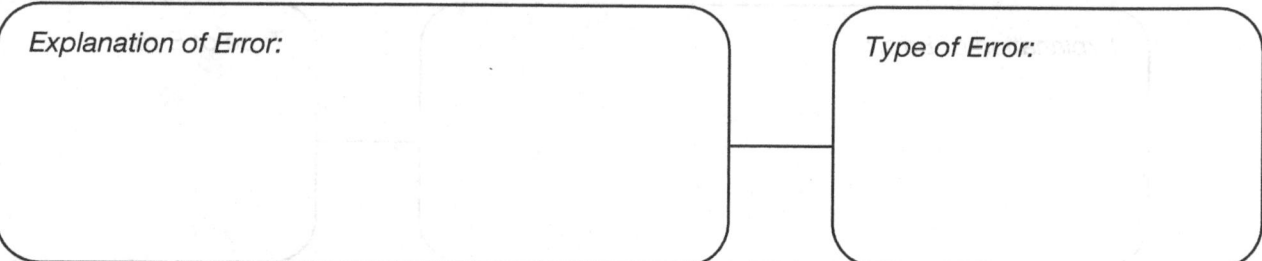

Prefix:

Definition:

Root:

inherent

Worksheet 16

Suffix:

What it Looks Like:

Analogous Exercise:

inherent : eye color

______________ : social habits

Why? Nature of the Relationship:

Original Analogy Using the Vocabulary Word:

Worksheet 16

Name:_____ Date:_____

Ungrammatical Sentence:

Irregardless of the number of years that he has played
the clarinet, Reggie still considers himself a musical <u>novice</u>.

Explanation of Error: | Type of Error:

Prefix:

Definition:

Root:

novice

Worksheet 17

Suffix:

What it Looks Like:

Analogous Exercise:

indubitable : expert   _____ : novice

Why? Nature of the Relationship: | Original Analogy Using the Vocabulary Word:

Ungrammatical Sentence:

Neither the local car dealership nor the traveling circus demonstrate <u>parity</u> in terms of how much money employees are paid relative to one another.

Explanation of Error:

Type of Error:

Prefix:

Definition:

Root:

parity

Worksheet 18

Suffix:

What it Looks Like:

Analogous Exercise:

equality : parity

_____ : bias

Why? Nature of the Relationship:

Original Analogy Using the Vocabulary Word:

Worksheet 18

Ungrammatical Sentence:

Some heads of orphanages in pre-Victorian England were <u>benevolent</u> but others had the reputation of being cruel and perhaps even unlawful.

Explanation of Error:		Type of Error:

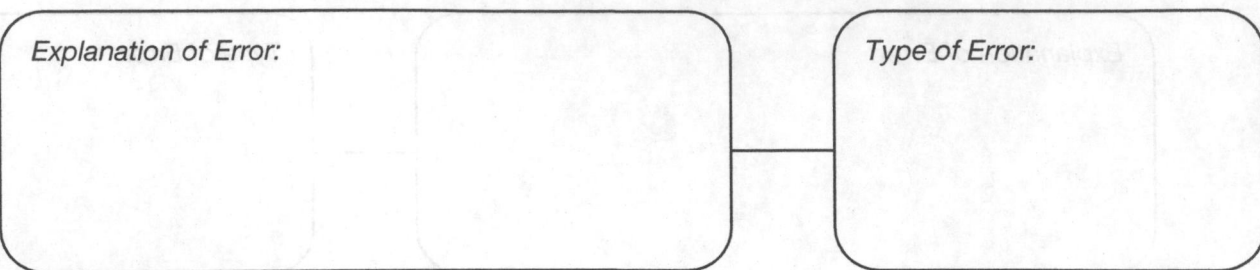

Prefix:

Definition:

Root:

benevolent

Worksheet 19

Suffix:

What it Looks Like:

Analogous Exercise:

ruthless dictator : benevolent   _____ : magnanimous

Why? Nature of the Relationship:	Original Analogy Using the Vocabulary Word:

Worksheet 19

Ungrammatical Sentence:

I was <u>doleful</u> after reading the final chapter of my favorite novel; but my spirits soon brightened when I purchased its sequel at the local bookstore.

Explanation of Error:

Type of Error:

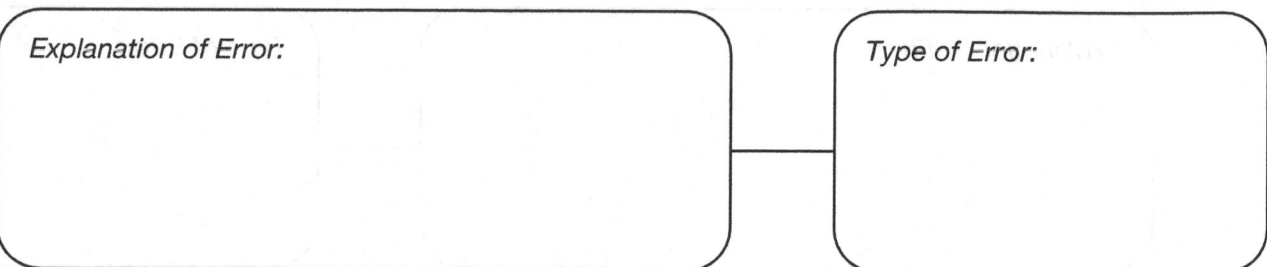

Prefix:

Definition:

Root:

doleful

Worksheet 20

Suffix:

What it Looks Like:

Analogous Exercise:

eulogy : doleful

_____ : cheerful

Why? Nature of the Relationship:

Original Analogy Using the Vocabulary Word:

Worksheet 20

Worksheet 21

Ungrammatical Sentence:

It is probably inaccurate too describe a chowder or soup as <u>fragmentary</u>, although some uncooked ingredients, separated on a table, would qualify.

Explanation of Error:

Type of Error:

Prefix:

Definition:

Root:

fragmentary

Worksheet 21

Suffix:

What it Looks Like:

Analogous Exercise:

fragmentary : complete

_____ : profuse

Why? Nature of the Relationship:

Original Analogy Using the Vocabulary Word:

Ungrammatical Sentence:

Every nation on Earth has a <u>capital</u> city, I am
unfortunately unable to name all of those places.

Explanation of Error:	*Type of Error:*

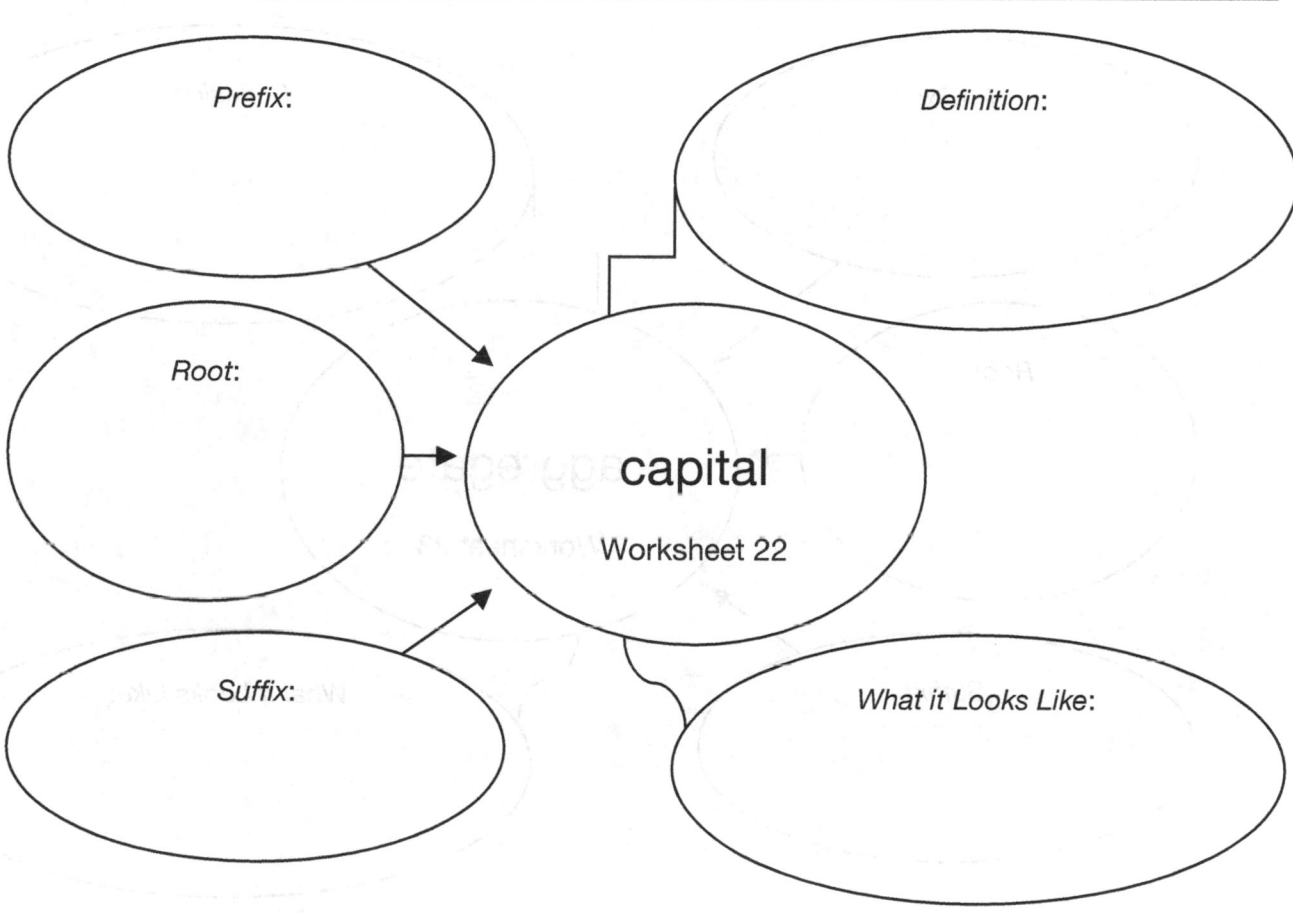

Analogous Exercise:

capital : hierarchy _____ : road

Why? Nature of the Relationship:	*Original Analogy Using the Vocabulary Word:*

Worksheet 22

Ungrammatical Sentence:

There are less assignments that count toward my friend's <u>aggregate</u> grade in his first period class than there are counted toward mine.

Explanation of Error:

Type of Error:

Prefix:

Definition:

Root:

aggregate

Worksheet 23

Suffix:

What it Looks Like:

Analogous Exercise:

high school : fragmentary   _____ : aggregate

Why? Nature of the Relationship:

Original Analogy Using the Vocabulary Word:

Worksheet 23

Name:______________________________ Date:____________

Ungrammatical Sentence:

For homework, I read poems by Walt Whitman, William Shakespeare, and Emily Dickinson, but I describe the tone of only one of those as <u>diffident</u>.

Explanation of Error:

Type of Error:

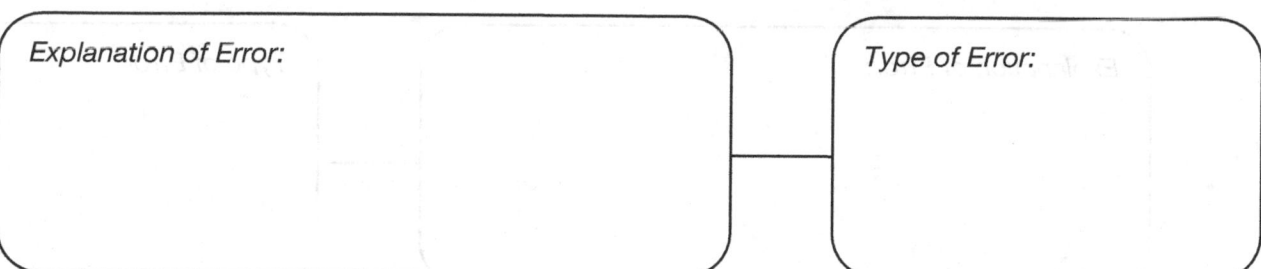

Prefix:

Definition:

Root:

diffident

Worksheet 24

Suffix:

What it Looks Like:

Analogous Exercise:

diffident : lively ____________: convivial

Why? Nature of the Relationship:

Original Analogy Using the Vocabulary Word:

Worksheet 24

Ungrammatical Sentence:

If a given teacher is unwilling to <u>remit</u> their policy concerning penalties applied to late homework assignments, then students' grades might suffer.

Explanation of Error:

Type of Error:

Prefix:

Definition:

Root:

remit

Worksheet 25

Suffix:

What it Looks Like:

Analogous Exercise:

remit : second

_____ : first

Why? Nature of the Relationship:

Original Analogy Using the Vocabulary Word:

Perfect 800: SAT Verbal © Prufrock Press Inc. • Permission is granted to photocopy or reproduce this page for single classroom use only.

Name:_____ Date:_____

Ungrammatical Sentence:

The Boston Massacre of 1770 not only <u>expedited</u> the spreading resentment among New Englanders, it may have led directly to the Boston Tea Party.

Explanation of Error:

Type of Error:

Prefix:

Definition:

Root:

expedite
Worksheet 26

Suffix:

What it Looks Like:

Analogous Exercise:

traffic jam : delay   _____ : expedite

Why? Nature of the Relationship:

Original Analogy Using the Vocabulary Word:

Ungrammatical Sentence:

As the populace watched excitedly, the warring political factions <u>coalesced</u> into a unified government before their eyes on television.

Explanation of Error:

Type of Error:

Prefix:

Definition:

Root:

coalesce

Worksheet 27

Suffix:

What it Looks Like:

Analogous Exercise:

aggregate : coalesce   _____ : separate

Why? Nature of the Relationship:

Original Analogy Using the Vocabulary Word:

Name:_____ Date:_____

Ungrammatical Sentence:

Each of the <u>ambulatory</u> creatures of which I am aware have legs.

Explanation of Error:	Type of Error:

Prefix:

Definition:

Root:

ambulatory

Worksheet 28

Suffix:

What it Looks Like:

Analogous Exercise:

ambulatory : feet   _____ : hands

Why? Nature of the Relationship:	Original Analogy Using the Vocabulary Word:

Ungrammatical Sentence:

The <u>ineffable</u> joy felt by Tiny Tim's family corresponds with many other elements in the conclusion of Dickens's *A Christmas Carol*.

Explanation of Error:

Type of Error:

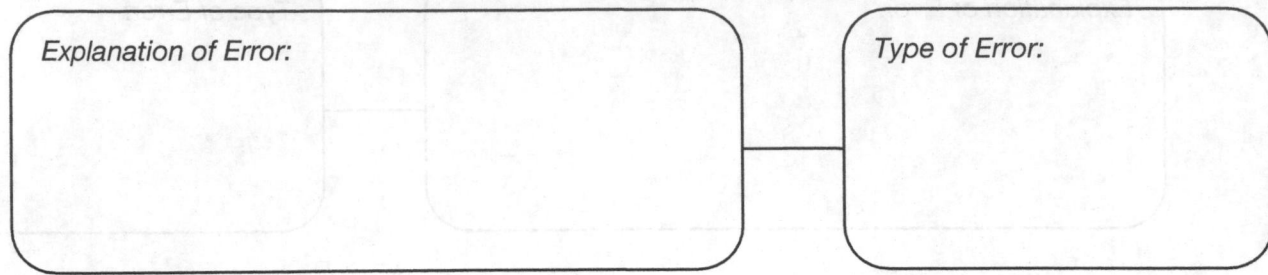

Prefix:

Definition:

Root:

ineffable

Worksheet 29

Suffix:

What it Looks Like:

Analogous Exercise:

words : ineffable

_____ : unimaginable

Why? Nature of the Relationship:

Original Analogy Using the Vocabulary Word:

Ungrammatical Sentence:

Many persons wish for <u>omniscience</u>,
but no humans actually demonstrate it.

Explanation of Error:

Type of Error:

Prefix:

Definition:

Root:

omniscience

Worksheet 30

Suffix:

What it Looks Like:

Analogous Exercise:

omniscience : humans

_____ : countries

Why? Nature of the Relationship:

Original Analogy Using the Vocabulary Word:

Worksheet 30

Name:______________________________ Date:__________

Ungrammatical Sentence:

The reason why many <u>misanthropes</u> are lonely is because they may not receive very many invitations to holiday parties.

Explanation of Error:

Type of Error:

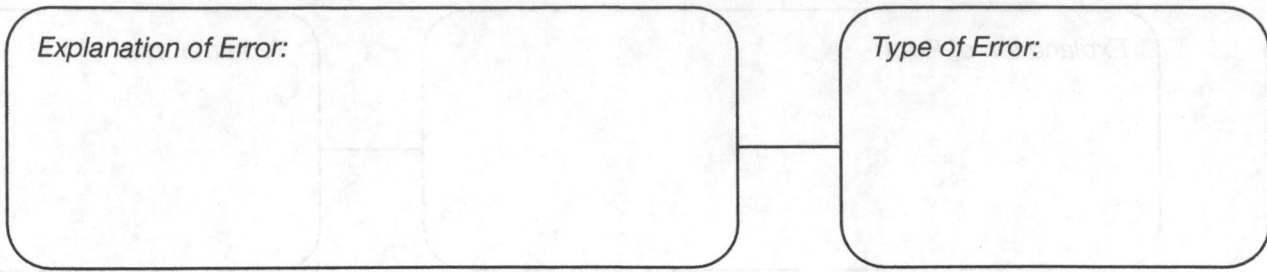

Prefix:

Definition:

Root:

misanthrope

Worksheet 31

Suffix:

What it Looks Like:

Analogous Exercise:

autonomy : misanthrope ____________ : film buff

Why? Nature of the Relationship:

Original Analogy Using the Vocabulary Word:

Ungrammatical Sentence:

The gentleman, although usually docile, strongly and loudly opposed the eminent <u>sequestration</u> of his personal property.

Explanation of Error:

Type of Error:

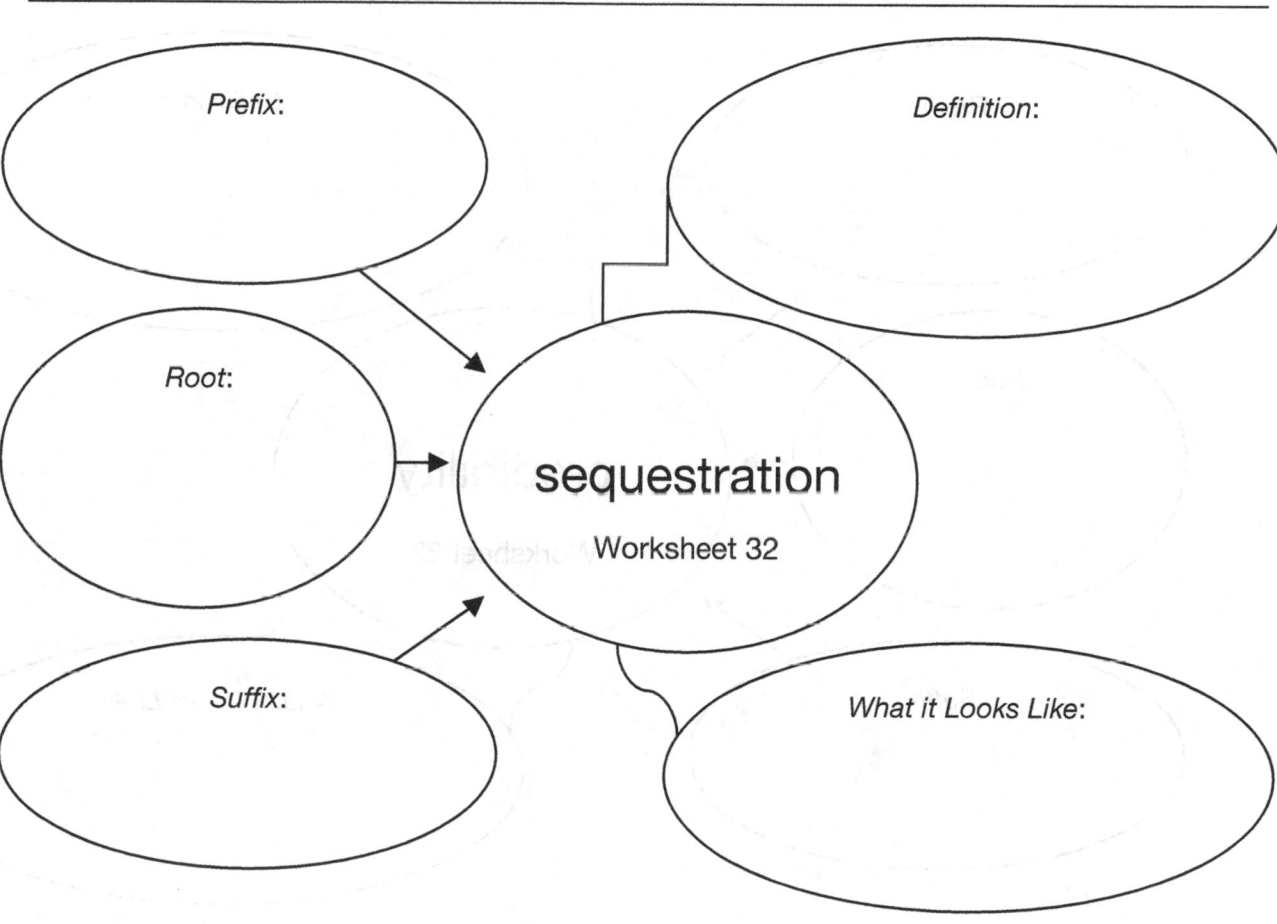

Prefix:

Definition:

Root:

sequestration
Worksheet 32

Suffix:

What it Looks Like:

Analogous Exercise:

sequestration : law   _____ : common sense

Why? Nature of the Relationship:

Original Analogy Using the Vocabulary Word:

Ungrammatical Sentence:

My friends and me are intelligent individuals, yet we lack <u>credibility</u> as experts in the field of prehistoric anthropology.

Explanation of Error:

Type of Error:

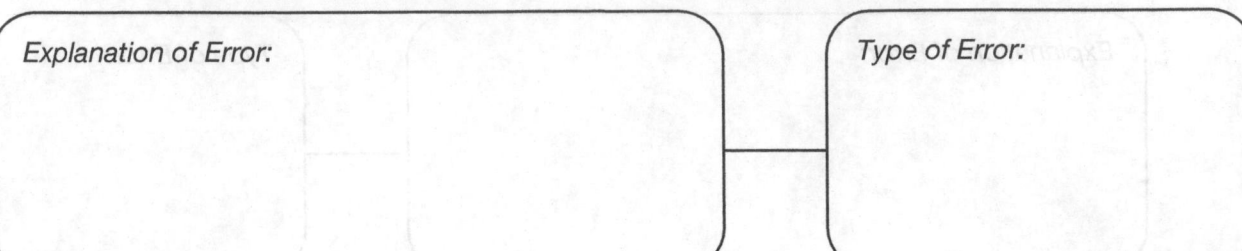

Prefix:

Definition:

Root:

credibility

Worksheet 33

Suffix:

What it Looks Like:

Analogous Exercise:

credibility : expert   _____ : novice

Why? Nature of the Relationship:

Original Analogy Using the Vocabulary Word:

Perfect 800: SAT Verbal © Prufrock Press Inc. • Permission is granted to photocopy or reproduce this page for single classroom use only.

Ungrammatical Sentence:

The political analyst's <u>prognosis</u> of our country's imminent
condition was: hopeful, cheerful, and well-received.

```
┌─────────────────────────────────┐   ┌─────────────────────────────────┐
│ Explanation of Error:           │   │ Type of Error:                  │
│                                 │───│                                 │
│                                 │   │                                 │
│                                 │   │                                 │
└─────────────────────────────────┘   └─────────────────────────────────┘
```

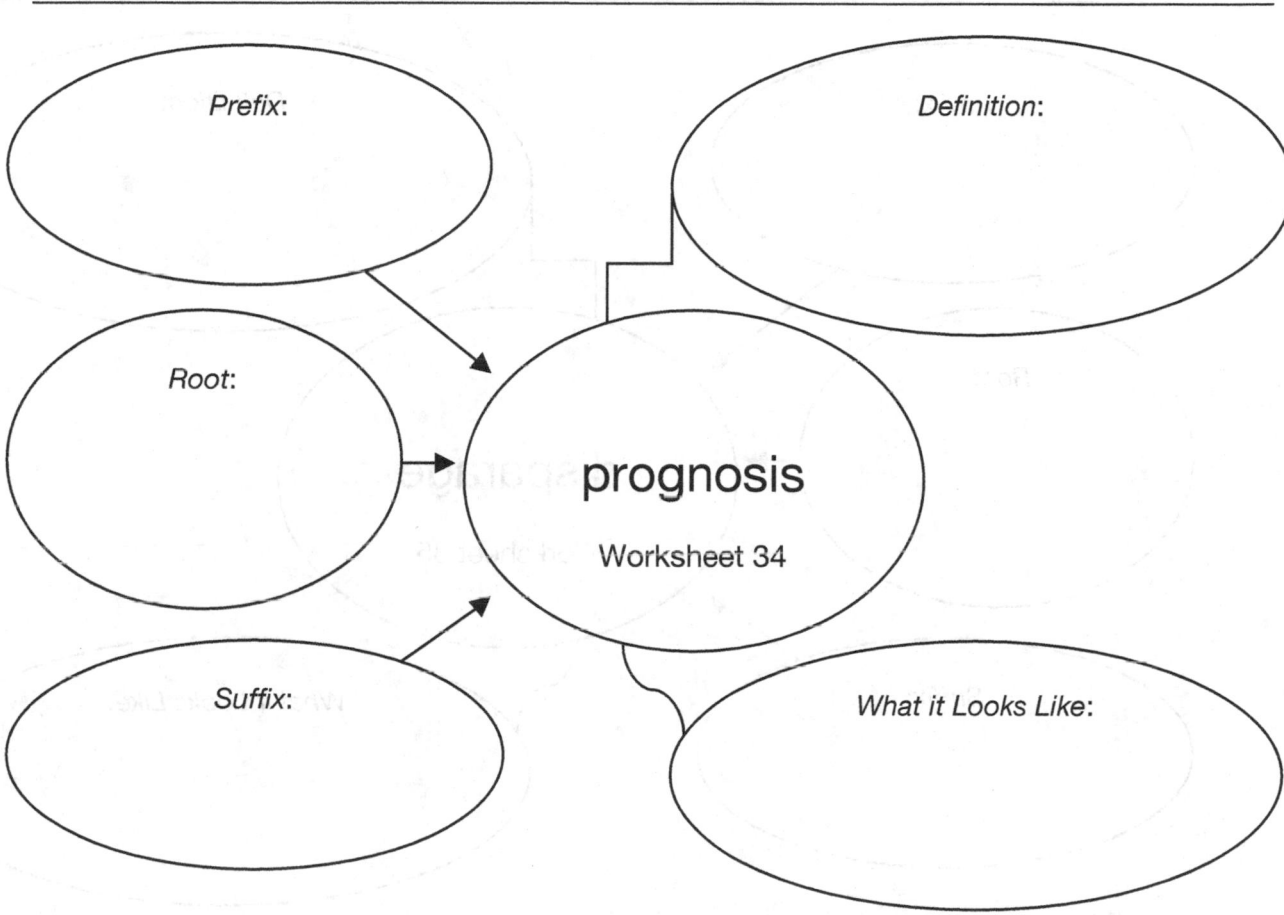

Prefix:

Definition:

Root:

prognosis

Worksheet 34

Suffix:

What it Looks Like:

Analogous Exercise:

prognosis : future   _____ : present

```
┌─────────────────────────────────┐   ┌─────────────────────────────────┐
│ Why? Nature of the Relationship:│   │ Original Analogy Using the      │
│                                 │   │ Vocabulary Word:                │
│                                 │───│                                 │
│                                 │   │                                 │
│                                 │   │                                 │
└─────────────────────────────────┘   └─────────────────────────────────┘
```

Worksheet 34

Name:_____ Date:_____

Ungrammatical Sentence:

During his belligerent monologue, the mayor apparently found
it quite impossible to <u>disparage</u> his opponent's ideas any farther.

Explanation of Error:

Type of Error:

Prefix:

Definition:

Root:

disparage

Worksheet 35

Suffix:

What it Looks Like:

Analogous Exercise:

misanthrope : disparage

_____ : applaud

Why? Nature of the Relationship:

Original Analogy Using the Vocabulary
Word:

Name:________________________________ Date:____________

Ungrammatical Sentence:

If you are someone who can be described as pugnacious, you might find yourself without many close friends.

Explanation of Error:

Type of Error:

Prefix:

Root:

Suffix:

pugnacious

Worksheet #36

Definition:

What it Looks Like:

Worksheet 36

Analogous Exercise:

pugnacious : belligerent

____________ : benevolent

Why? Nature of the Relationship:

Original Analogy Using the Vocabulary Word:

Ungrammatical Sentence:

Stories which involve spaceships and alien visitors
are often viewed as <u>apocryphal</u> by history teachers.

Explanation of Error:

Type of Error:

Prefix:

Definition:

Root:

apocryphal

Worksheet 37

Suffix:

What it Looks Like:

Analogous Exercise:

doubt : apocryphal   _____ : indubitable

Why? Nature of the Relationship:

Original Analogy Using the Vocabulary Word:

Worksheet 37

Name:______________________________ Date:__________

Ungrammatical Sentence:

Between the 12 of them, the members of the jury unanimously found it reasonable to <u>exonerate</u> the defendant of all wrongdoing.

Explanation of Error:

Type of Error:

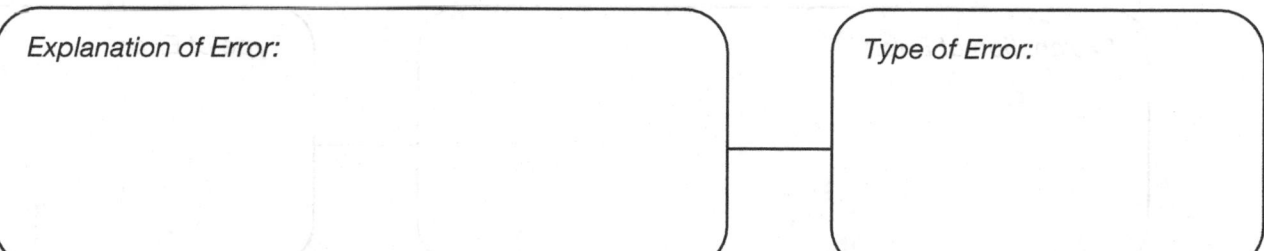

Prefix:

Definition:

Root:

exonerate

Worksheet 38

Suffix:

What it Looks Like:

Analogous Exercise:

exonerate : innocent

______________ : culpable

Why? Nature of the Relationship:

Original Analogy Using the Vocabulary Word:

Worksheet 38

Ungrammatical Sentence:

In marketing, <u>fervid</u> advertisement of reasonably priced products is perhaps the best way to affect an immediate upswing in sales.

Explanation of Error:		Type of Error:

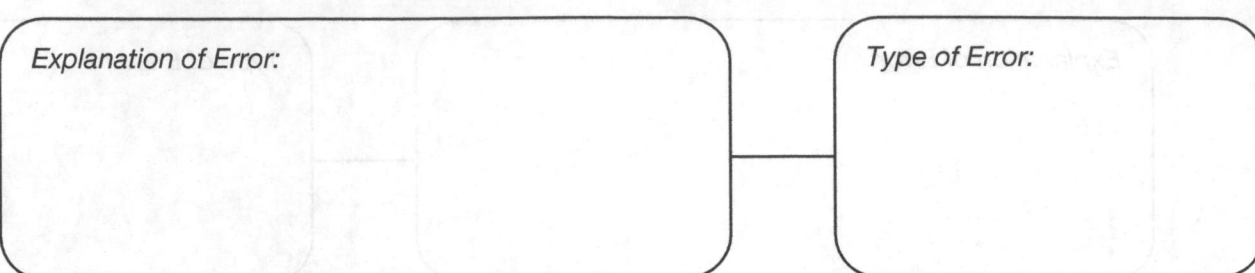

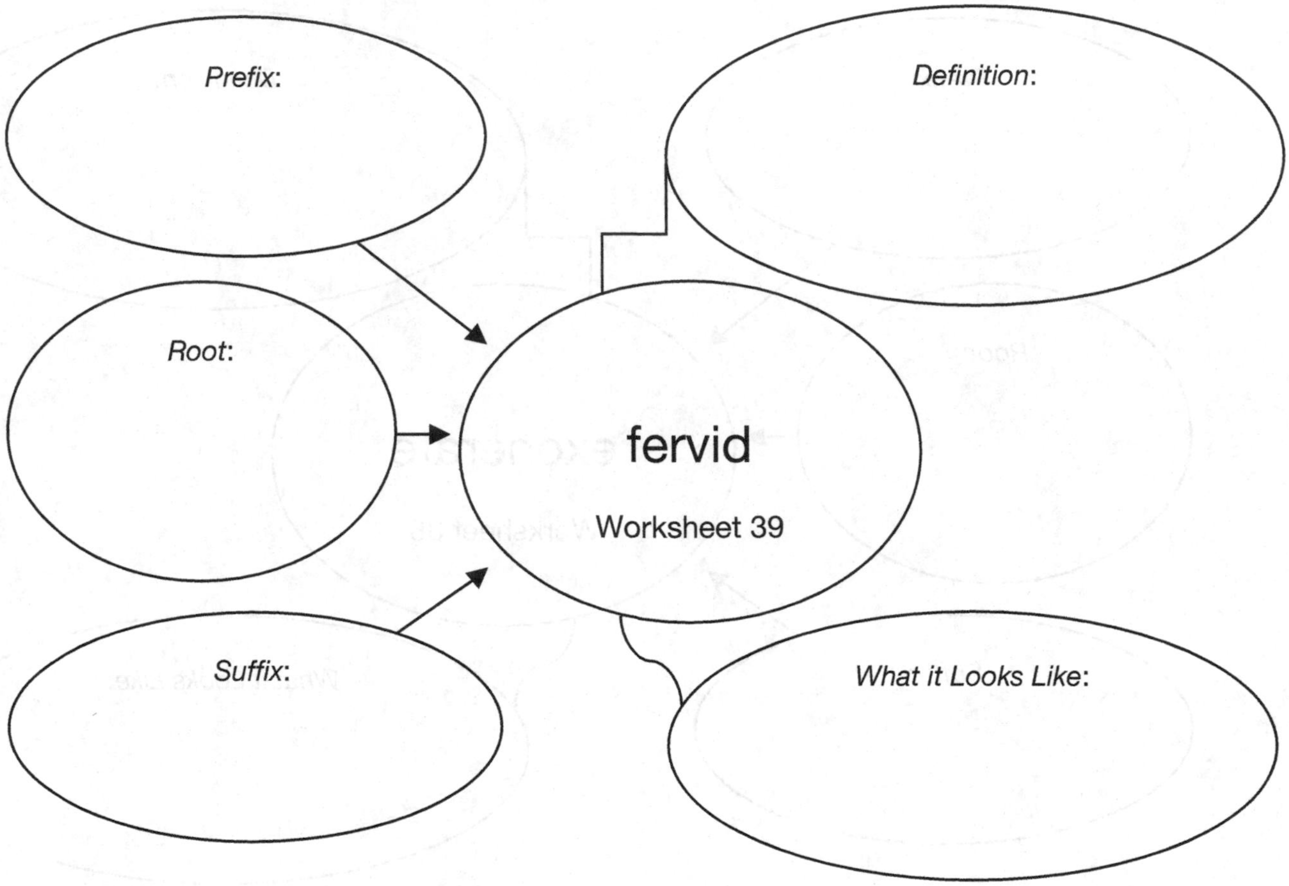

Prefix:

Root:

Suffix:

fervid

Worksheet 39

Definition:

What it Looks Like:

Worksheet 39

Analogous Exercise:

docile : fervid _____ : ambulatory

Why? Nature of the Relationship:	Original Analogy Using the Vocabulary Word:

Name:______________________________________ Date:__________

Ungrammatical Sentence:

The incredulous rumor about <u>intermittent</u> periods of taxation caused many employers to lose sleep because of worry.

Explanation of Error:

Type of Error:

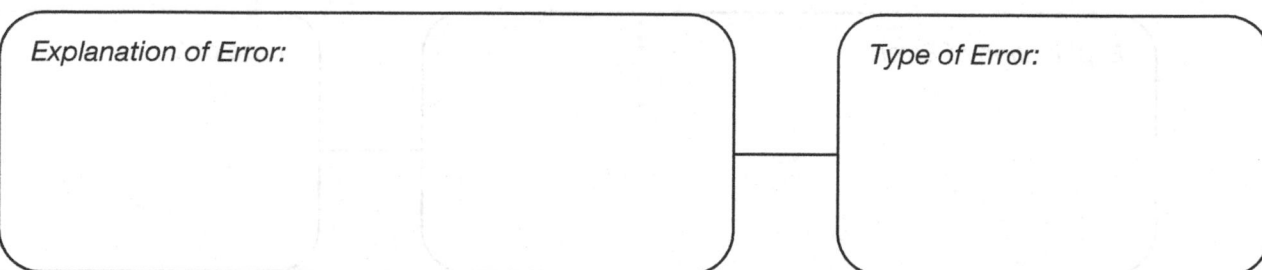

Prefix:

Definition:

Root:

intermittent

Worksheet 40

Suffix:

What it Looks Like:

Analogous Exercise:

Earth : constant ____________ : intermittent

Why? Nature of the Relationship:

Original Analogy Using the Vocabulary Word:

Worksheet 40

Ungrammatical Sentence:

Many people know the phrase <u>obstruction</u> of justice from television programs, but few actually recognize its purpose in courts of law.

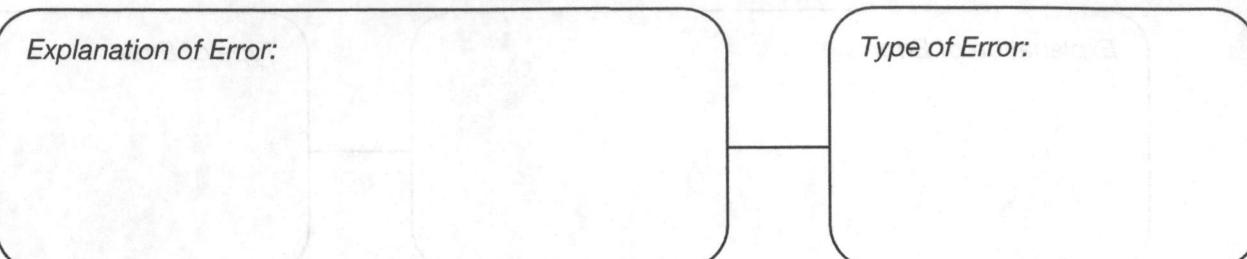

Explanation of Error:		Type of Error:

Prefix:

Definition:

Root:

obstruction

Worksheet 41

Suffix:

What it Looks Like:

Analogous Exercise:

obstruction : delay _____ : exacerbate

Why? Nature of the Relationship:

Original Analogy Using the Vocabulary Word:

Worksheet 41

Name:____ Date:__________

Ungrammatical Sentence:

The judge might of considered the reformed burglar a credible witness and assumed the <u>verity</u> of his testimony, but for the power of reputation.

Explanation of Error:

Type of Error:

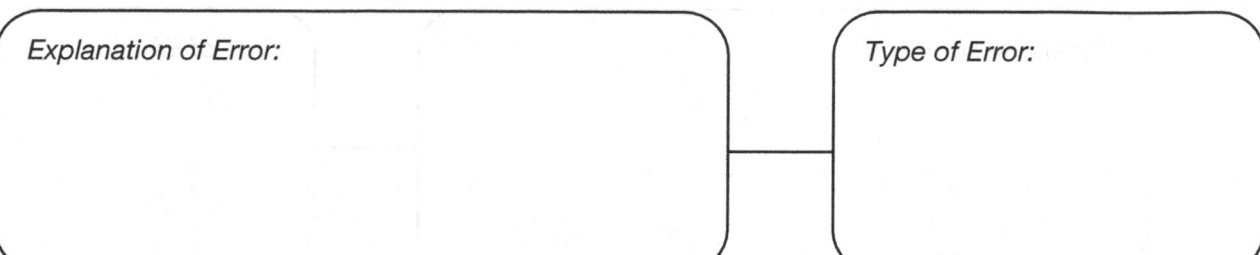

Prefix:

Definition:

Root:

verity

Worksheet 42

Suffix:

What it Looks Like:

Worksheet 42

Analogous Exercise:

verity : apocryphal

__________ : large

Why? Nature of the Relationship:

Original Analogy Using the Vocabulary Word:

Name:____ Date:____________

Ungrammatical Sentence:

Although practical, my teacher's plan to use petitions in order to <u>advocate</u> for taller schools statewide seemed to have little actual purpose.

Explanation of Error:

Type of Error:

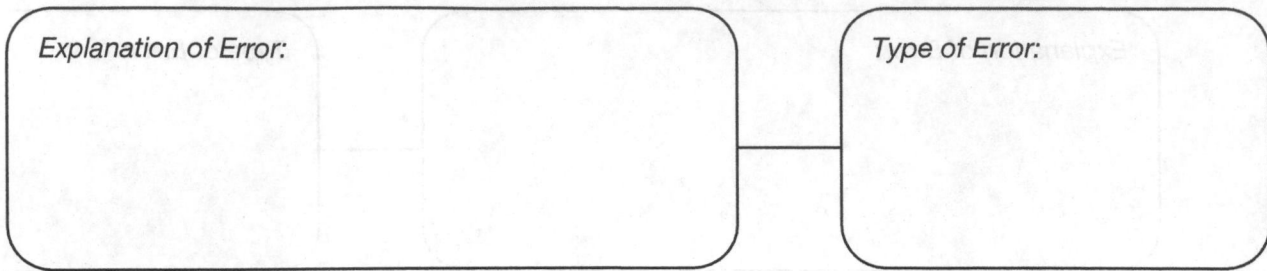

Prefix:

Definition:

Root:

advocate

Worksheet 43

Suffix:

What it Looks Like:

Analogous Exercise:

ally : advocate ____________ : disparage

Why? Nature of the Relationship:

Original Analogy Using the Vocabulary Word:

Worksheet 43

Ungrammatical Sentence:

I know Albert Einstein must have delivered some of his
less famous lectures with only <u>perfunctory</u> preparation.

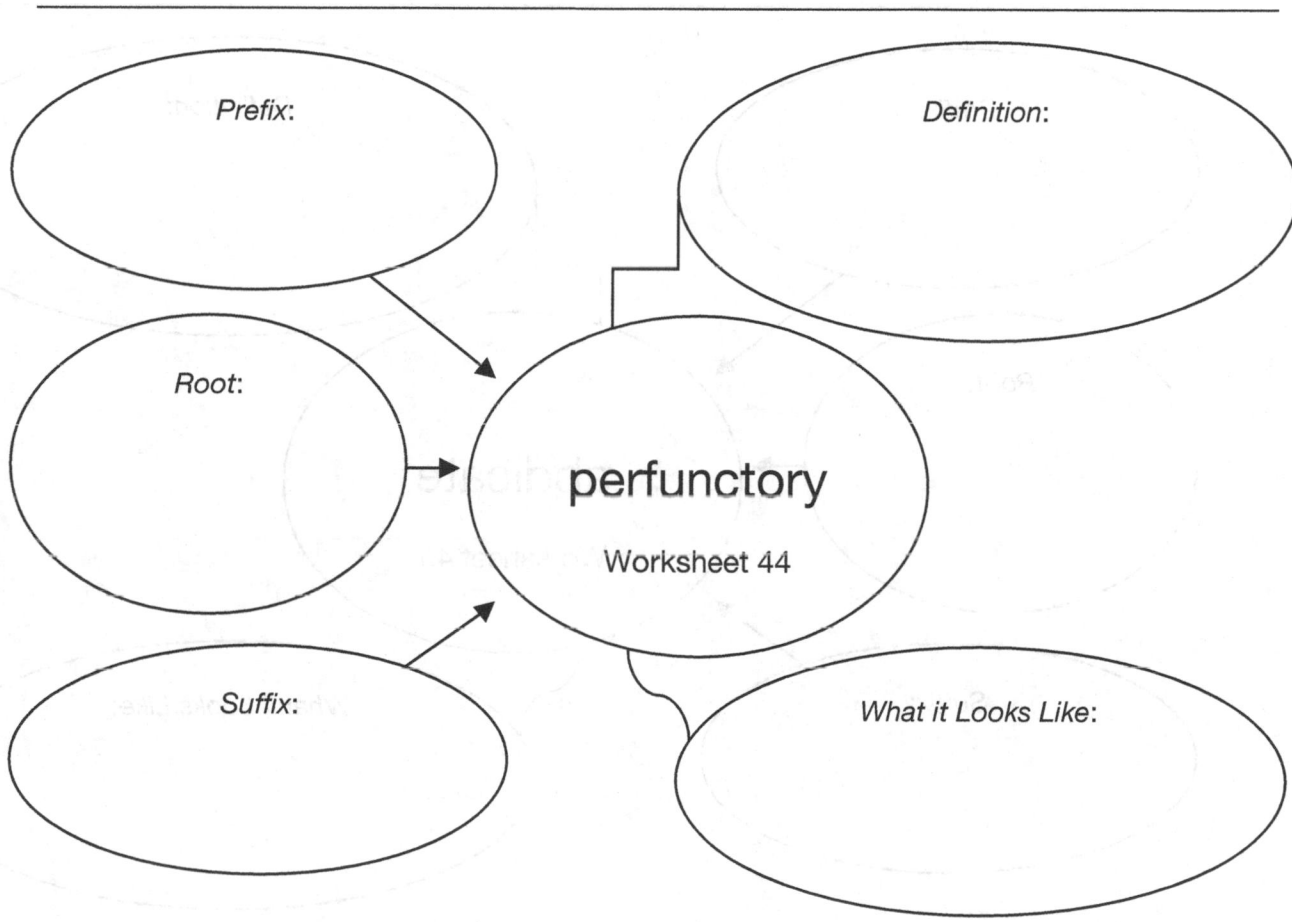

Explanation of Error:

Type of Error:

Prefix:

Definition:

Root:

perfunctory

Worksheet 44

Suffix:

What it Looks Like:

Analogous Exercise:

brushing teeth : perfunctory _____ : fervid

Why? Nature of the Relationship:

Original Analogy Using the Vocabulary Word:

Ungrammatical Sentence:

During the early 70's, President Richard Nixon chose to <u>abdicate</u>
his position rather than face the possibility of impeachment.

Explanation of Error:

Type of Error:

Prefix:

Definition:

Root:

abdicate

Worksheet 45

Suffix:

What it Looks Like:

Analogous Exercise:

authority : abdicate   _____ : remit

Why? Nature of the Relationship:

Original Analogy Using the Vocabulary Word:

Perfect 800: SAT Verbal © Prufrock Press Inc. • Permission is granted to photocopy or reproduce this page for single classroom use only.

Ungrammatical Sentence:

As phrased by Shakespeare and as evidenced by many <u>conjugal</u> pairings, it is probable that, "the course of true love never did run smooth."

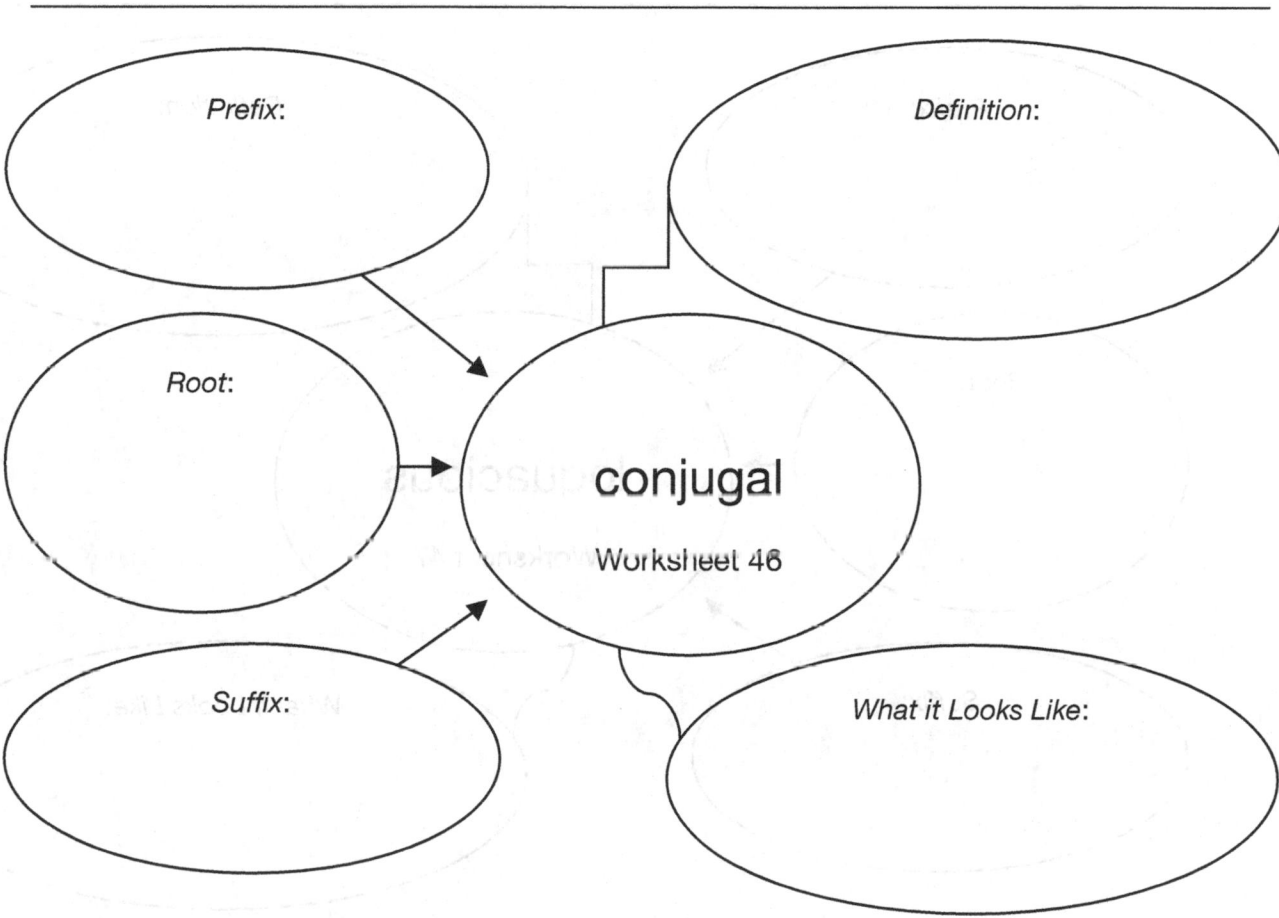

Explanation of Error:	Type of Error:

Prefix:

Definition:

Root:

conjugal

Worksheet 46

Suffix:

What it Looks Like:

Analogous Exercise:

together : conjugal

_____ : fragmentary

Why? Nature of the Relationship:

Original Analogy Using the Vocabulary Word:

Name:______________________________ Date:____________

Ungrammatical Sentence:

Sorrowful eulogists and comedians are doleful and <u>loquacious</u>, respectfully.

Explanation of Error:

Type of Error:

Prefix:

Definition:

Root:

loquacious

Worksheet 47

Suffix:

What it Looks Like:

Analogous Exercise:

loquacious : ineffable ____________ : unthinkable

Why? Nature of the Relationship:

Original Analogy Using the Vocabulary Word:

Name:______________________________ Date:__________

Ungrammatical Sentence:

The student could not help dozing off during the lecture, about which he was very disinterested, even when his teacher made <u>derogatory</u> remarks.

Explanation of Error:

Type of Error:

Prefix:

Root:

Suffix:

derogatory

Worksheet 48

Definition:

What it Looks Like:

Analogous Exercise:

derogatory : disparage

______________ : advocate

Why? Nature of the Relationship:

Original Analogy Using the Vocabulary Word:

Worksheet 48

Ungrammatical Sentence:

In 1918, influenza was <u>pandemic</u>, though experts now believe bacterial, rather than viral, infections to be what most American citizens died from.

Explanation of Error:

Type of Error:

Prefix:

Definition:

Root:

pandemic

Worksheet 49

Suffix:

What it Looks Like:

Analogous Exercise:

pandemic : all

_____ : some

Why? Nature of the Relationship:

Original Analogy Using the Vocabulary Word:

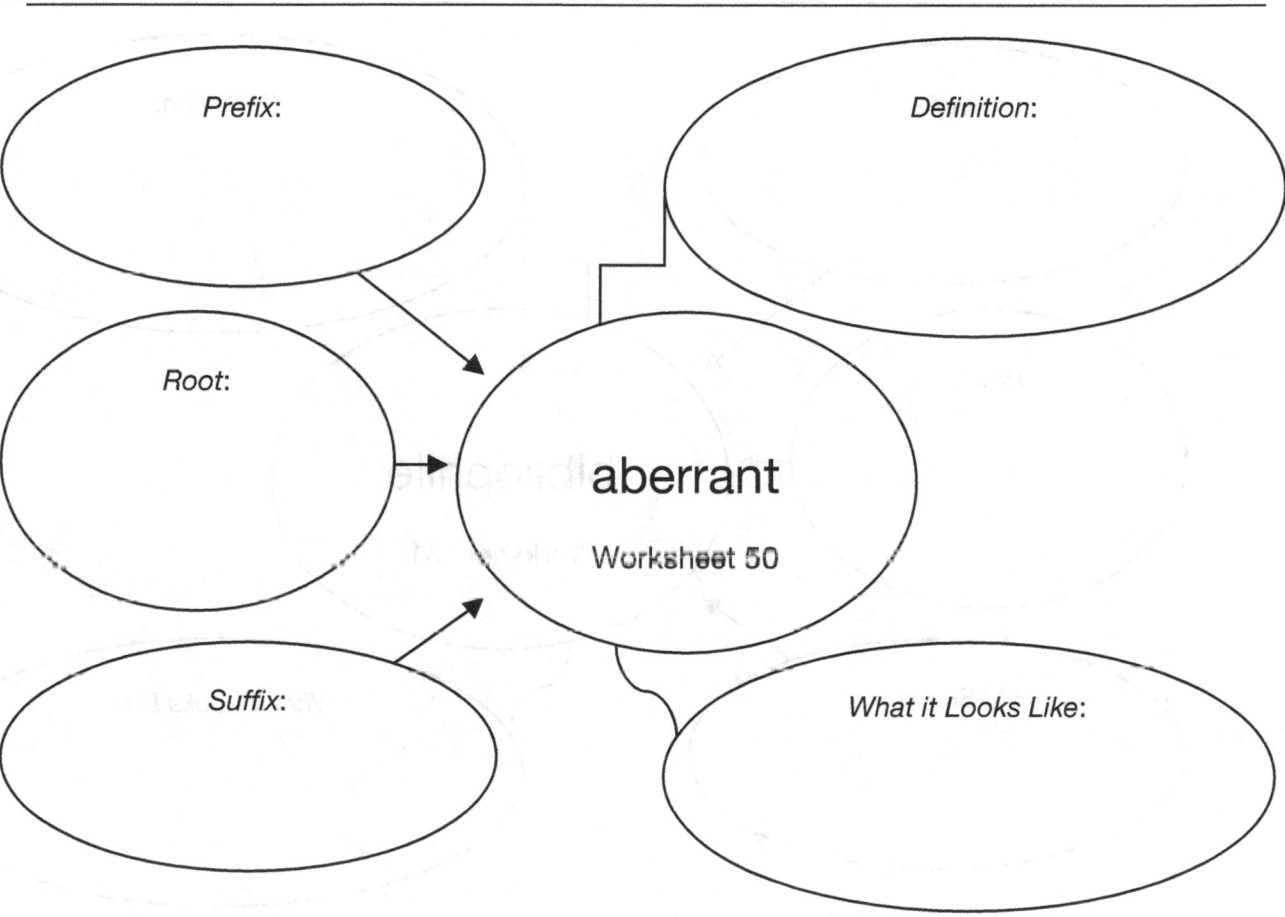

Name:_____ Date:_____

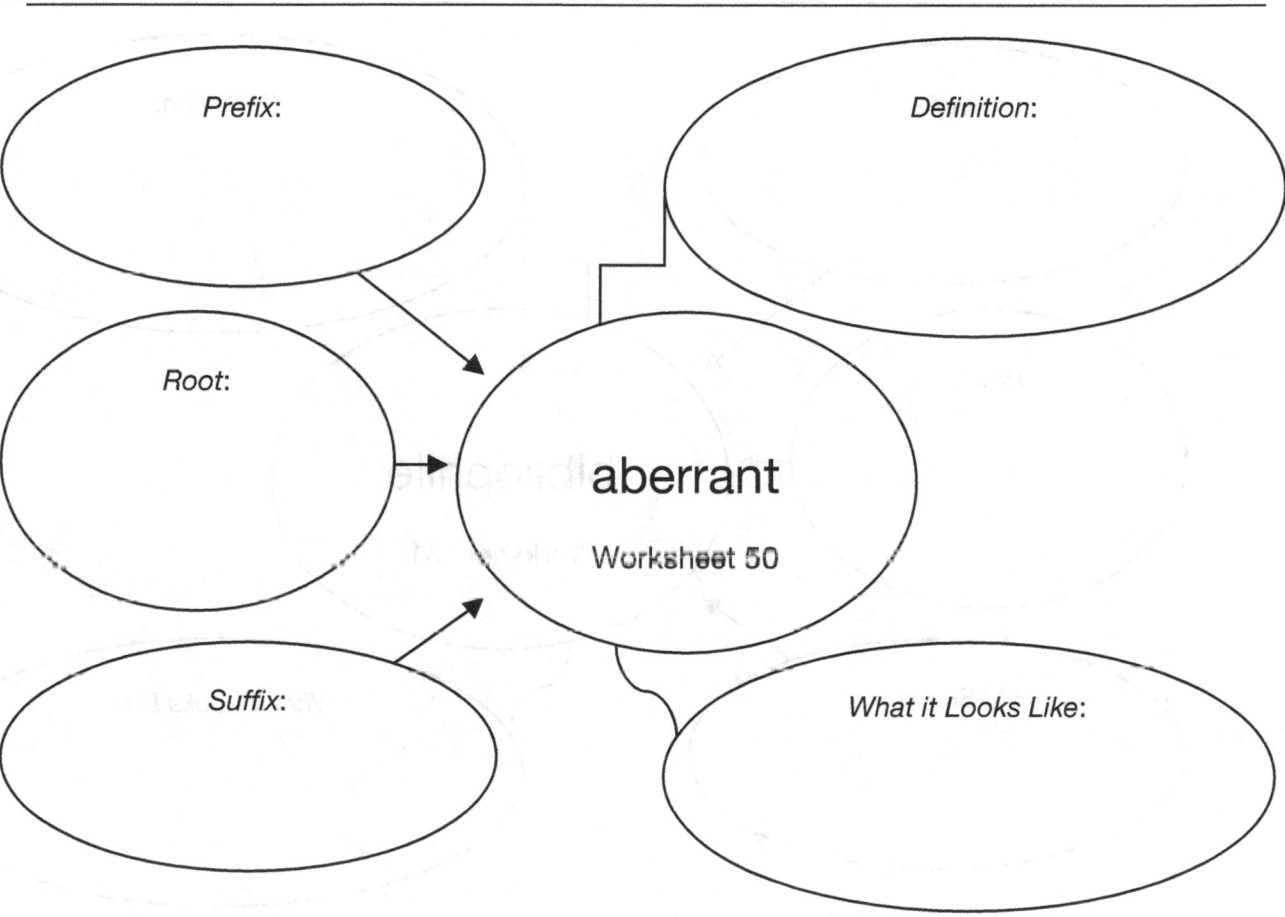

Ungrammatical Sentence:

In the words of my grandfather, "his decision not to go
into the family business was <u>aberrant</u> in every way."

Explanation of Error:

Type of Error:

Prefix:

Definition:

Root:

aberrant

Worksheet 50

Suffix:

What it Looks Like:

Analogous Exercise:

aberrant : routine   _____ : excellent

Why? Nature of the Relationship:

Original Analogy Using the Vocabulary
Word:

Worksheet 50

Ungrammatical Sentence:

For Dutch theologian Desiderius Erasmus famously noted his choice of books over food and clothes, and can thus be described as a <u>bibliophile</u>.

Explanation of Error:

Type of Error:

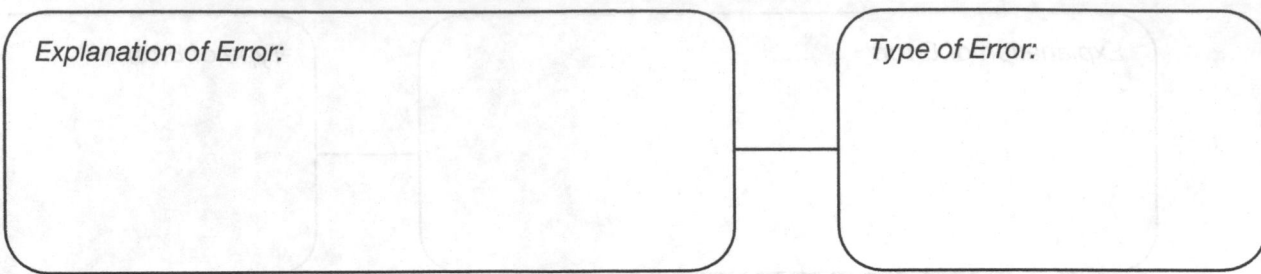

Prefix:

Definition:

Root:

bibliophile

Worksheet 51

Suffix:

What it Looks Like:

Analogous Exercise:

library : bibliophile

_____ : pedagogue

Why? Nature of the Relationship:

Original Analogy Using the Vocabulary Word:

Worksheet 51

Name:____ Date:__________

Ungrammatical Sentence:

It is a stereotypical belief that the conclusion of most Shakespearean tragedies resemble an <u>apoplexy</u> of death and sorrow.

Explanation of Error:

Type of Error:

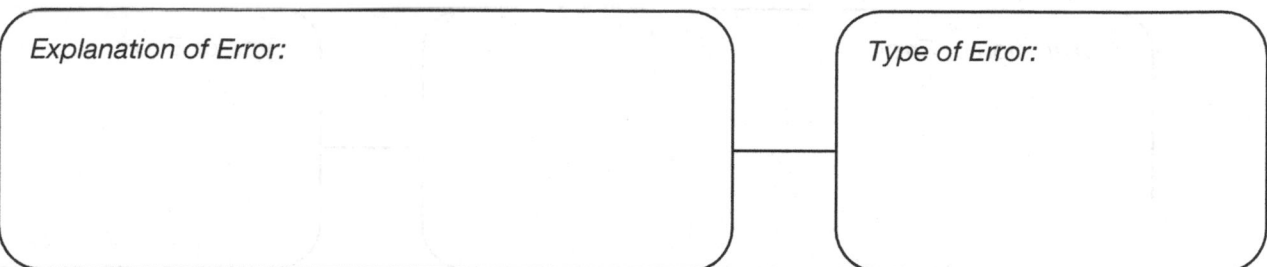

Prefix:

Definition:

Root:

apoplexy

Worksheet 52

Suffix:

What it Looks Like:

Analogous Exercise:

apoplexy : pugnacious

______________ : benevolent

Why? Nature of the Relationship:

Original Analogy Using the Vocabulary Word:

Worksheet 52

Ungrammatical Sentence:

The <u>viability</u> of changing your legal name to The Excellent Chairman
and Regent of Grammar and Morphology is probably small.

Explanation of Error:

Type of Error:

Prefix:

Definition:

Root:

viability

Worksheet 53

Suffix:

What it Looks Like:

Worksheet 53

Analogous Exercise:

viability : obstruction   _____ : miscalculation

Why? Nature of the Relationship:

Original Analogy Using the Vocabulary Word:

Perfect 800: SAT Verbal © Prufrock Press Inc. • Permission is granted to photocopy or reproduce this page for single classroom use only.

Ungrammatical Sentence:

Tchaikovsky was never <u>ambivalent</u> about the structures of his sonatas; those pieces have been played millions of times by countless musicians.

Explanation of Error:

Type of Error:

Prefix:

Definition:

Root:

ambivalent

Worksheet 54

Suffix:

What it Looks Like:

Analogous Exercise:

confusion : ambivalent

_____ : doleful

Why? Nature of the Relationship:

Original Analogy Using the Vocabulary Word:

Ungrammatical Sentence:

I was able to imply from the <u>predictive</u> almanac that wisteria vines and crape myrtle trees should be pruned after this February's snowfall.

Explanation of Error:	Type of Error:

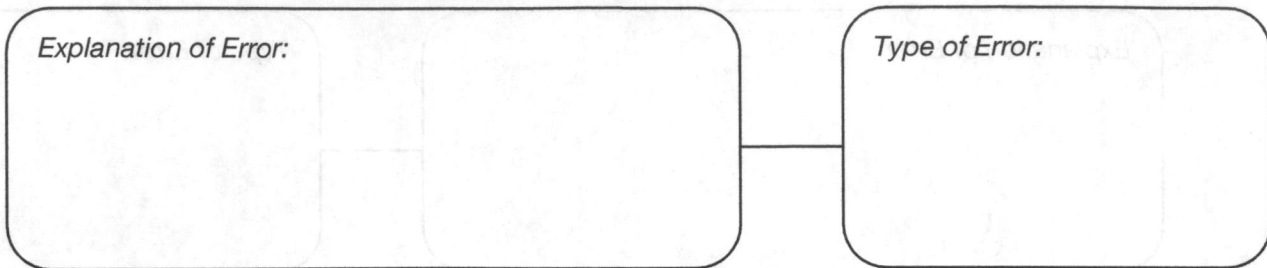

Prefix:

Root:

Suffix:

predictive

Worksheet 55

Definition:

What it Looks Like:

Analogous Exercise:

predictive : prognosis   _____ : reminiscence

Why? Nature of the Relationship:	Original Analogy Using the Vocabulary Word:

Ungrammatical Sentence:

Although good writers and investigators contribute weekly to
my local newspaper, the credibility of some of it's stories is <u>dubious</u>.

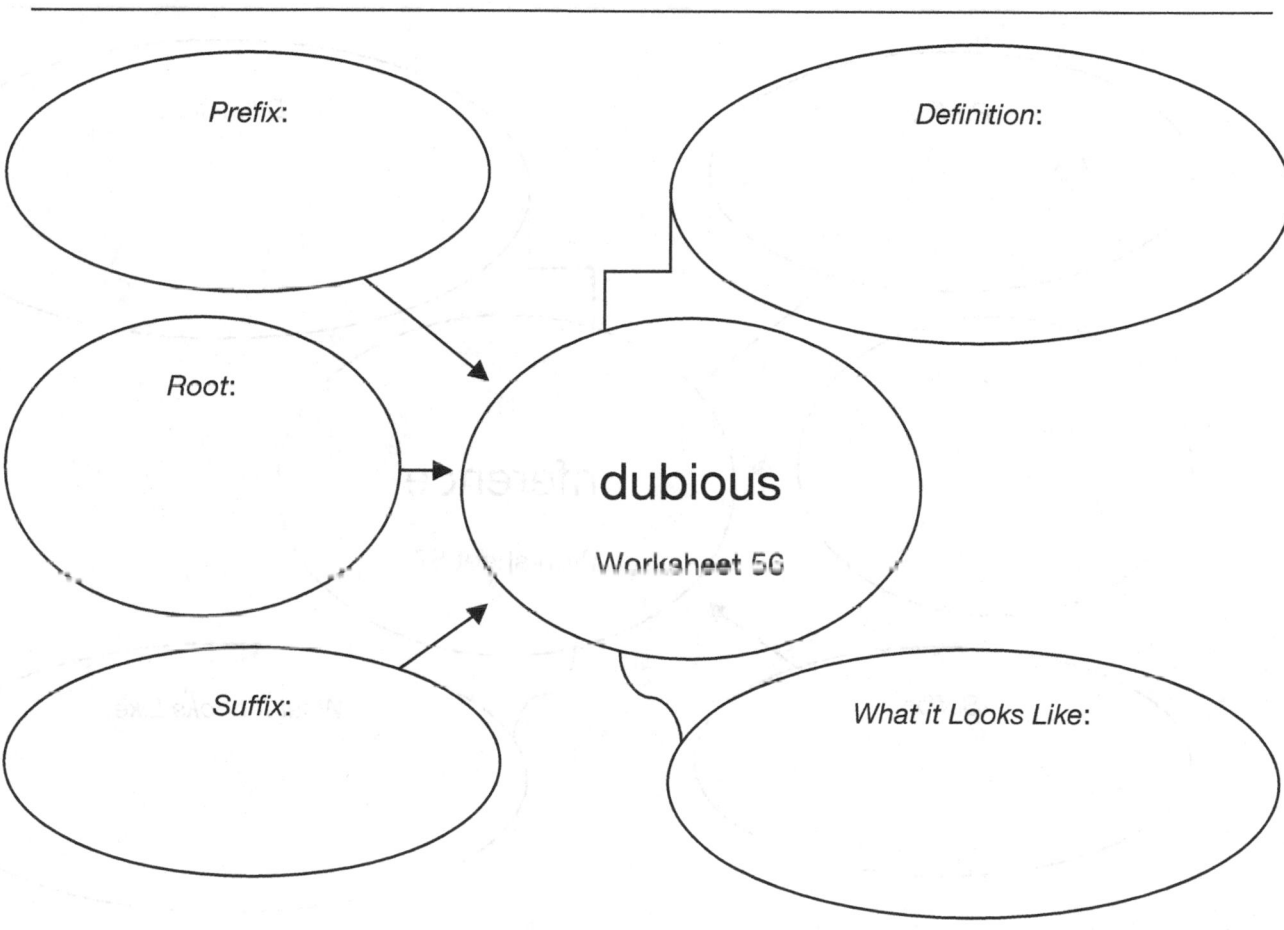

Explanation of Error:

Type of Error:

Prefix:

Definition:

Root:

dubious

Worksheet 56

Suffix:

What it Looks Like:

Analogous Exercise:

dubious : ambivalent   _____ : multitalented

Why? Nature of the Relationship:

Original Analogy Using the Vocabulary Word:

Ungrammatical Sentence:

And furthermore, it appears that our <u>inference</u> regarding
the speckled band was perhaps correct, Dr. Watson.

Explanation of Error:

Type of Error:

Prefix:

Definition:

Root:

inference

Worksheet 57

Suffix:

What it Looks Like:

Analogous Exercise:

viability : inference

_____ : statement of fact

Why? Nature of the Relationship:

Original Analogy Using the Vocabulary Word:

Perfect 800: SAT Verbal © Prufrock Press Inc. • Permission is granted to photocopy or reproduce this page for single classroom use only.

(sidebar) **Worksheet 57**

Ungrammatical Sentence:

The <u>refractory</u> inmates attempted to advocate for themselves yet neither the warden nor the chief guard was willing to listen to their outburst.

Explanation of Error:

Type of Error:

Prefix:

Definition:

Root:

refractory

Worksheet 58

Suffix:

What it Looks Like:

Analogous Exercise:

togetherness : conjugal   _____ : refractory

Why? Nature of the Relationship:

Original Analogy Using the Vocabulary Word:

Ungrammatical Sentence:

You must recognize the eminent architect's idea concerning the
<u>homogeneousness</u> of building materials is both plausible and attractive.

Explanation of Error:

Type of Error:

Prefix:

Definition:

Root:

homogeneousness

Worksheet 59

Suffix:

What it Looks Like:

Analogous Exercise:

one : homogeneousness   _____ : amorphousness

Why? Nature of the Relationship:

Original Analogy Using the Vocabulary Word:

Perfect 800: SAT Verbal © Prufrock Press Inc. • Permission is granted to photocopy or reproduce this page for single classroom use only.

Ungrammatical Sentence:

Not only did the New York Giants refuse to <u>capitulate</u> in 1951,
they won the pennant from the rival Dodgers in a dramatic fashion.

Explanation of Error:

Type of Error:

Prefix:

Definition:

Root:

capitulate

Worksheet 60

Suffix:

What it Looks Like:

Analogous Exercise:

capitulate : surrender   _____ : apoplexy

Why? Nature of the Relationship:

Original Analogy Using the Vocabulary Word:

Ungrammatical Sentence:

Regardless of the profuse number of inconsistencies in the starlet's testimony, the imminent attorney refused to believe in her <u>duplicity</u>.

Explanation of Error:

Type of Error:

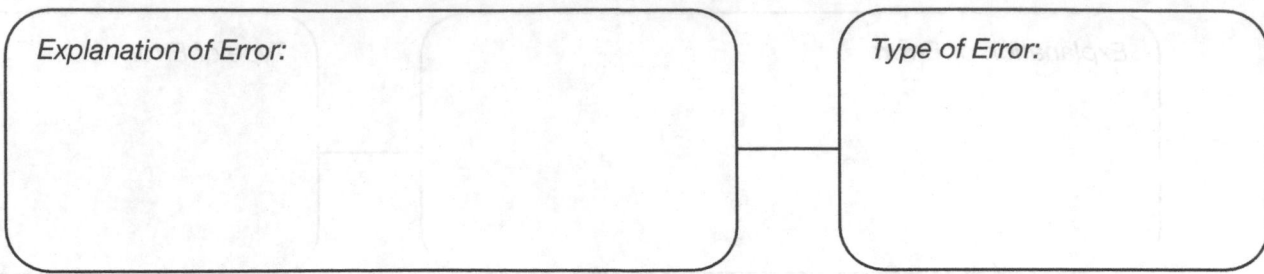

Prefix:

Definition:

Root:

duplicity

Worksheet 61

Suffix:

What it Looks Like:

Analogous Exercise:

duplicity : homogeneousness   _____ : gymnast

Why? Nature of the Relationship:

Original Analogy Using the Vocabulary Word:

Perfect 800: SAT Verbal © Prufrock Press Inc. • Permission is granted to photocopy or reproduce this page for single classroom use only.

Name:_____ Date:_____

Ungrammatical Sentence:

Nat King Cole, who many jazz aficionados cite as a favorite vocalist, had an absolutely <u>mellifluous</u> tone to his crooning voice.

Explanation of Error:

Type of Error:

Prefix:

Definition:

Root:

mellifluous

Worksheet 62

Suffix:

What it Looks Like:

Analogous Exercise:

mellifluous : traffic jam   _____ : skunk

Why? Nature of the Relationship:

Original Analogy Using the Vocabulary Word:

Ungrammatical Sentence:

The reason why certain chemical compounds are <u>transmutative</u> may be because their coalescence allows for both amorphous and material states.

Explanation of Error:	Type of Error:

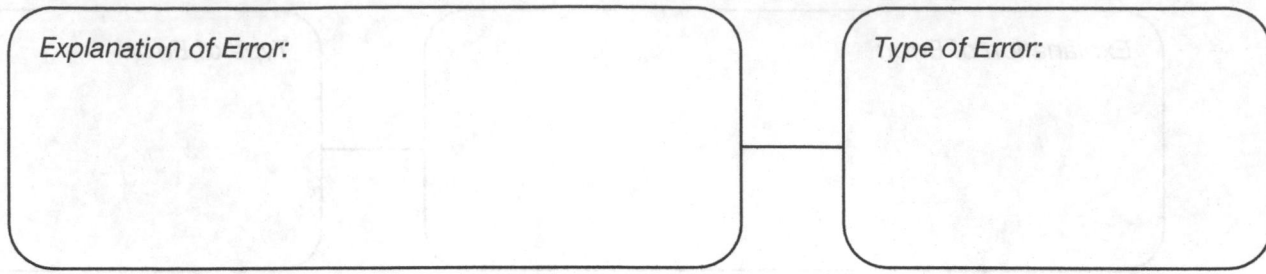

Prefix:

Definition:

Root:

transmutative

Worksheet 63

Suffix:

What it Looks Like:

Analogous Exercise:

transmutative : water   _____ : plastic

Why? Nature of the Relationship:	Original Analogy Using the Vocabulary Word:

Perfect 800: SAT Verbal © Prufrock Press Inc. • Permission is granted to photocopy or reproduce this page for single classroom use only.

Ungrammatical Sentence:

The loquacious <u>interlocutor</u> identified himself as Barnaby, he was
a very interesting individual with whom to hold a conversation.

Explanation of Error:

Type of Error:

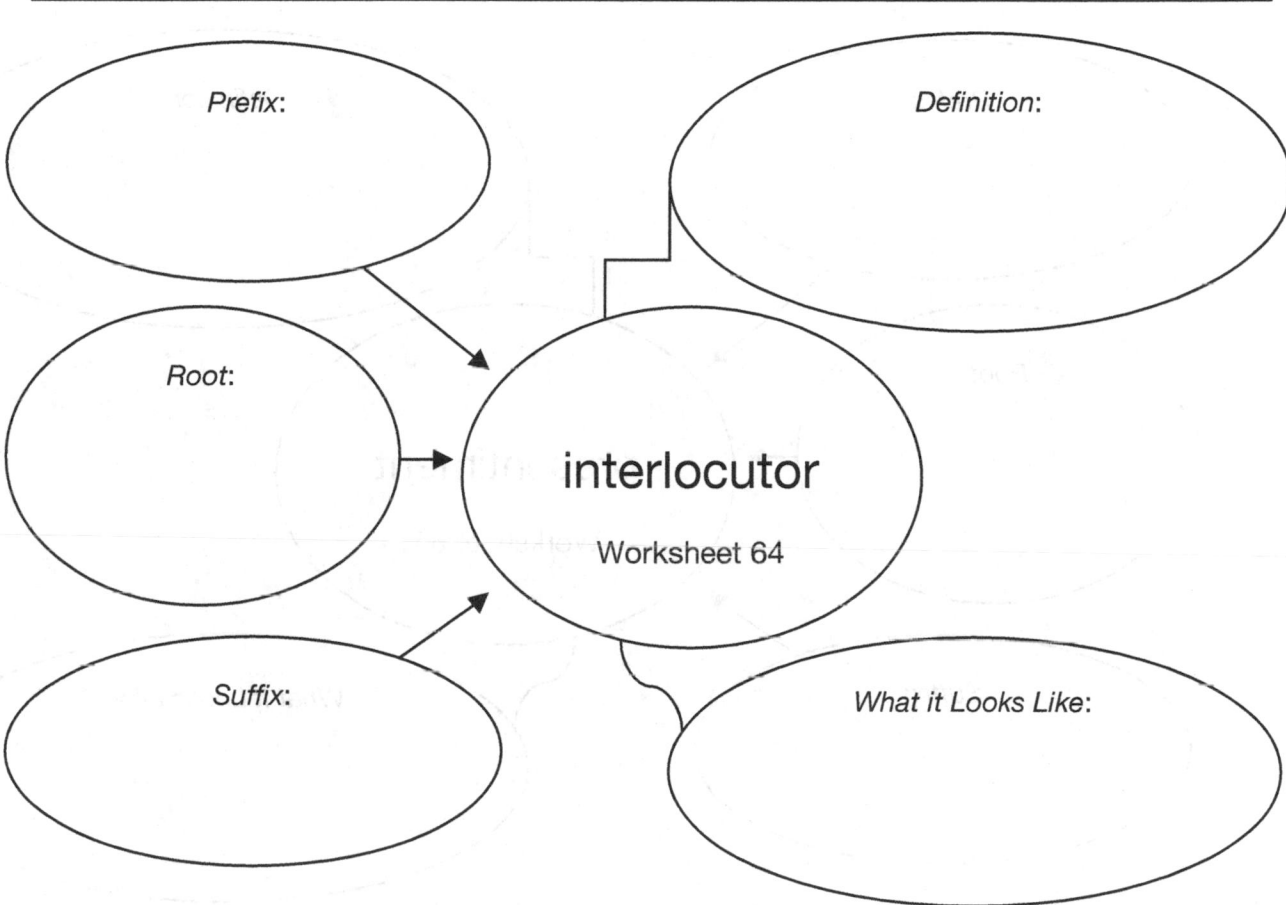

Prefix:

Definition:

Root:

interlocutor

Worksheet 64

Suffix:

What it Looks Like:

Analogous Exercise:

interlocuter : loquacious   _____ : refractory

Why? Nature of the Relationship:

Original Analogy Using the Vocabulary Word:

Ungrammatical Sentence:

My sister has a <u>presentiment</u> that figure skating will appear on television tonight, tomorrow, and she thinks that it may also be on next weekend.

Explanation of Error:

Type of Error:

Prefix:

Definition:

Root:

presentiment

Worksheet 65

Suffix:

What it Looks Like:

Analogous Exercise:

observation : inference

_____ : presentiment

Why? Nature of the Relationship:

Original Analogy Using the Vocabulary Word:

Name:____ Date:__________

Ungrammatical Sentence:

The <u>philanthropist</u> gave generously to the needy widow because she was very kind.

Explanation of Error:

Type of Error:

Prefix:

Root:

Suffix:

Definition:

What it Looks Like:

philanthropist

Worksheet 66

Analogous Exercise:

philanthropist : magnanimous

______________ : mellifluous

Why? Nature of the Relationship:

Original Analogy Using the Vocabulary Word:

Worksheet 66

Ungrammatical Sentence:

I have read that it was difficult for bootleggers, flappers, and stockbrokers to demonstrate emotional <u>equanimity</u> during the Roaring 20's.

Explanation of Error:

Type of Error:

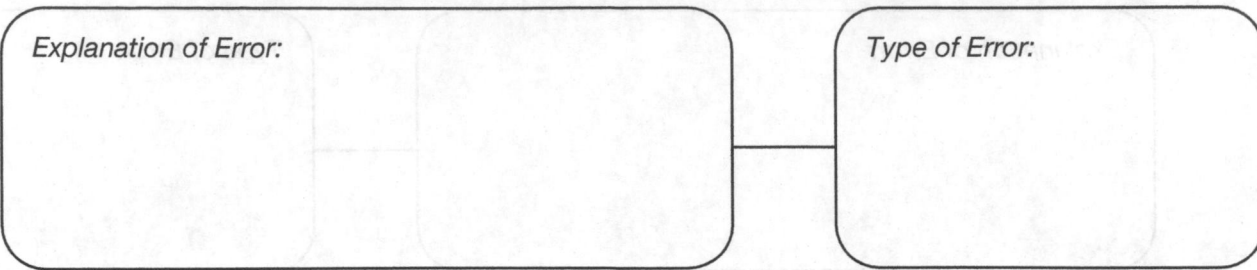

Prefix:

Definition:

Root:

equanimity

Worksheet 67

Suffix:

What it Looks Like:

Analogous Exercise:

flat : equanimity   _____ : aberrance

Why? Nature of the Relationship:

Original Analogy Using the Vocabulary Word:

Ungrammatical Sentence:

Narrators who demonstrate omniscience rarely make <u>tentative</u> predictions concerning their respective novels's outcomes.

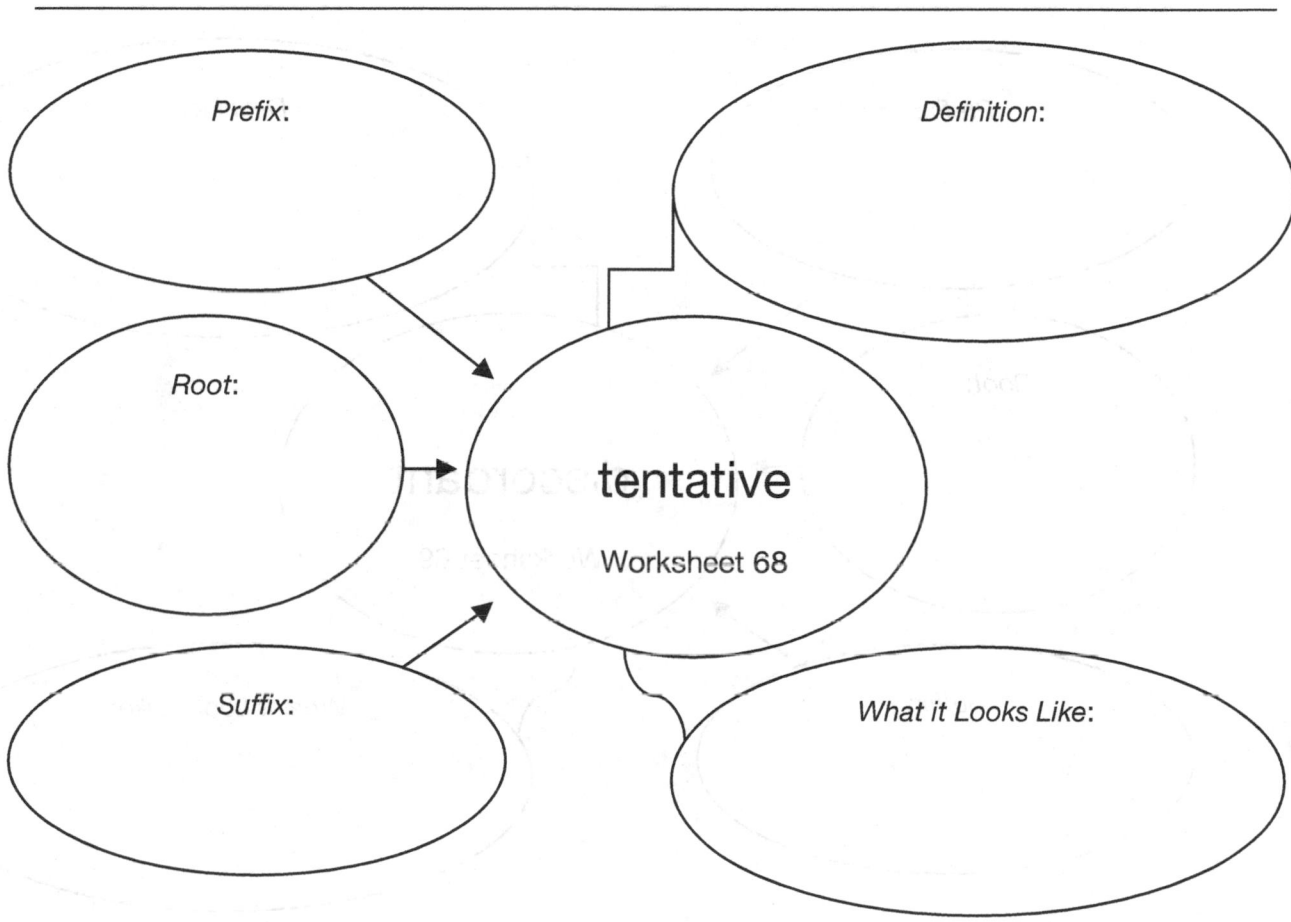

| Explanation of Error: | Type of Error: |

Prefix:

Definition:

Root:

tentative

Worksheet 68

Suffix:

What it Looks Like:

Analogous Exercise:

predictive : tentative   _____ : definite

| Why? Nature of the Relationship: | Original Analogy Using the Vocabulary Word: |

Name:____ Date:___________

Ungrammatical Sentence:

An extremely <u>discordant</u> noise arose between the orchestral instruments situated within the pit.

Explanation of Error:

Type of Error:

Prefix:

Root:

Suffix:

discordant

Worksheet 69

Definition:

What it Looks Like:

Analogous Exercise:

coalesce : discordant ______________ : unified

Why? Nature of the Relationship:

Original Analogy Using the Vocabulary Word:

Worksheet 69

Ungrammatical Sentence:

Transmutative creatures are <u>polymorphous,</u>
and I am somewhat scared of those.

Explanation of Error:	Type of Error:

Prefix:

Definition:

Root:

polymorphous

Worksheet 70

Suffix:

What it Looks Like:

Analogous Exercise:

duplicity : polymorphous   _____ : homogeneous

Why? Nature of the Relationship:	Original Analogy Using the Vocabulary Word:

Worksheet 70

Ungrammatical Sentence:

Thomas Edison's creative <u>inclination</u> allowed him less hours of leisure time than hours spent experimenting and tinkering laboriously.

Explanation of Error:

Type of Error:

Prefix:

Definition:

Root:

inclination
Worksheet 71

Suffix:

What it Looks Like:

Analogous Exercise:

inclination : triangle   _____ : square

Why? Nature of the Relationship:

Original Analogy Using the Vocabulary Word:

Ungrammatical Sentence:

The patient's apoplexy was anything but <u>quiescent</u>, for its
severity actually frightened the nurse whom she was assigned to.

Explanation of Error:

Type of Error:

Prefix:

Definition:

Root:

quiescent
Worksheet 72

Suffix:

What it Looks Like:

Analogous Exercise:

bibliophile : quiescent   _____ : ambulatory

Why? Nature of the Relationship:

Original Analogy Using the Vocabulary Word:

Ungrammatical Sentence:

I do not actually know if the mysterious visitor was <u>cognizant</u> of my dog and I; I rather imagine that the dark night shrouded us well from sight.

Explanation of Error:

Type of Error:

Prefix:

Definition:

Root:

cognizant

Worksheet 73

Suffix:

What it Looks Like:

Analogous Exercise:

cognizant : credibility _____ : apocryphalness

Why? Nature of the Relationship:

Original Analogy Using the Vocabulary Word:

Worksheet 73

Name:_____ Date:_____

Ungrammatical Sentence:

The county's chief authority on taxation and fiscal accountability stated clearly that, "<u>heterodox</u> bookkeeping methods exacerbate problems."

Explanation of Error:

Type of Error:

Prefix:

Definition:

Root:

heterodox

Worksheet 74

Suffix:

What it Looks Like:

Analogous Exercise:

heterodox : discordant

_____ : agreeable

Why? Nature of the Relationship:

Original Analogy Using the Vocabulary Word:

Name:____ Date:___________

Ungrammatical Sentence:

The belligerent pedagogue's methodology was quite an <u>impediment</u> too my achievement in his class!

Explanation of Error:

Type of Error:

Prefix:

Definition:

Root:

impediment

Worksheet 75

Suffix:

What it Looks Like:

Analogous Exercise:

obstruction : impediment ______________ : purple

Why? Nature of the Relationship:

Original Analogy Using the Vocabulary Word:

Name:_____ Date:_____

Ungrammatical Sentence:

Benedict Arnold's <u>egregious</u> duplicity during The Revolutionary War gained him lasting infamy, at least in the United States of America.

Explanation of Error:

Type of Error:

Prefix:

Definition:

Root:

egregious

Worksheet 76

Suffix:

What it Looks Like:

Analogous Exercise:

egregious : capitulate

_____ : sing along

Why? Nature of the Relationship:

Original Analogy Using the Vocabulary Word:

Name:________________________________ Date:____________

Ungrammatical Sentence:

The politician's indubitable verity was at least for her an <u>anomaly</u>; most things that she said were, at the very least, apocryphal.

Explanation of Error:

Type of Error:

Prefix:

Definition:

Root:

anomaly

Worksheet 77

Suffix:

What it Looks Like:

Analogous Exercise:

heterodox : anomaly

______________ : normality

Why? Nature of the Relationship:

Original Analogy Using the Vocabulary Word:

Name:_____ Date:_____

Ungrammatical Sentence:

Watching the tennis match I witnessed parity <u>recede</u> before the superiority of experience; needless to say, the novice player lost handily.

Explanation of Error:

Type of Error:

Prefix:

Definition:

Root:

recede

Worksheet 78

Suffix:

What it Looks Like:

Analogous Exercise:

recede : tide   _____ : sun

Why? Nature of the Relationship:

Original Analogy Using the Vocabulary Word:

Ungrammatical Sentence:

The essay for English class and the scientific experiment were completed <u>concurrently</u> by the impressively talented student.

Explanation of Error:

Type of Error:

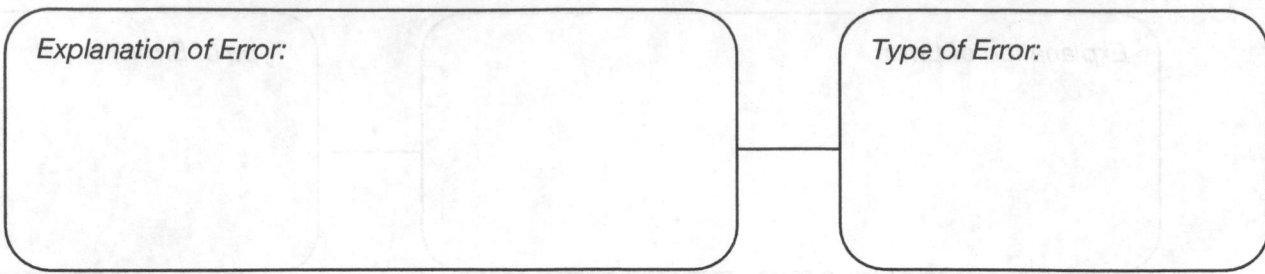

Prefix:

Definition:

Root:

concurrently

Worksheet 79

Suffix:

What it Looks Like:

Analogous Exercise:

interstate highway : concurrently   _____ : intermittently

Why? Nature of the Relationship:

Original Analogy Using the Vocabulary Word:

Perfect 800: SAT Verbal © Prufrock Press Inc. • Permission is granted to photocopy or reproduce this page for single classroom use only.

Ungrammatical Sentence:

Tabloid newspapers are often exonerated easy when
they are accused by angry celebrities of <u>defamation</u>.

Explanation of Error:

Type of Error:

Prefix:

Definition:

Root:

defamation

Worksheet 80

Suffix:

What it Looks Like:

Analogous Exercise:

ineffable : defamation   _____ : physical violence

Why? Nature of the Relationship:

Original Analogy Using the Vocabulary Word:

Worksheet 80

Name:______________________________ Date:__________

Ungrammatical Sentence:

Providence is a word with several related denotations: religious, civic, and intellectual.

Explanation of Error:

Type of Error:

Prefix:

Definition:

Root:

providence

Worksheet 81

Suffix:

What it Looks Like:

Analogous Exercise:

thought : providence ____________ : luck

Why? Nature of the Relationship:

Original Analogy Using the Vocabulary Word:

Ungrammatical Sentence:

Even though fears of a lethal pandemic were international, but the frightening avian flu outbreak of 1997 was, in truth, relatively <u>innocuous</u>.

Explanation of Error:

Type of Error:

Prefix:

Definition:

Root:

innocuous

Worksheet 82

Suffix:

What it Looks Like:

Analogous Exercise:

innocuous : tea   _____ : bacon

Why? Nature of the Relationship:

Original Analogy Using the Vocabulary Word:

Worksheet 82

Name:_____ Date:_____

Ungrammatical Sentence:

Pugnacious rioters probably <u>contravene</u> laws
more then docile bibliophiles do.

Explanation of Error:

Type of Error:

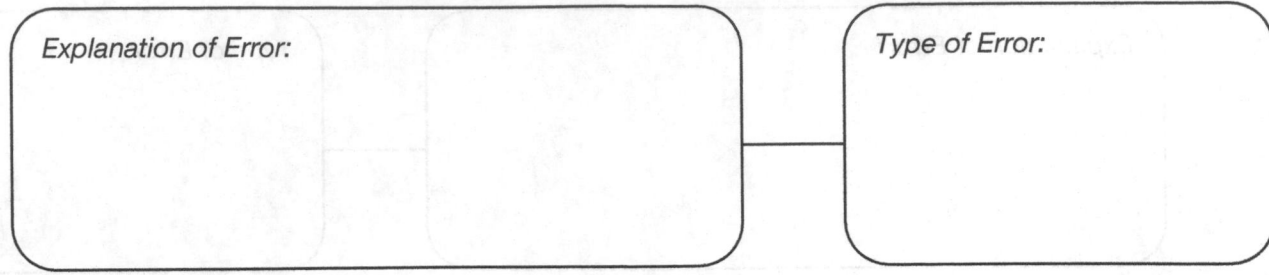

Prefix:

Definition:

Root:

contravene

Worksheet 83

Suffix:

What it Looks Like:

Analogous Exercise:

discordant : contravene

_____ : capitulate

Why? Nature of the Relationship:

Original Analogy Using the Vocabulary Word:

Perfect 800: SAT Verbal © Prufrock Press Inc. • Permission is granted to photocopy or reproduce this page for single classroom use only.

Ungrammatical Sentence:

Colonial Williamsburg is an impressive <u>anachronism</u>; an outdoor museum, it employs more colonial tradesmen than any other educational institution.

Explanation of Error:	Type of Error:

Prefix:

Definition:

Root:

anachronism
Worksheet 84

Suffix:

What it Looks Like:

Analogous Exercise:

anachronism : 1990   _____ : Bombay, India

Why? Nature of the Relationship:	Original Analogy Using the Vocabulary Word:

Ungrammatical Sentence:

The well known theorist considers <u>hereditary</u> physical traits fully controllable with scientific aid; his idea's viability is slightly dubious.

Explanation of Error:

Type of Error:

Prefix:

Definition:

Root:

hereditary

Worksheet 85

Suffix:

What it Looks Like:

Analogous Exercise:

wild guess : presentiment _____ : hereditary

Why? Nature of the Relationship:

Original Analogy Using the Vocabulary Word:

Ungrammatical Sentence:

I tried to confidently converse with the <u>magniloquent</u> philanthropist, but found myself completely intimidated by his dignified manner.

Explanation of Error:	*Type of Error:*

Prefix:

Definition:

Root:

magniloquent

Worksheet 86

Suffix:

What it Looks Like:

Analogous Exercise:

magniloquent : mellifluous   _____ : sweet-smelling

Why? Nature of the Relationship:	*Original Analogy Using the Vocabulary Word:*

Ungrammatical Sentence:

Overlooking Saint Peter's Square, the Pope offered a <u>benediction</u> to the thousands of persons who had gathered to hear him speak.

Explanation of Error:

Type of Error:

Prefix:

Definition:

Root:

benediction

Worksheet 87

Suffix:

What it Looks Like:

Analogous Exercise:

gossip tabloids : defamation

_____ : benediction

Why? Nature of the Relationship:

Original Analogy Using the Vocabulary Word:

Worksheet 87

Ungrammatical Sentence:

Hearing his own mellifluousness, the newscaster stated that "his tone rings like a knife cuts through butter," which was an <u>ambiguous</u> description.

Explanation of Error:

Type of Error:

Prefix:

Definition:

Root:

ambiguous

Worksheet 88

Suffix:

What it Looks Like:

Analogous Exercise:

ambiguous : poetry

_____ : maze

Why? Nature of the Relationship:

Original Analogy Using the Vocabulary Word:

Worksheet 88

Ungrammatical Sentence:

No aberrant student has ever tried to <u>litigate</u> to defend their claim that Isaac Newton developed calculus before Gottfried Leibniz did.

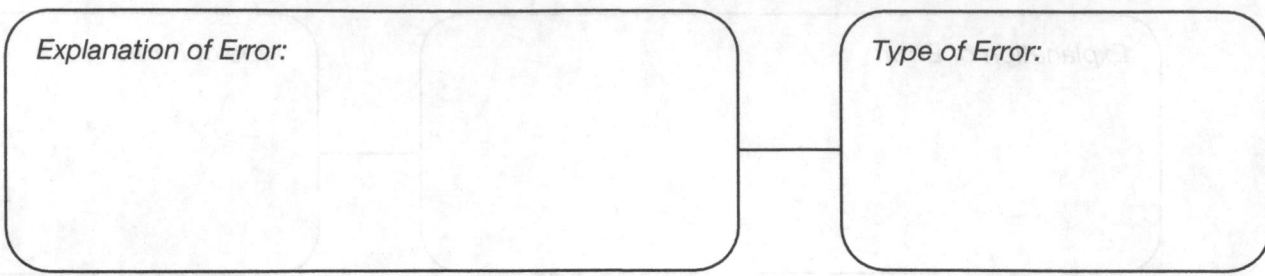

Explanation of Error:

Type of Error:

Prefix:

Definition:

Root:

litigate

Worksheet 89

Suffix:

What it Looks Like:

Analogous Exercise:

litigate : judge

_____ : referee

Why? Nature of the Relationship:

Original Analogy Using the Vocabulary Word:

Name:____ Date:___________

Ungrammatical Sentence:

The art of <u>cryptography</u> corresponds with those areas of the human brain that are able to make inferences and communicate in heterodox ways.

Explanation of Error:

Type of Error:

Prefix:

Definition:

Root:

cryptography

Worksheet 90

Suffix:

What it Looks Like:

Analogous Exercise:

elementary school : multiplication ______________ : cryptography

Why? Nature of the Relationship:

Original Analogy Using the Vocabulary Word:

Worksheet 90

Ungrammatical Sentence:

<u>Dejected</u> and incredible, the stunned snowboarder simply would not admit that he had actually lost the contest to a novice from Jamaica.

Explanation of Error:

Type of Error:

Prefix:

Definition:

Root:

Suffix:

dejected

Worksheet 91

What it Looks Like:

Analogous Exercise:

dejected : quiescent   _____ : magniloquent

Why? Nature of the Relationship:

Original Analogy Using the Vocabulary Word:

Ungrammatical Sentence:

Many innocuous things can be described as <u>luminous</u>,
including: fireflies, streetlights, and the sun.

Explanation of Error:

Type of Error:

Prefix:

Definition:

Root:

luminous

Worksheet 92

Suffix:

What it Looks Like:

Analogous Exercise:

luminous : stars

_____ : seas

Why? Nature of the Relationship:

Original Analogy Using the Vocabulary Word:

Worksheet 92

Name:____ Date:__________

Ungrammatical Sentence:

The painting by Albrecht Durer and my little brother's favorite song are ambiguous and reductive, respectfully; I greatly prefer the painting.

Explanation of Error:

Type of Error:

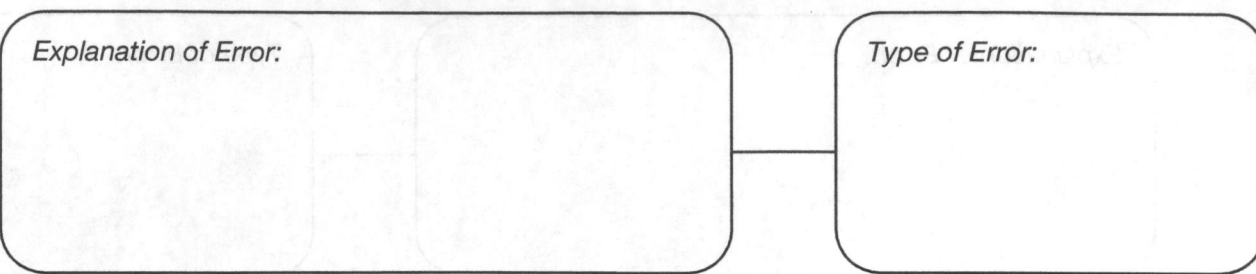

Prefix:

Definition:

Root:

reductive

Worksheet 93

Suffix:

What it Looks Like:

Analogous Exercise:

encyclopedia : thorough ____________ : reductive

Why? Nature of the Relationship:

Original Analogy Using the Vocabulary Word:

Worksheet 93

Name:_____ Date:_____

Ungrammatical Sentence:

I imagine that it is difficult to indoctrinate dolphins with
human-like communicative capabilities, although.

Explanation of Error:

Type of Error:

Prefix:

Definition:

Root:

indoctrinate

Worksheet 94

Suffix:

What it Looks Like:

Analogous Exercise:

pedagogue : indoctrinate   _____ : capitulate

Why? Nature of the Relationship:

Original Analogy Using the Vocabulary
Word:

Ungrammatical Sentence:

The headmaster's lecture to the truant boy was neither innocuous or lighthearted, but quite filled with <u>degradation</u> and defamation.

Explanation of Error:

Type of Error:

Prefix:

Definition:

Root:

degradation

Worksheet 95

Suffix:

What it Looks Like:

Analogous Exercise:

doleful : degradation

_____ : benediction

Why? Nature of the Relationship:

Original Analogy Using the Vocabulary Word:

Ungrammatical Sentence:

The idea of <u>eugenics</u> is a controversial one, to say the least; since Adolf Hitler long ago expressed a desire for homogeneousness among men.

Explanation of Error:		Type of Error:

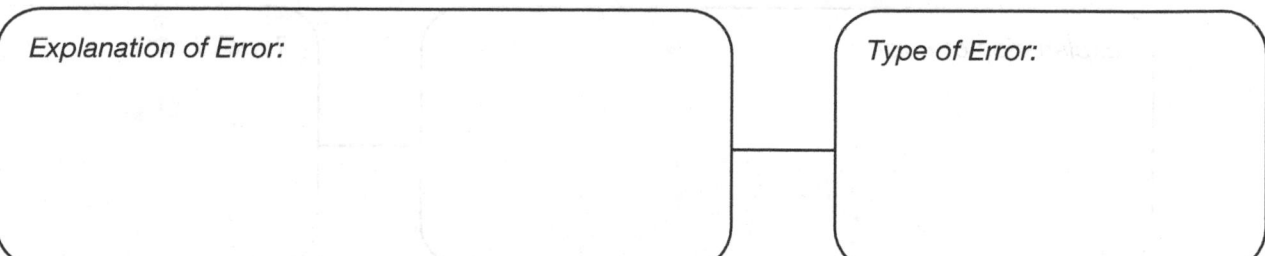

Prefix:

Definition:

Root:

eugenics

Worksheet 96

Suffix:

What it Looks Like:

Analogous Exercise:

eugenics : hereditary   _____ : anomalous

Why? Nature of the Relationship:	Original Analogy Using the Vocabulary Word:

Name:____ Date:____________

Ungrammatical Sentence:

If pursuing litigation, a plaintiff's lack of total <u>fidelity</u> to the facts of a case can effect an impediment to justice, irregardless of his or her motive.

Explanation of Error:

Type of Error:

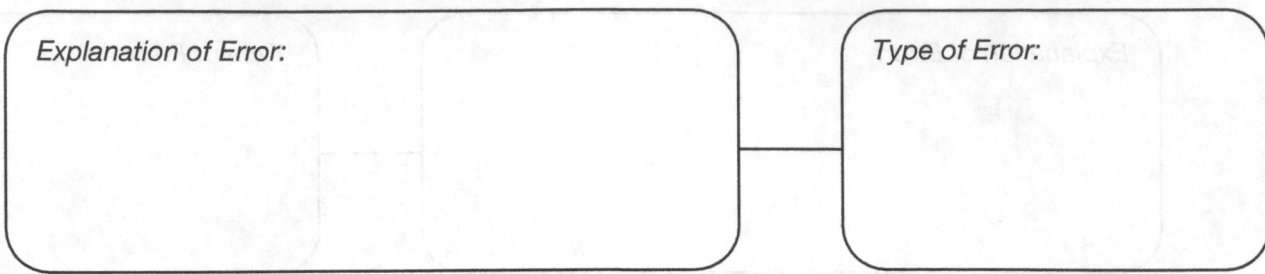

Prefix:

Definition:

Root:

fidelity

Worksheet 97

Suffix:

What it Looks Like:

Analogous Exercise:

conjugal : fidelity ______________ : duplicity

Why? Nature of the Relationship:

Original Analogy Using the Vocabulary Word:

Worksheet 97

Ungrammatical Sentence:

Some readers believe that it is nearly impossible to <u>elucidate</u> thematic meaning in William Blake's poetry, which was incredibly complicated.

Explanation of Error:

Type of Error:

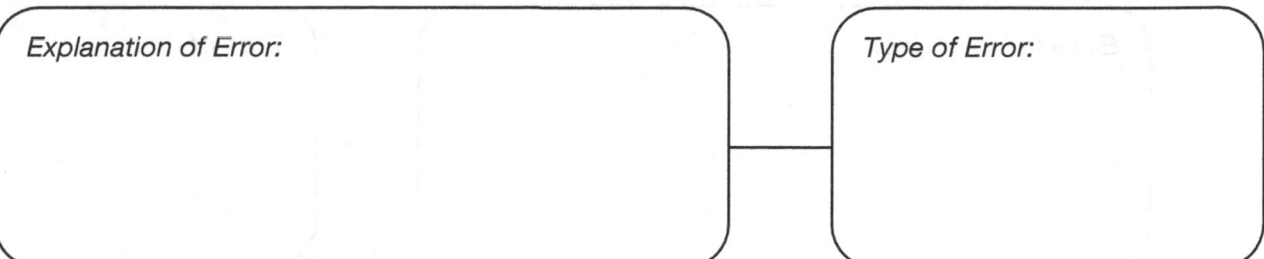

Prefix:

Definition:

Root:

elucidate
Worksheet 98

Suffix:

What it Looks Like:

Analogous Exercise:

elucidate : ambiguous   _____ : reductive

Why? Nature of the Relationship:

Original Analogy Using the Vocabulary Word:

Ungrammatical Sentence:

When the verdict was announced, utter <u>pandemonium</u> erupted in the courtroom as the uninterested judge and jury members fled for their lives.

Explanation of Error:	Type of Error:

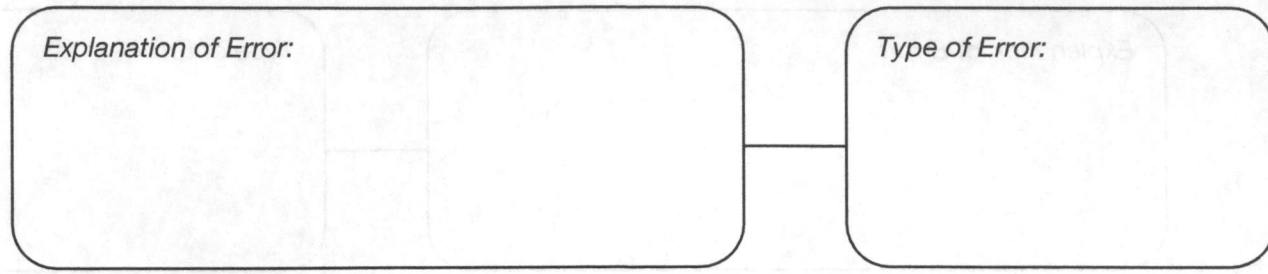

Prefix:

Definition:

Root:

pandemonium

Worksheet 99

Suffix:

What it Looks Like:

Analogous Exercise:

pandemonium : distance   _____ : time

Why? Nature of the Relationship:	Original Analogy Using the Vocabulary Word:

Name:______________________________ Date:__________

Ungrammatical Sentence:

As the teacher announces that her pop quiz is not worth many points, each of the students in the very large classroom demonstrate impassivity.

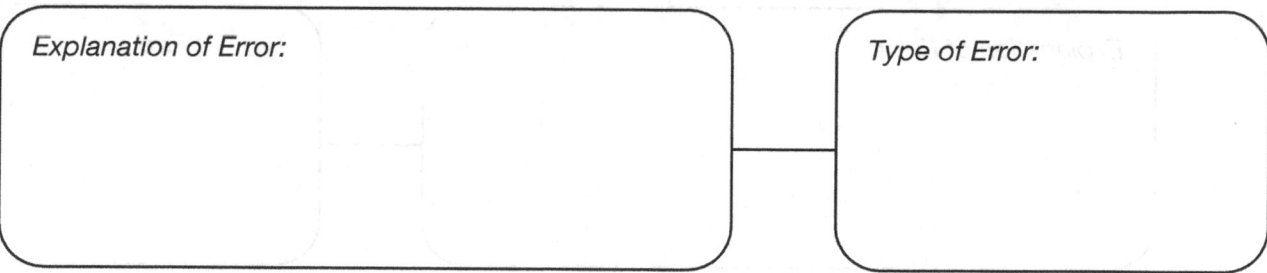

Explanation of Error:

Type of Error:

Prefix:

Definition:

Root:

impassivity

Worksheet 100

Suffix:

What it Looks Like:

Analogous Exercise:

impassivity : recede

__________ : arise

Why? Nature of the Relationship:

Original Analogy Using the Vocabulary Word:

Worksheet 100

Name:____ Date:__________

Ungrammatical Sentence:

The Battle of the Alamo effected the Texas Revolution greatly, adding <u>acrimonious</u> fire to an already hot political issue.

Explanation of Error:

Type of Error:

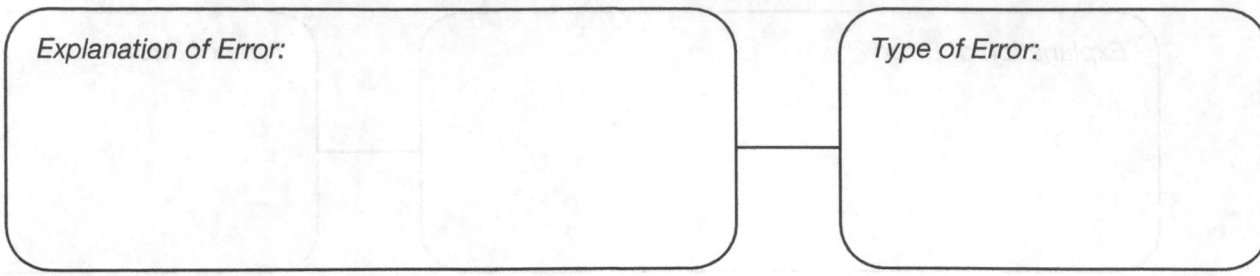

Prefix:

Definition:

Root:

acrimonious

Worksheet 101

Suffix:

What it Looks Like:

Analogous Exercise:

quiescence : apoplexy

____________ : acrimonious

Why? Nature of the Relationship:

Original Analogy Using the Vocabulary Word:

Worksheet 101

Name:_____ Date:_____

Ungrammatical Sentence:

Neither <u>condolence</u> nor quiescence are appropriate responses to one's first personal encounter with any of the famous wonders of the world.

Explanation of Error:

Type of Error:

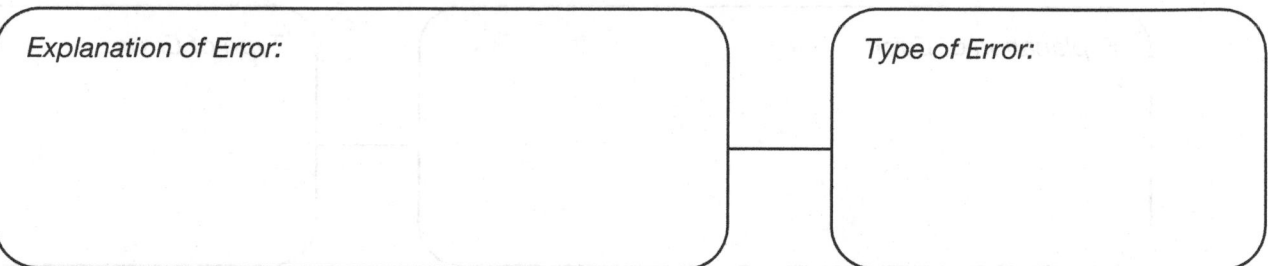

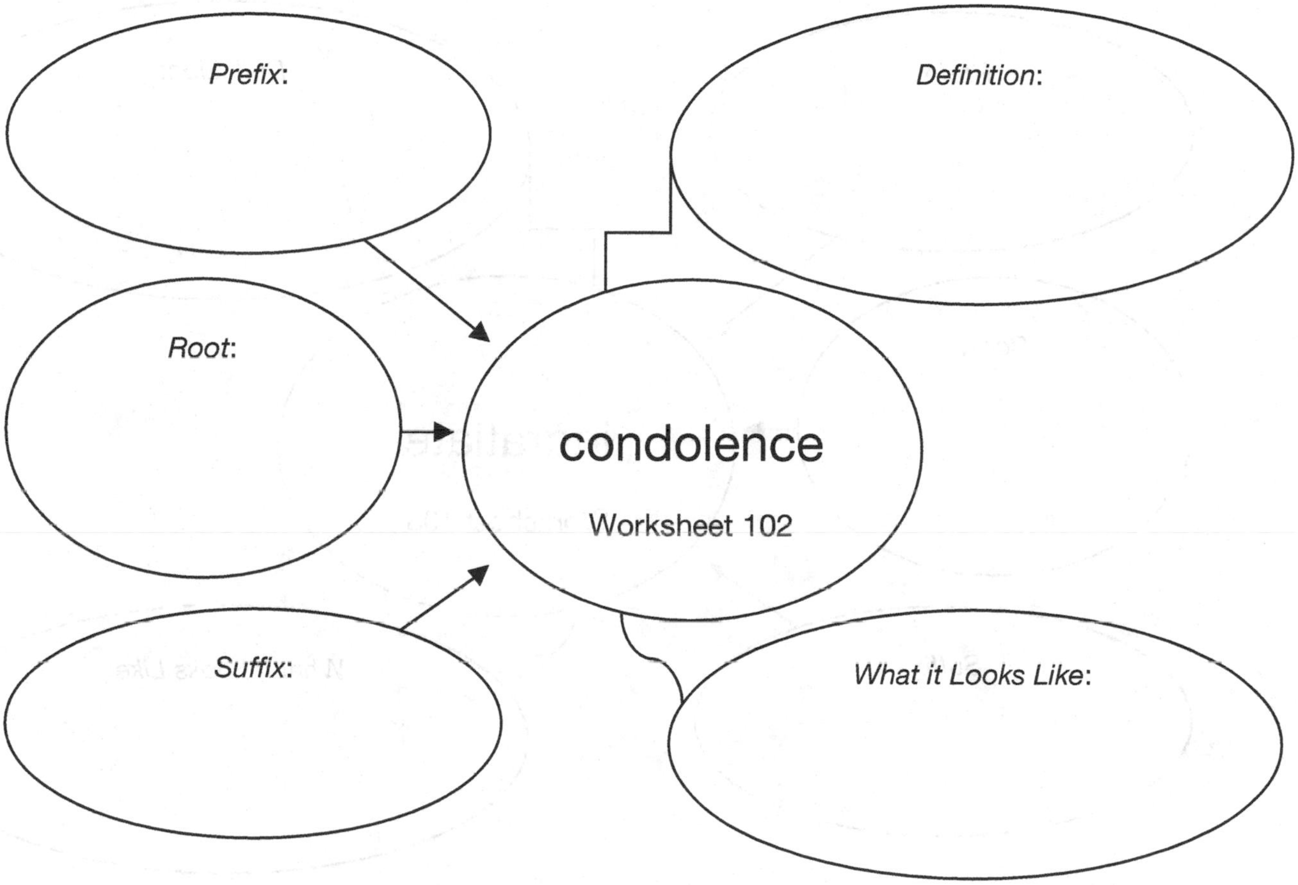

Prefix:

Definition:

Root:

condolence

Worksheet 102

Suffix:

What it Looks Like:

Analogous Exercise:

eulogy : condolence   _____ : litigation

Why? Nature of the Relationship:

Original Analogy Using the Vocabulary Word:

Ungrammatical Sentence:

In 1945, Ho Chi Minh was repeatedly unable to <u>ingratiate</u> himself with President Truman, farther escalating the potential for rebellion in Vietnam.

<table>
<tr><td>

Explanation of Error:

</td><td>

Type of Error:

</td></tr>
</table>

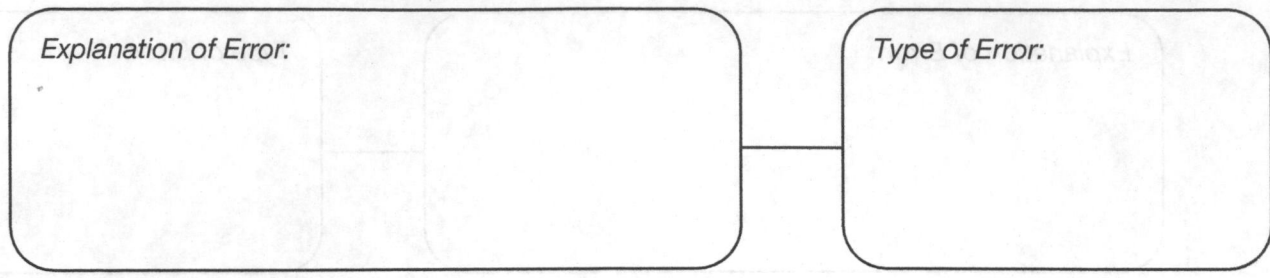

Prefix:

Definition:

Root:

ingratiate

Worksheet 103

Suffix:

What it Looks Like:

Analogous Exercise:

magniloquence : ingratiate   _____ : disparage

<table>
<tr><td>

Why? Nature of the Relationship:

</td><td>

Original Analogy Using the Vocabulary Word:

</td></tr>
</table>

Ungrammatical Sentence:

Relying on the <u>tenuousness</u> of memory, the scientist presented his idea to preserve the blue whale from extinction to the audience in the theater.

Explanation of Error:

Type of Error:

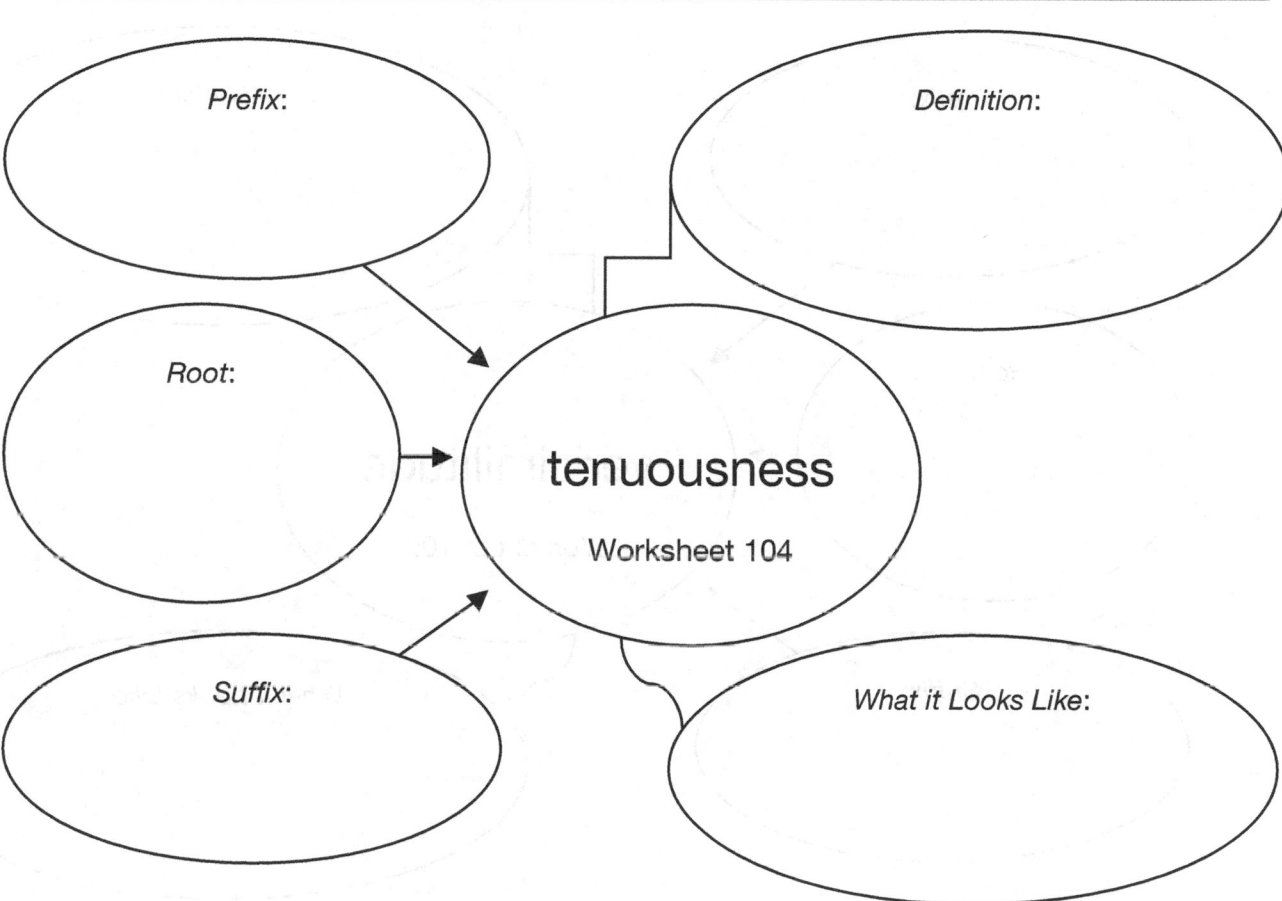

Prefix:

Definition:

Root:

tenuousness

Worksheet 104

Suffix:

What it Looks Like:

Analogous Exercise:

tenuousness : thin   _____ : thick

Why? Nature of the Relationship:

Original Analogy Using the Vocabulary Word:

Worksheet 104

Name:________________________ Date:__________

Ungrammatical Sentence:

Computer-generated special effects which appear in blockbuster movies often provide audiences with the <u>verisimilitude</u> of magic.

Explanation of Error:

Type of Error:

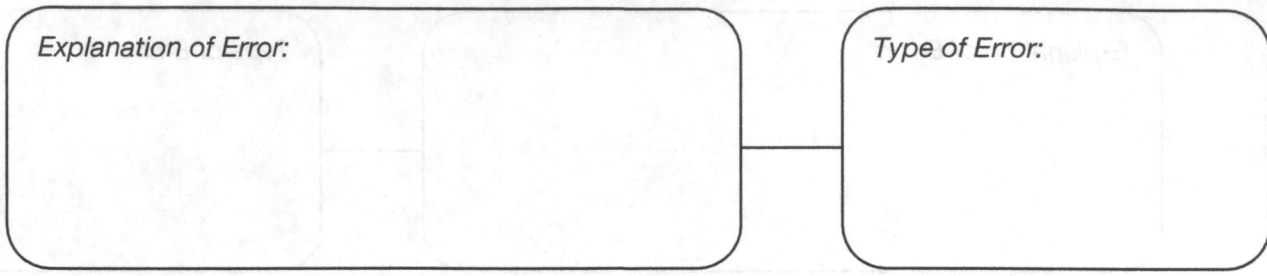

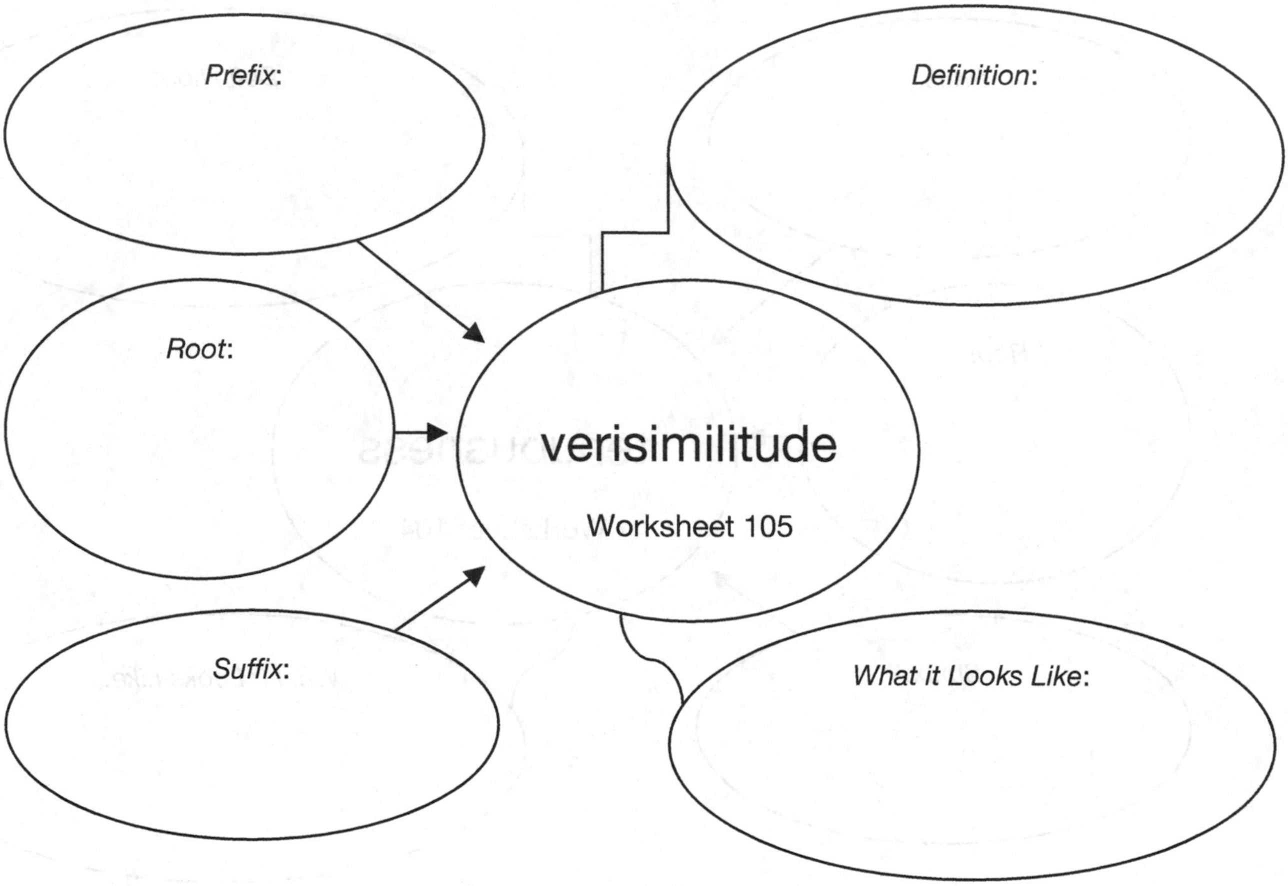

Prefix:
Definition:
Root:
verisimilitude
Worksheet 105
Suffix:
What it Looks Like:

Analogous Exercise:

complete : reductive   ____________ : verisimilitude

Why? Nature of the Relationship:

Original Analogy Using the Vocabulary Word:

Name:____________________________________ Date:____________

Ungrammatical Sentence:

South Carolina's <u>secession</u> from the Union in 1860 could of been prevented, Confederate politicians claimed, had Lincoln not been elected.

Explanation of Error:

Type of Error:

Prefix:

Definition:

Root:

secession

Worksheet 106

Suffix:

What it Looks Like:

Worksheet 106

Analogous Exercise:

move : secession _______________ : fidelity

Why? Nature of the Relationship:

Original Analogy Using the Vocabulary Word:

Name:_____ Date:_____

Ungrammatical Sentence:

If you are <u>nescient</u> of basic microeconomic theory, you might be unprepared for even perfunctory negotiations to purchase a used car.

Explanation of Error:

Type of Error:

Prefix:

Definition:

Root:

nescient

Worksheet 107

Suffix:

What it Looks Like:

Analogous Exercise:

newborn : nescient   _____ : omniscient

Why? Nature of the Relationship:

Original Analogy Using the Vocabulary Word:

Perfect 800: SAT Verbal © Prufrock Press Inc. • Permission is granted to photocopy or reproduce this page for single classroom use only.

Name:______________________________ Date:__________

Ungrammatical Sentence:

The Founding Fathers hoped that beginning the United States Constitution with a philosophical preamble was both a good idea and totally practical.

Explanation of Error:

Type of Error:

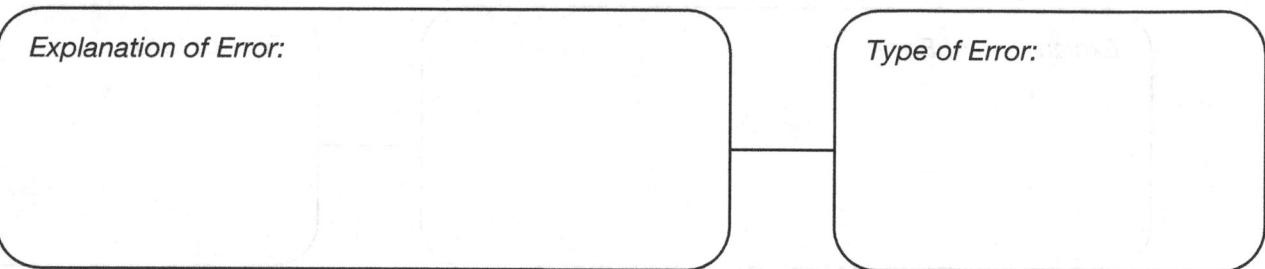

Prefix:

Definition:

Root:

preamble

Worksheet 108

Suffix:

What it Looks Like:

Analogous Exercise:

preamble : early   ______________ : late

Why? Nature of the Relationship:

Original Analogy Using the Vocabulary Word:

Worksheet 108

Name:_____ Date:_____

Ungrammatical Sentence:

The insurance company, which insured five of the motorists involved in yesterday's accidents, were unable to <u>exculpate</u> its clients from blame.

Explanation of Error:	*Type of Error:*

Prefix:

Definition:

Root:

exculpate

Worksheet 109

Suffix:

What it Looks Like:

Analogous Exercise:

culpability : exculpate _____ : elucidate

Why? Nature of the Relationship:	*Original Analogy Using the Vocabulary Word:*

Name:______________________________ Date:__________

Ungrammatical Sentence:

The eminent professor demonstrating an indignant manner was unwilling to comment for the newspaper reporter's story.

Explanation of Error:

Type of Error:

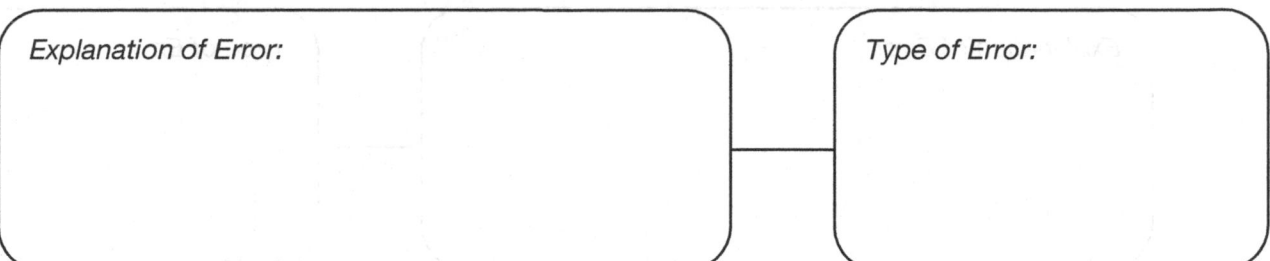

Prefix:

Root:

Suffix:

indignant

Worksheet 110

Definition:

What it Looks Like:

Analogous Exercise:

indignant : acrimonious ____________ : dejected

Why? Nature of the Relationship:

Original Analogy Using the Vocabulary Word:

Name:______________________________ Date:__________

Ungrammatical Sentence:

I imagine that circus performers require several traits, including: <u>flamboyance</u>, fearlessness, and a sense of humor.

Explanation of Error:

Type of Error:

Prefix:

Definition:

Root:

flamboyance

Worksheet 111

Suffix:

What it Looks Like:

Analogous Exercise:

impassivity : flamboyance ____________ : color

Why? Nature of the Relationship:

Original Analogy Using the Vocabulary Word:

Ungrammatical Sentence:

Upset by the Major General's suggestion of professional incompetence and <u>ignominy</u>, the Lieutenant Colonel refused to attend his ceremony.

Explanation of Error:

Type of Error:

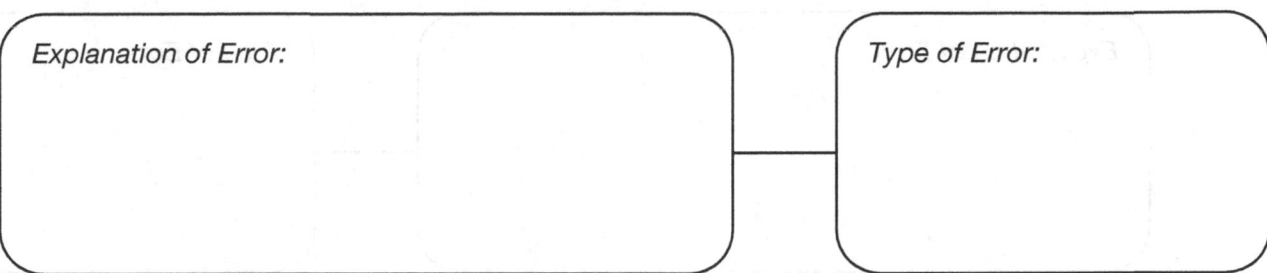

Prefix:

Definition:

Root:

ignominy

Worksheet 112

Suffix:

What it Looks Like:

Analogous Exercise:

defamation : ignominy _____ : dignity

Why? Nature of the Relationship:

Original Analogy Using the Vocabulary Word:

Ungrammatical Sentence:

For many adults, the inherent and predictable outcome of any algebraic equation, especially when it's variables are multitudinous, is <u>perplexity</u>.

Explanation of Error:

Type of Error:

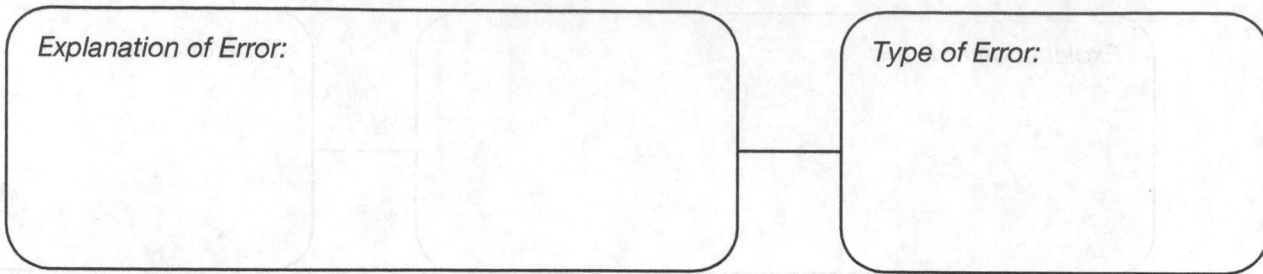

Prefix:

Definition:

Root:

perplexity

Worksheet 113

Suffix:

What it Looks Like:

Analogous Exercise:

elucidate : perplexity

_____ : impediment

Why? Nature of the Relationship:

Original Analogy Using the Vocabulary Word:

Ungrammatical Sentence:

A <u>circumspect</u> real estate agent is always investigating every conceivable difficulty that their clients might encounter during the purchasing process.

Explanation of Error:	Type of Error:

Prefix:

Definition:

Root:

circumspect

Worksheet 114

Suffix:

What it Looks Like:

Analogous Exercise:

circumspect : cognizant   _____ : naïve

Why? Nature of the Relationship:	Original Analogy Using the Vocabulary Word:

Ungrammatical Sentence:

I assume that fewer persons have a <u>predilection</u> for ordering steak at fashionable French restaurants than for ordering escargot.

Explanation of Error:	Type of Error:

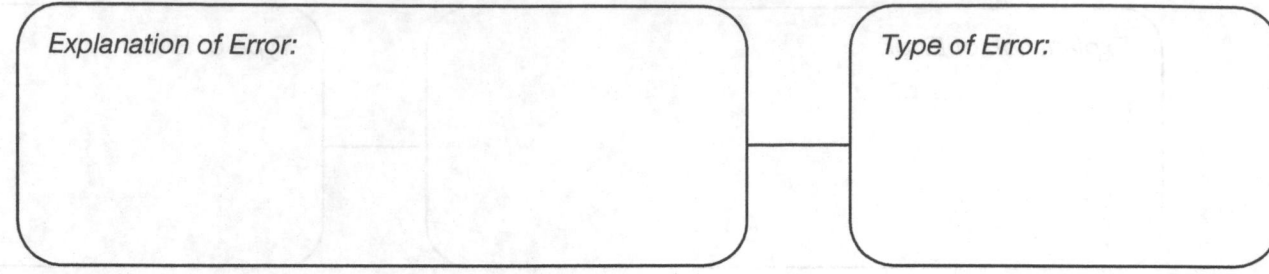

Prefix:

Definition:

Root:

predilection

Worksheet 115

Suffix:

What it Looks Like:

Analogous Exercise:

prognosis : predilection   _____ : preamble

Why? Nature of the Relationship:	Original Analogy Using the Vocabulary Word:

Worksheet 115

Ungrammatical Sentence:

The secession and effective independence of the Confederate States of America from 1861 to 65 went far beyond vocal <u>remonstrance</u>.

Explanation of Error:

Type of Error:

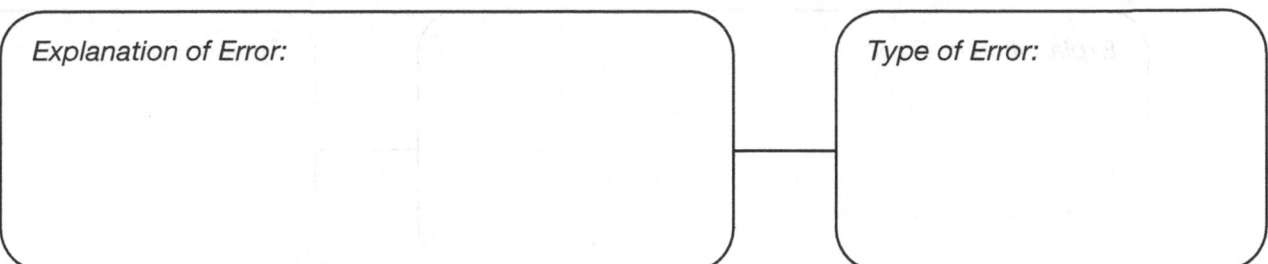

Prefix:

Definition:

Root:

remonstrance

Worksheet 116

Suffix:

What it Looks Like:

Analogous Exercise:

fidelity : secession   _____ : remonstrance

Why? Nature of the Relationship:

Original Analogy Using the Vocabulary Word:

Ungrammatical Sentence:

Shakespeare included less stage directions than characters in his scripts, perhaps because he did not want to <u>obfuscate</u> focal human issues.

Explanation of Error:

Type of Error:

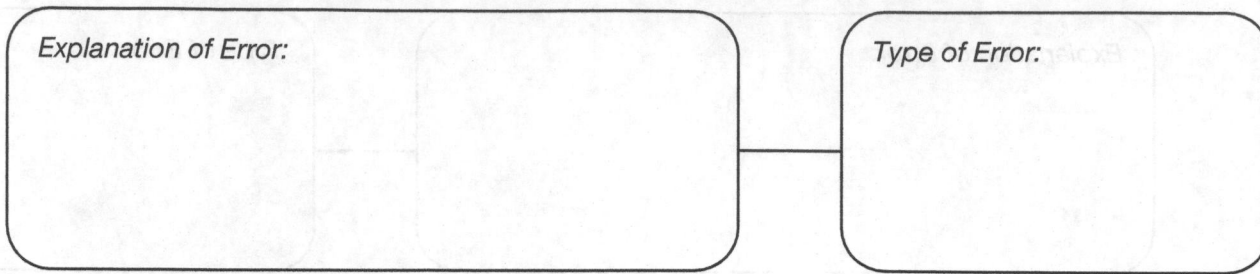

Prefix:

Definition:

Root:

obfuscate

Worksheet 117

Suffix:

What it Looks Like:

Analogous Exercise:

muddy : obfuscate

_____ : elucidate

Why? Nature of the Relationship:

Original Analogy Using the Vocabulary Word:

Worksheet 117

Name:____ Date:__________

Ungrammatical Sentence:

Silent and impassive, my not quite awake little brother refused to <u>synchronize</u> his alarm clock with mine.

Explanation of Error:

Type of Error:

Prefix:

Definition:

Root:

synchronize

Worksheet 118

Suffix:

What it Looks Like:

Analogous Exercise:

synchronize : concurrently

__________ : independently

Why? Nature of the Relationship:

Original Analogy Using the Vocabulary Word:

Worksheet 118

Ungrammatical Sentence:

<u>Introspection</u> and hypnosis are buzzwords among psychiatrists and people who study the various ways in which the human mind reacts to tragedy.

Explanation of Error:	Type of Error:

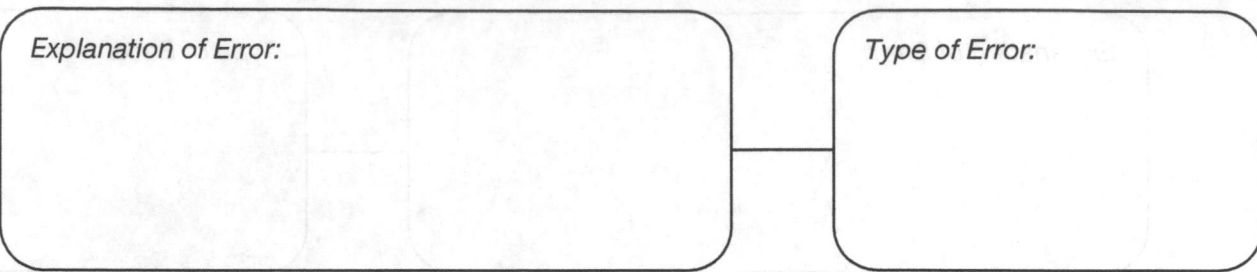

Prefix:

Definition:

Root:

introspection

Worksheet 119

Suffix:

What it Looks Like:

Analogous Exercise:

circumspection : introspection   _____ : self

Why? Nature of the Relationship:	Original Analogy Using the Vocabulary Word:

Worksheet 119

Ungrammatical Sentence:

I knew Yauncey Hill Preparatory School had a tremendous reputation for academic rigor, but I did not realize its true difficulty until I <u>matriculate</u>d.

Explanation of Error:	Type of Error:

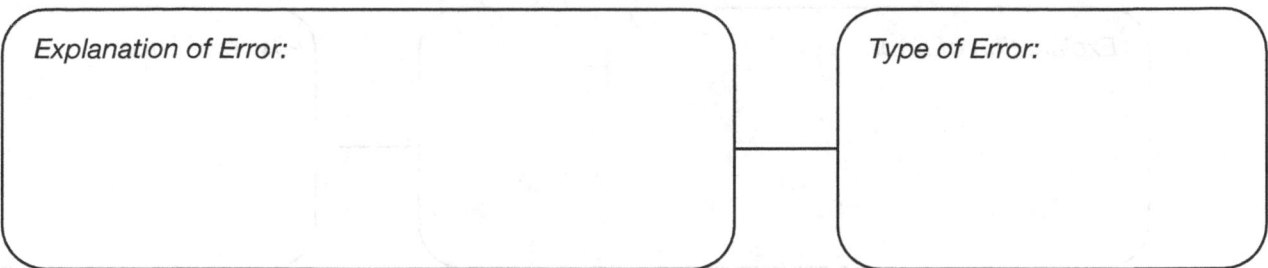

Prefix:

Definition:

Root:

matriculate

Worksheet 120

Suffix:

What it Looks Like:

Analogous Exercise:

ignite : matriculate   _____ : indoctrinate

Why? Nature of the Relationship:	Original Analogy Using the Vocabulary Word:

Worksheet 120

Ungrammatical Sentence:

Few things on this planet are as <u>immutable</u> as rocks are, yet even those can become sand as time and environmental factors exert their powers.

Explanation of Error:

Type of Error:

Prefix:

Definition:

Root:

immutable

Worksheet 121

Suffix:

What it Looks Like:

Analogous Exercise:

transmutative : immutable   _____ : impassivity

Why? Nature of the Relationship:

Original Analogy Using the Vocabulary Word:

Worksheet 121

Ungrammatical Sentence:

Trying hard to make a successfully <u>discursive</u> argument the debater used evidence from every source of information that he could recall.

Explanation of Error:	Type of Error:

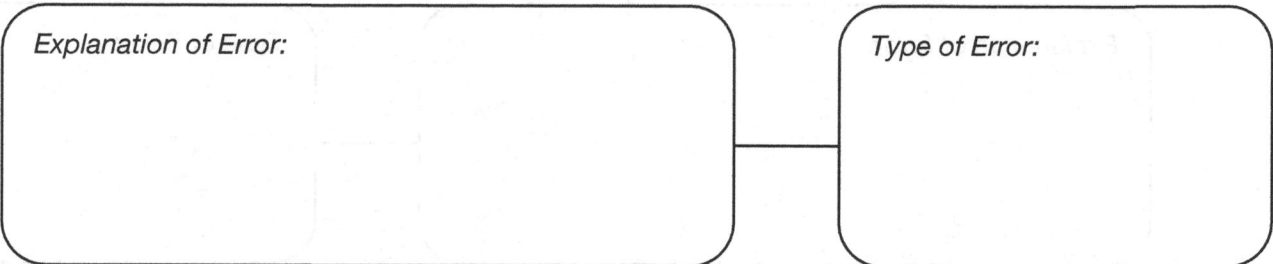

Prefix:

Definition:

Root:

discursive

Worksheet 122

Suffix:

What it Looks Like:

Analogous Exercise:

Equator : coastline _____ : discursive

Why? Nature of the Relationship:	Original Analogy Using the Vocabulary Word:

Name:____ Date:__________

Ungrammatical Sentence:

Training for the marathon, my out-of-shape uncle and the popular varsity athlete were an <u>abject</u> failure and a successful competitor, respectfully.

Explanation of Error:

Type of Error:

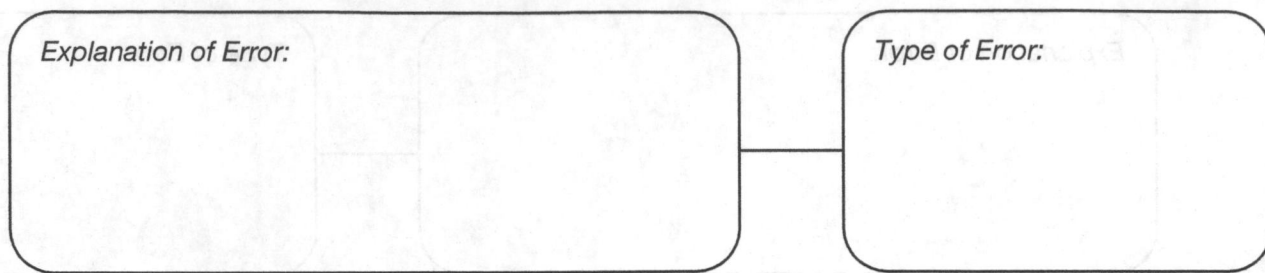

Prefix:

Definition:

Root:

abject

Worksheet 123

Suffix:

What it Looks Like:

Analogous Exercise:

inject : abject

__________ : ignominy

Why? Nature of the Relationship:

Original Analogy Using the Vocabulary Word:

Worksheet 123

Ungrammatical Sentence:

Video games, irregardless of their incredible popularity, are responsible for introducing very few <u>neologism</u>s to popular linguistic culture.

Explanation of Error:

Type of Error:

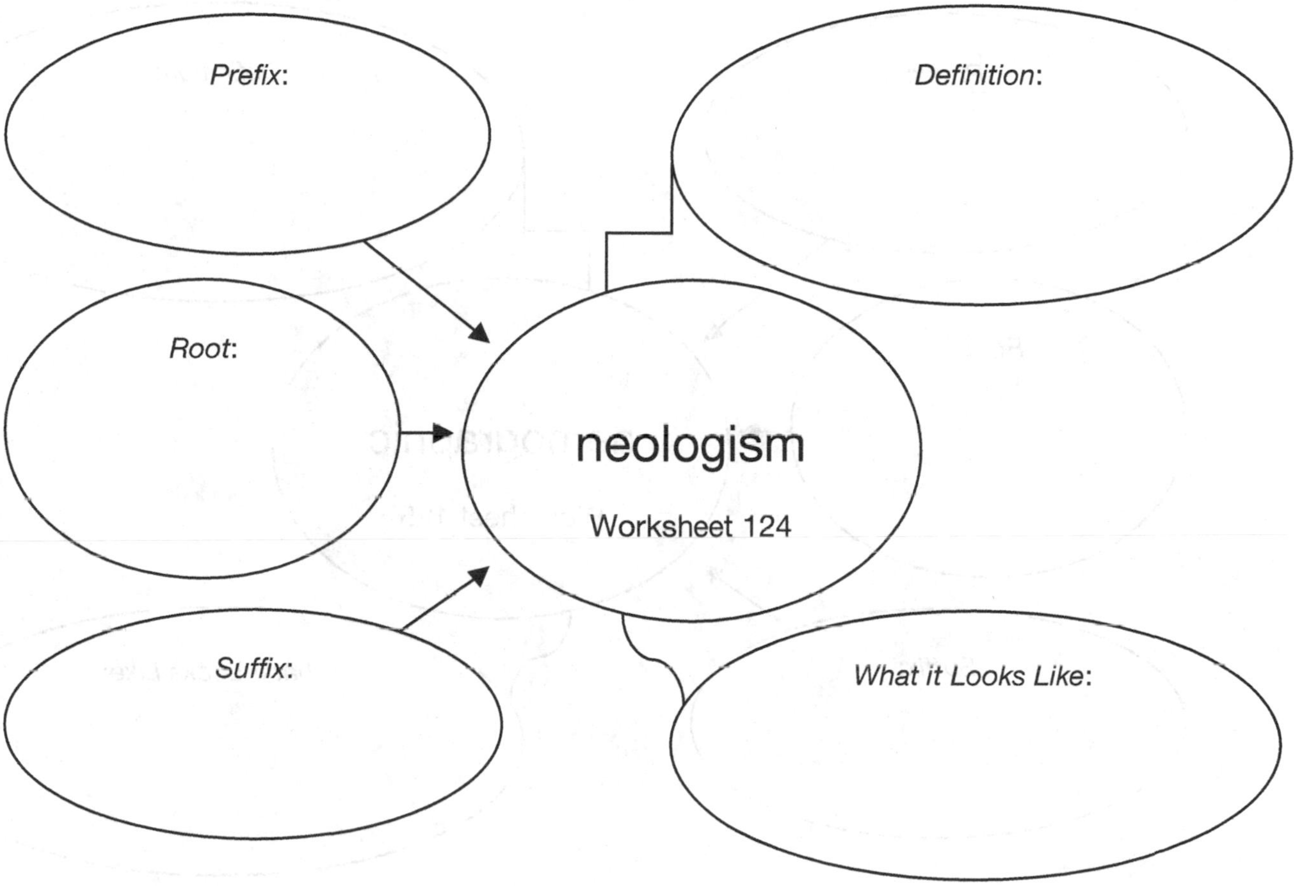

Prefix:

Definition:

Root:

Suffix:

neologism

Worksheet 124

What it Looks Like:

Analogous Exercise:

anomaly : neologism   _____ : dictionary

Why? Nature of the Relationship:

Original Analogy Using the Vocabulary Word:

Ungrammatical Sentence:

A <u>demographic</u> study was conducted by the National Endowment for the Arts, in conjunction with a wealthy, anonymous philanthropist.

Explanation of Error:	Type of Error:

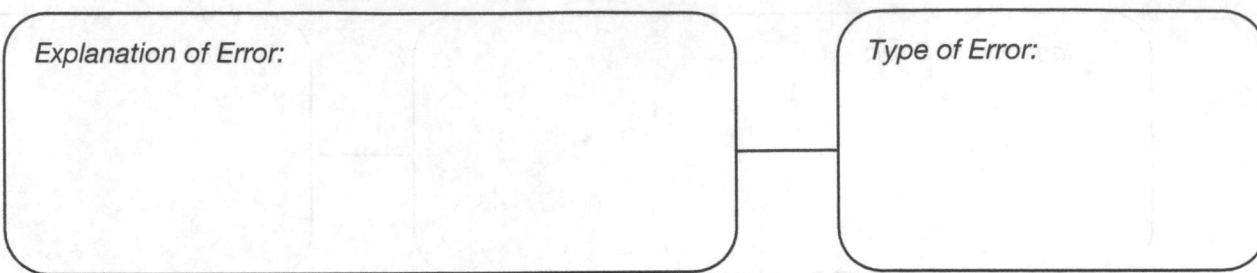

Prefix:

Definition:

Root:

demographic

Worksheet 125

Suffix:

What it Looks Like:

Analogous Exercise:

cryptographic : demographic _____ : people

Why? Nature of the Relationship:	Original Analogy Using the Vocabulary Word:

Ungrammatical Sentence:

Despite the poem's utter ambiguity and the class' nescient comprehension of metaphors, everyone could appreciate the poet's playful <u>effervescence</u>.

Explanation of Error:

Type of Error:

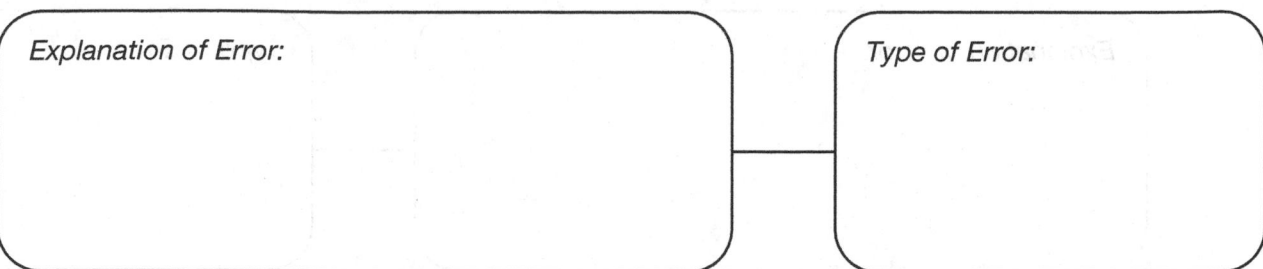

Prefix:

Definition:

Root:

effervescence

Worksheet 126

Suffix:

What it Looks Like:

Analogous Exercise:

flamboyance : effervescence   _____ : autonomy

Why? Nature of the Relationship:

Original Analogy Using the Vocabulary Word:

Ungrammatical Sentence:

The <u>conflagration</u>, which moved ominously down the sylvan hillside, threatened to destroy more then one neighborhood.

| Explanation of Error: | | Type of Error: |

Prefix:

Definition:

Root:

conflagration

Worksheet 127

Suffix:

What it Looks Like:

Analogous Exercise:

pandemonium : conflagration _____ : fire

| Why? Nature of the Relationship: | | Original Analogy Using the Vocabulary Word: |

Name:______________________________ Date:____________

Ungrammatical Sentence:

"Plain" and "plane" are <u>homonyms</u>, yet neither of the words' definitions are liable to cause perplexity.

Explanation of Error:

Type of Error:

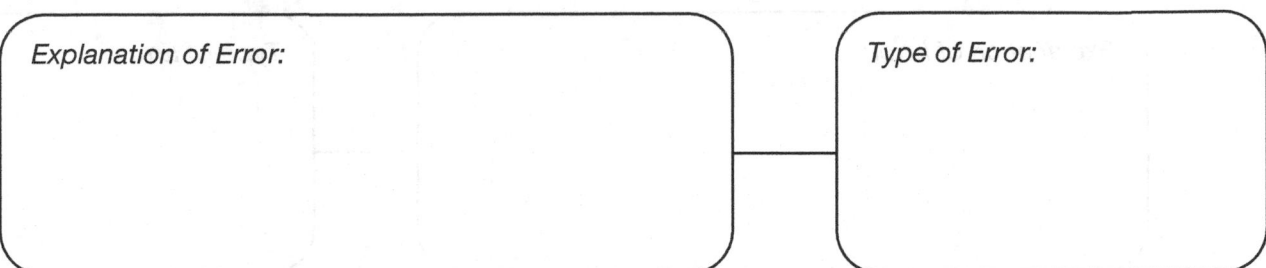

Prefix:

Definition:

Root:

homonym

Worksheet 128

Suffix:

What it Looks Like:

Analogous Exercise:

verity : verisimilitude

______________ : homonym

Why? Nature of the Relationship:

Original Analogy Using the Vocabulary Word:

Ungrammatical Sentence:

During the Age of Imperialism, European countries which attempted to <u>subjugate</u> foreign nations included France, Germany, and Belgium.

Explanation of Error:

Type of Error:

Prefix:

Definition:

Root:

subjugate

Worksheet 129

Suffix:

What it Looks Like:

Analogous Exercise:

advocate : subjugate

_____ : below

Why? Nature of the Relationship:

Original Analogy Using the Vocabulary Word:

Name:____ Date:__________

Ungrammatical Sentence:

It seemed to my classmates and I that our lecturer was not only magniloquent, but amicable as well.

Explanation of Error:

Type of Error:

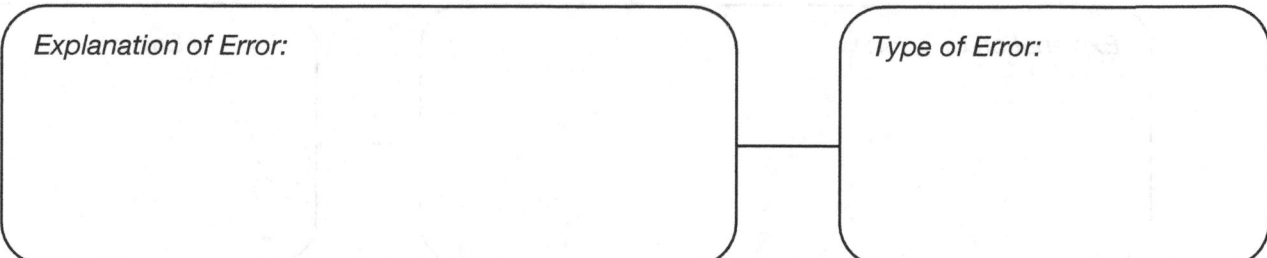

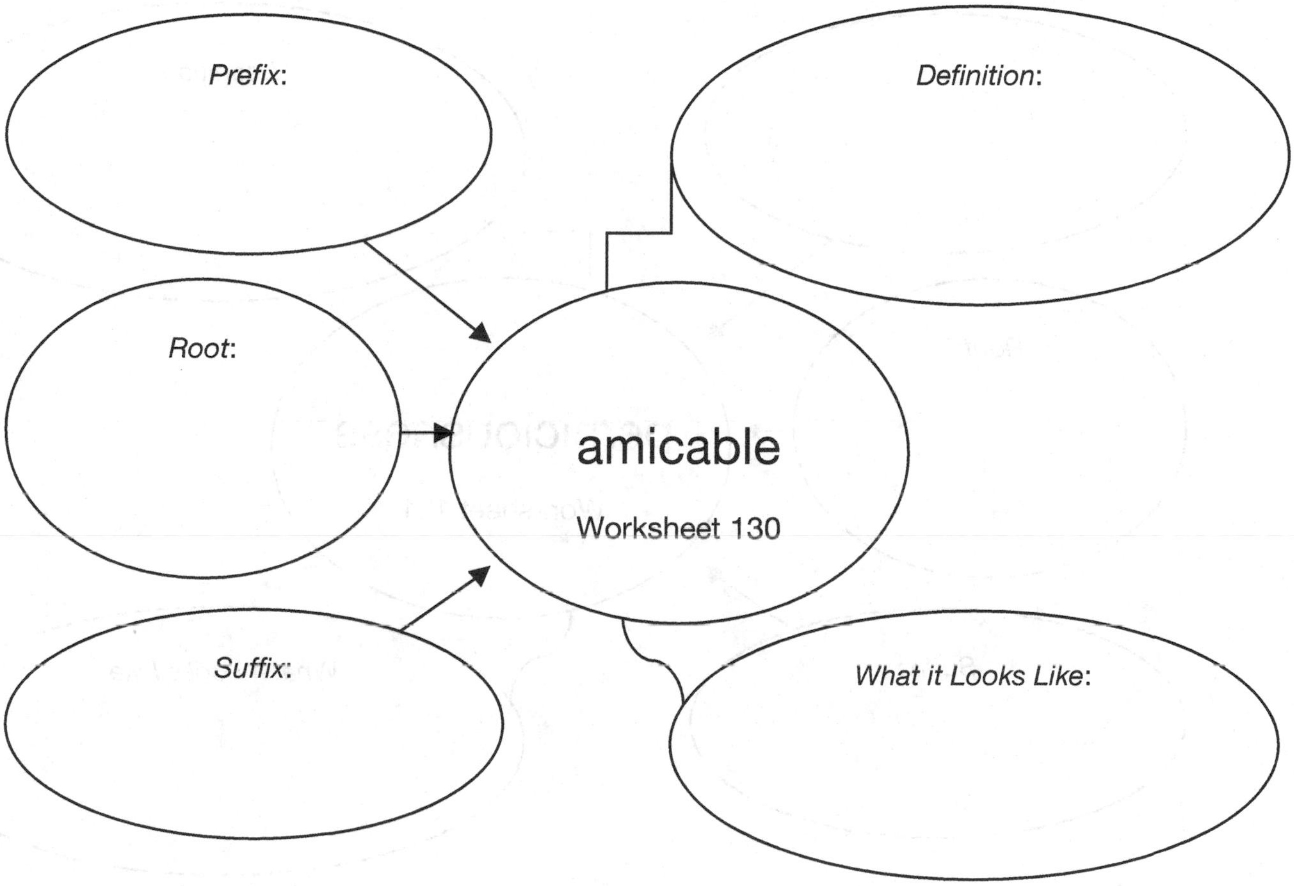

Prefix:
Definition:
Root:
amicable
Worksheet 130
Suffix:
What it Looks Like:

Analogous Exercise:

amicable : pugnacious   ______________ : belligerent

Why? Nature of the Relationship:

Original Analogy Using the Vocabulary Word:

Ungrammatical Sentence:

For "<u>perniciousness</u>" is a word that one could use accurately to describe the effects of various trade sanctions and tariffs imposed without cause.

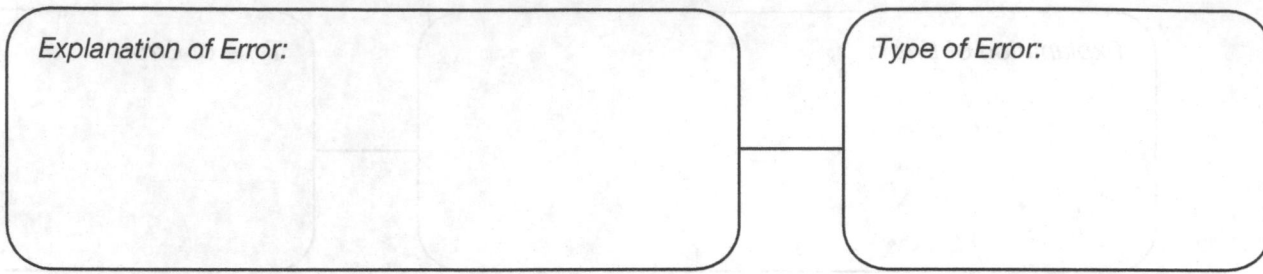

Explanation of Error:

Type of Error:

Prefix:

Definition:

Root:

perniciousness

Worksheet 131

Suffix:

What it Looks Like:

Analogous Exercise:

exonerate : benevolence   _____ : perniciousness

Why? Nature of the Relationship:

Original Analogy Using the Vocabulary Word:

Ungrammatical Sentence:

Despite the incredulous efforts that Ptolemy put into his astronomical observations, his geocentric theories were essentially <u>erroneous</u>.

Explanation of Error:

Type of Error:

Prefix:

Definition:

Root:

erroneous

Worksheet 132

Suffix:

What it Looks Like:

Analogous Exercise:

nescience : erroneous   _____ : correct

Why? Nature of the Relationship:

Original Analogy Using the Vocabulary Word:

Worksheet 132

Name:____ Date:____________

Ungrammatical Sentence:

Several popular musicians have recently written songs that remonstrate against the <u>superfluity</u> of television channels, which there are many of.

Explanation of Error:

Type of Error:

Prefix:

Definition:

Root:

superfluity

Worksheet 133

Suffix:

What it Looks Like:

Analogous Exercise:

superfluity : profuse ______________ : reductive

Why? Nature of the Relationship:

Original Analogy Using the Vocabulary Word:

Worksheet 133

Name:_____ Date:_____

Ungrammatical Sentence:

To win the board game, I had to avoid neologisms, but still think creatively
and quick in order to list viable <u>synonym</u>s for uncommon words.

Explanation of Error:

Type of Error:

Prefix:

Definition:

Root:

synonym

Worksheet 134

Suffix:

What it Looks Like:

Analogous Exercise:

words : synonym   synchronization : _____

Why? Nature of the Relationship:

*Original Analogy Using the Vocabulary
Word:*

Worksheet 134

Ungrammatical Sentence:

Sheriff Pat Garrett surely felt <u>antipathy</u> for Billy the Kid, but conjecture that the lawman killed Billy is tenuous, indubitable proof does not exist.

Explanation of Error:

Type of Error:

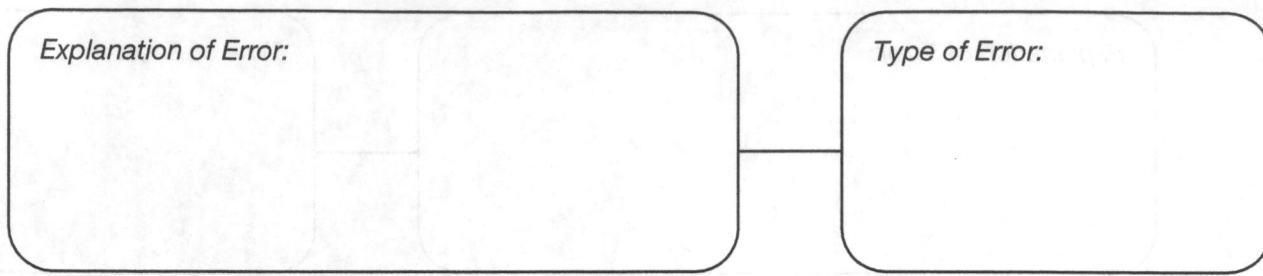

Prefix:

Definition:

Root:

antipathy

Worksheet 135

Suffix:

What it Looks Like:

Analogous Exercise:

acrimonious : antipathy   _____ : effervescence

Why? Nature of the Relationship:

Original Analogy Using the Vocabulary Word:

Worksheet 135

Name:______________________________ Date:__________

Ungrammatical Sentence:

I could imply from the <u>diffuseness</u> of sunflower seeds about the room that my parakeets had somehow escaped from their cages.

Explanation of Error:

Type of Error:

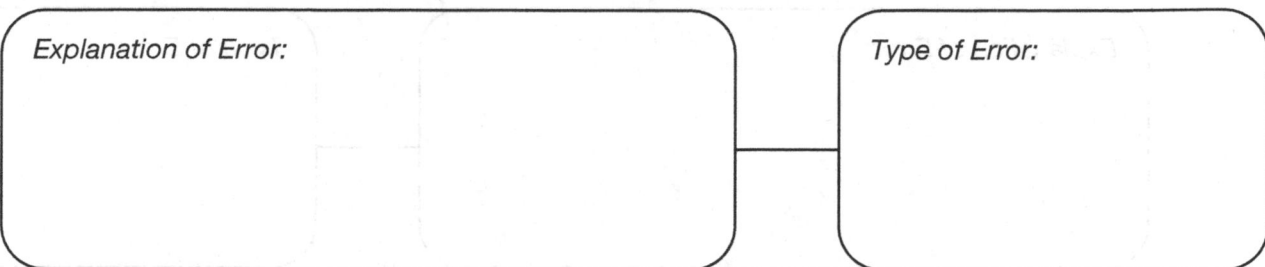

Prefix:

Definition:

Root:

diffuseness

Worksheet 136

Suffix:

What it Looks Like:

Analogous Exercise:

diffuseness : circumspection :: ______________ : introspection

Why? Nature of the Relationship:

Original Analogy Using the Vocabulary Word:

Worksheet 136

Name:_____ Date:_____

All members of the <u>electorate</u>, a group exercising vocally aberrant
flamboyance, is able to decide the fates of candidates for public offices.

Explanation of Error:	Type of Error:

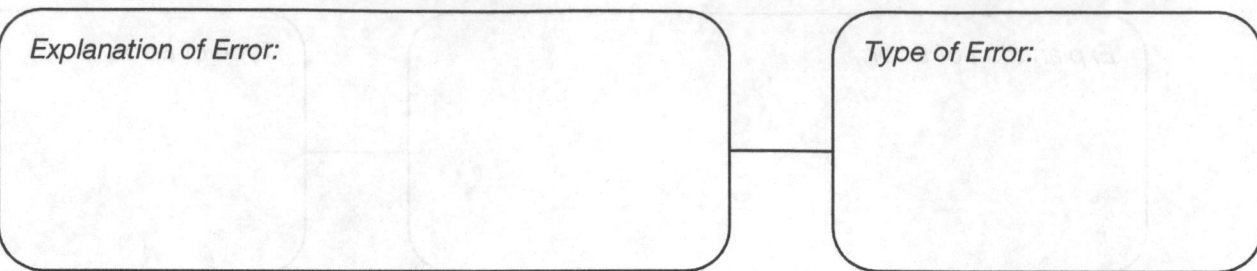

Prefix:

Definition:

Root:

electorate

Worksheet 137

Suffix:

What it Looks Like:

Analogous Exercise:

electorate : aggregate   _____ : diffuse

Why? Nature of the Relationship:	Original Analogy Using the Vocabulary Word:

Worksheet 137 (side tab)

Name:____ Date:__________

Ungrammatical Sentence:

Socrates was the antecedent of both Plato and Aristotle; and Confucius was the philosophical forefather of Mencius.

Explanation of Error:

Type of Error:

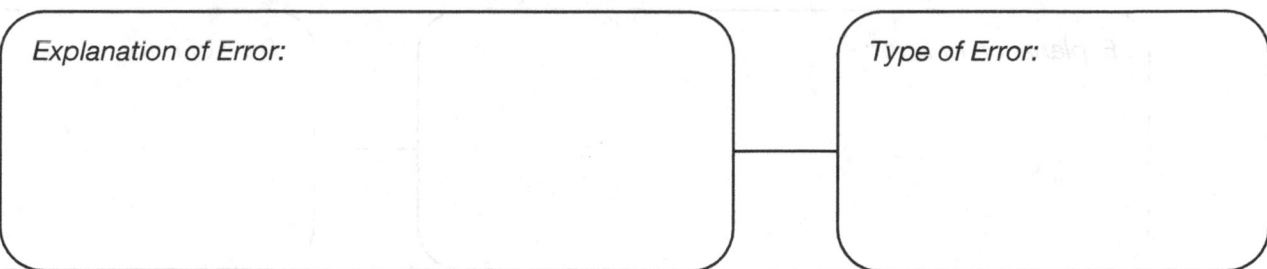

Prefix:

Definition:

Root:

antecedent

Worksheet 138

Suffix:

What it Looks Like:

Analogous Exercise:

document : preamble

__________ : antecedent

Why? Nature of the Relationship:

Original Analogy Using the Vocabulary Word:

Worksheet 138

Ungrammatical Sentence:

<u>Transgress</u>ing his own professional code, the ignominious medical doctor not only tried to extort money from the hospital, but falsified documents.

Explanation of Error:

Type of Error:

Prefix:

Definition:

Root:

transgress

Worksheet 139

Suffix:

What it Looks Like:

Analogous Exercise:

perniciousness : transgress

_____ : matriculate

Why? Nature of the Relationship:

Original Analogy Using the Vocabulary Word:

Ungrammatical Sentence:

The United Nations is a <u>heterogeneous</u> conglomerate of countries, between the many representatives of which there is sometimes acrimonious debate.

Explanation of Error:

Type of Error:

Prefix:

Definition:

Root:

heterogeneous

Worksheet 140

Suffix:

What it Looks Like:

Analogous Exercise:

heterogeneous : homogeneous   _____ : synonym

Why? Nature of the Relationship:

Original Analogy Using the Vocabulary Word:

Ungrammatical Sentence:

Irrespective of whether she should be labeled Queen of Egypt or Pharaoh, it is inarguable that Cleopatra was an imminent <u>matriarchal</u> leader.

Explanation of Error:	*Type of Error:*

Prefix:

Definition:

Root:

matriarchal

Worksheet 141

Suffix:

What it Looks Like:

Analogous Exercise:

mother : matriarchal   _____ : misanthropic

Why? Nature of the Relationship:	*Original Analogy Using the Vocabulary Word:*

Worksheet 141

Ungrammatical Sentence:

<u>Gastronomic</u> connoisseurs probably take more pleasure in investigating, discovering, and the taste of fine food than other citizens do.

Explanation of Error:

Type of Error:

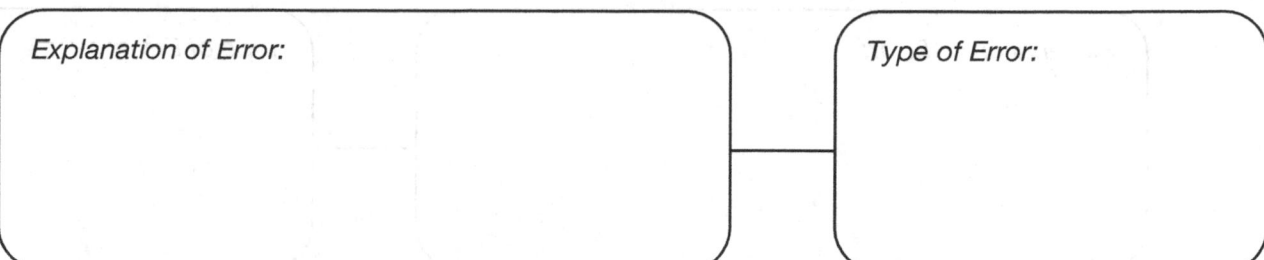

Prefix:

Definition:

Root:

gastronomic

Worksheet 142

Suffix:

What it Looks Like:

Analogous Exercise:

demographic : gastronomic   _____ : food

Why? Nature of the Relationship:

Original Analogy Using the Vocabulary Word:

Ungrammatical Sentence:

As its overall monetary value fell further each week, my portfolio of stocks steadily <u>degenerated</u> into almost abject worthlessness.

Explanation of Error:

Type of Error:

Prefix:

Definition:

Root:

degenerate

Worksheet 143

Suffix:

What it Looks Like:

Analogous Exercise:

improve : degenerate

_____ : recession

Why? Nature of the Relationship:

Original Analogy Using the Vocabulary Word:

Ungrammatical Sentence:

<u>Antebellum</u> Richmond was among the finest and most mannerly of Southern cities though its approval of slavery was an ethical shortcoming.

Explanation of Error:	Type of Error:

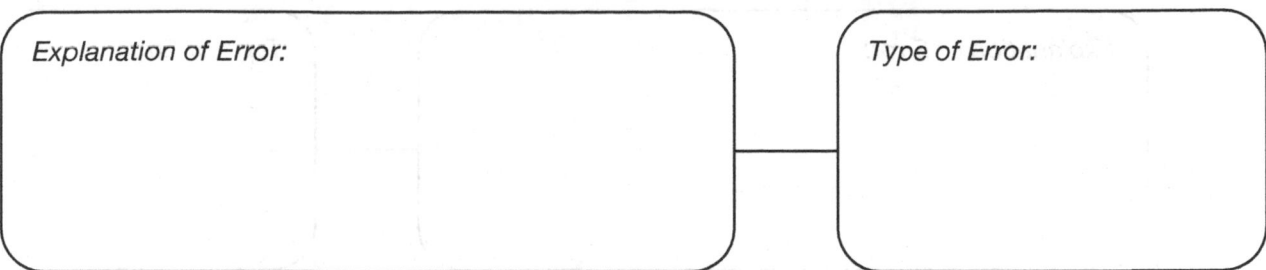

Prefix:

Definition:

Root:

antebellum

Worksheet 144

Suffix:

What it Looks Like:

Analogous Exercise:

antebellum : secession _____ : sunrise

Why? Nature of the Relationship:	Original Analogy Using the Vocabulary Word:

Name:____ Date:__________

Ungrammatical Sentence:

The film star's <u>extenuation</u> of his illegal activities did little to change the immutable dejection of his fans, whom were no longer able to trust him.

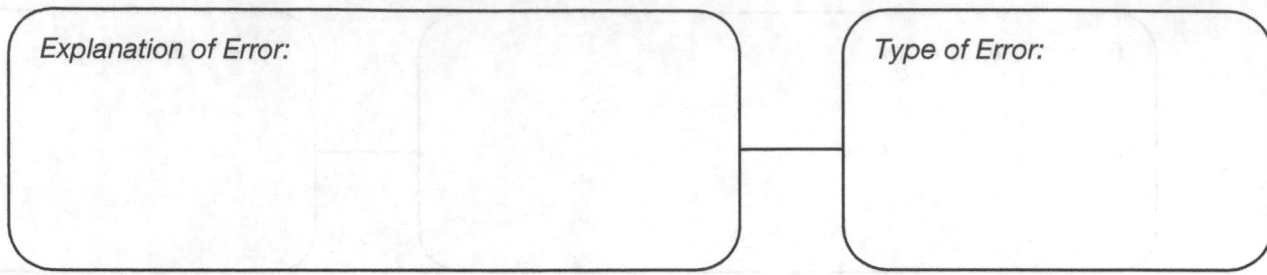

Explanation of Error:

Type of Error:

Prefix:

Definition:

Root:

extenuation

Worksheet 145

Suffix:

What it Looks Like:

Analogous Exercise:

extenuation : transgress ____________ : earning "A" grades

Why? Nature of the Relationship:

Original Analogy Using the Vocabulary Word:

Worksheet 145

Ungrammatical Sentence:

If Nostradamus actually did experience a circumspect <u>premonition</u> of the world's future, why have many of his apocryphal predictions not occurred?

Explanation of Error:

Type of Error:

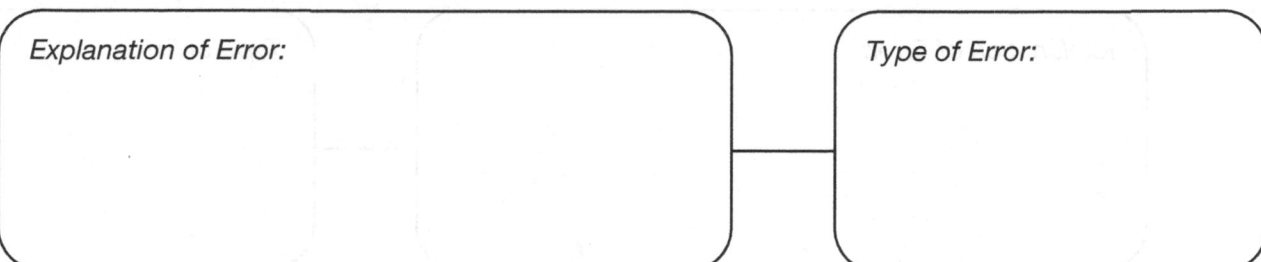

Prefix:

Definition:

Root:

premonition

Worksheet 146

Suffix:

What It Looks Like:

Analogous Exercise:

premonition : antecedent

_____ : superfluity

Why? Nature of the Relationship:

Original Analogy Using the Vocabulary Word:

Worksheet 146

Ungrammatical Sentence:

The reason why young children often find a gastronomic delicacy like escargot to be <u>repugnant</u> is because it perplexes novice palates.

Explanation of Error:

Type of Error:

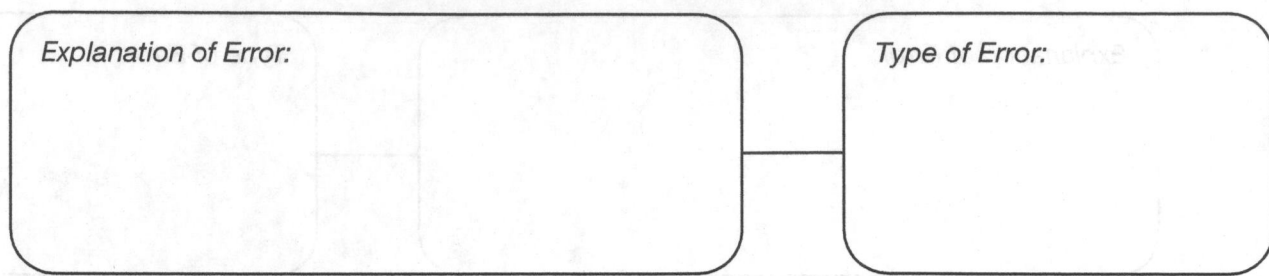

Prefix:

Definition:

Root:

repugnant

Worksheet 147

Suffix:

What it Looks Like:

Analogous Exercise:

repugnant : antipathy   _____ : amicability

Why? Nature of the Relationship:

Original Analogy Using the Vocabulary Word:

Name:____ Date:____________

Ungrammatical Sentence:

When I saw the fine that the public library wished to charge me for three overdue books, my <u>incredulity</u> made it hard for me to simply capitulate.

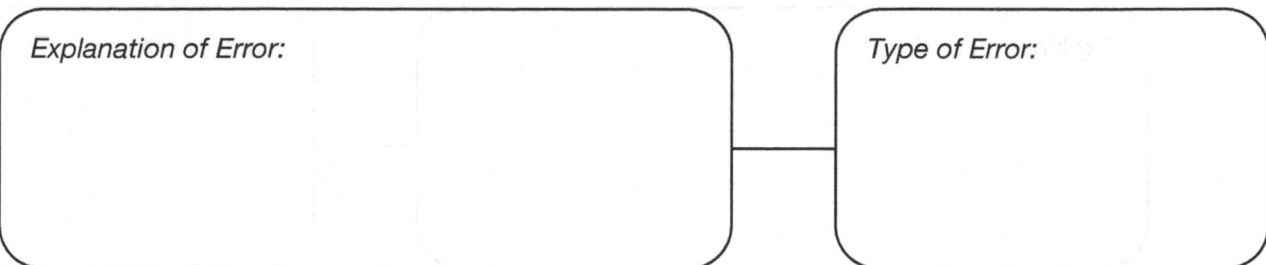

Explanation of Error:

Type of Error:

Prefix:

Definition:

Root:

incredulity

Worksheet 148

Suffix:

What it Looks Like:

Analogous Exercise:

erroneous : incredulity ______________ : indignity

Why? Nature of the Relationship:

Original Analogy Using the Vocabulary Word:

Worksheet 148

Ungrammatical Sentence:

There was little <u>concordance</u> between the amoebae's failure to multiply and the abnormality observed by the scientist under the microscope.

Explanation of Error:

Type of Error:

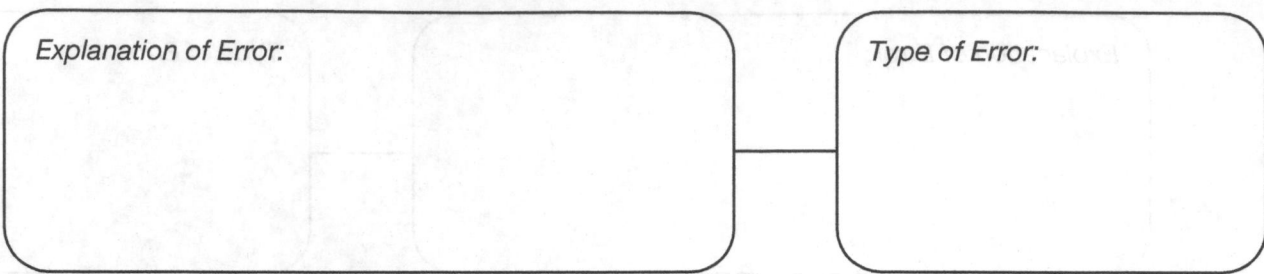

Prefix:

Definition:

Root:

concordance
Worksheet 149

Suffix:

What it Looks Like:

Analogous Exercise:

concordance : synchronized   _____ : diffused

Why? Nature of the Relationship:

Original Analogy Using the Vocabulary Word:

Ungrammatical Sentence:

The number of <u>prerogative</u>s enjoyed by an executive corresponds directly with his or her professional status on the company's hierarchy.

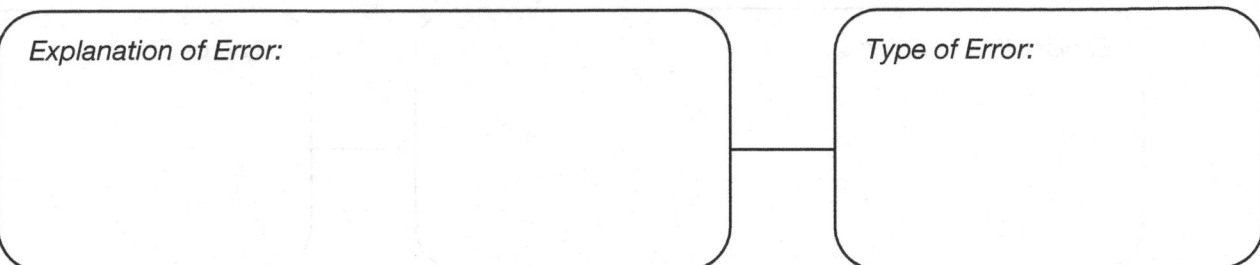

Explanation of Error:

Type of Error:

Prefix:

Definition:

Root:

prerogative

Worksheet 150

Suffix:

What It Looks Like:

Analogous Exercise:

matriarch : prerogative _____ : subjugation

Why? Nature of the Relationship:

Original Analogy Using the Vocabulary Word:

Name:_____ Date:_____

Ungrammatical Sentence:

In *Beowulf*, the monster Grendel demonstrated a <u>proclivity</u> for nightly perniciousness and egregious transgression of medieval Danish laws.

Explanation of Error:

Type of Error:

Prefix:

Definition:

Root:

proclivity

Worksheet 151

Suffix:

What it Looks Like:

Analogous Exercise:

proclivity : predilection   _____ : luminous

Why? Nature of the Relationship:

Original Analogy Using the Vocabulary Word:

Ungrammatical Sentence:

The "humanness" of computerized artificial intelligence is apocryphal, for it is unclear if robots display more <u>sentient</u> characteristics than rocks.

Explanation of Error:

Type of Error:

Prefix:

Root:

Suffix:

Definition:

sentient

Worksheet 152

What it Looks Like:

Analogous Exercise:

mountain : sentient

_____ : immutable

Why? Nature of the Relationship:

Original Analogy Using the Vocabulary Word:

Ungrammatical Sentence:

Even though <u>anarchic</u> grassroots revolutionaries have a history of initial political success, partly due to their inherent diffuseness across society.

| *Explanation of Error:* | *Type of Error:* |

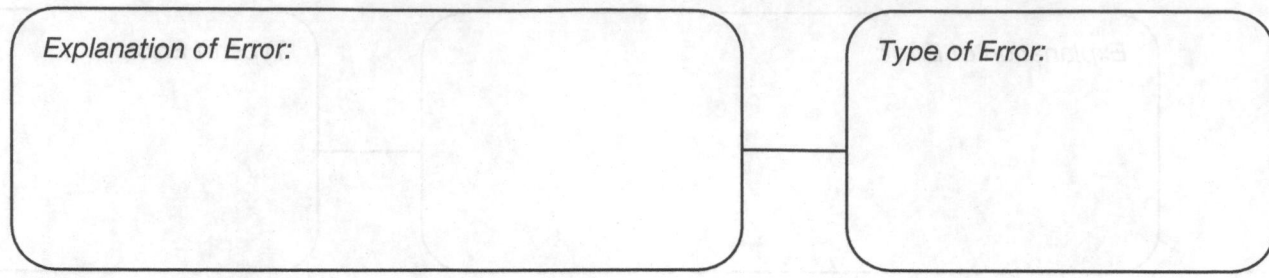

Prefix:

Definition:

Root:

anarchic

Worksheet 153

Suffix:

What it Looks Like:

Analogous Exercise:

pandemonium : anarchic   _____ : gastronomic

Why? Nature of the Relationship:

Original Analogy Using the Vocabulary Word:

Worksheet 153

Name:_____ Date:_____

Ungrammatical Sentence:

The visiting team's coach so upset the uninterested referee that the latter actually became <u>vociferous</u> when calling a technical foul.

Explanation of Error:	Type of Error:

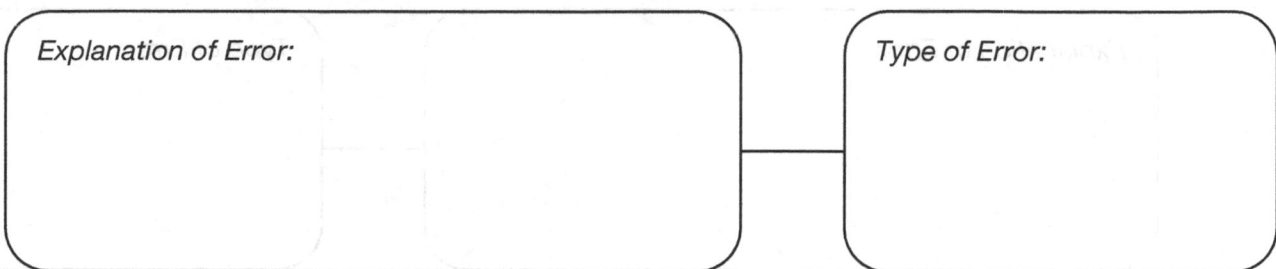

Prefix:

Root:

Suffix:

vociferous

Worksheet 154

Definition:

What it Looks Like:

Analogous Exercise:

mellifluous : vociferous   _____ : repugnant

Why? Nature of the Relationship:	Original Analogy Using the Vocabulary Word:

Ungrammatical Sentence:

In the United States, offering a waiter or waitress a <u>gratuity</u> composed of lira or rubles is probably not practicable, though I suppose it possible.

Explanation of Error:

Type of Error:

Prefix:

Definition:

Root:

gratuity

Worksheet 155

Suffix:

What it Looks Like:

Analogous Exercise:

docile : apoplexy

_____ : gratuity

Why? Nature of the Relationship:

Original Analogy Using the Vocabulary Word:

Worksheet 155

Name:____ Date:____________

Ungrammatical Sentence:

On his way to Italy, Hannibal could neither <u>circumvent</u> or ignore the Alps' geographic impediment, so he famously used elephants to cross them.

Explanation of Error:

Type of Error:

Prefix:

Definition:

Root:

circumvent

Worksheet 156

Suffix:

What it Looks Like:

Analogous Exercise:

obstruction : circumvent ______________ : extenuate

Why? Nature of the Relationship:

Original Analogy Using the Vocabulary Word:

Worksheet 156

Ungrammatical Sentence:

With ridiculous <u>circumlocution</u>, the mayor described his landslide defeat as "a minor setback that might delay his political agenda for a little while."

Explanation of Error:	*Type of Error:*

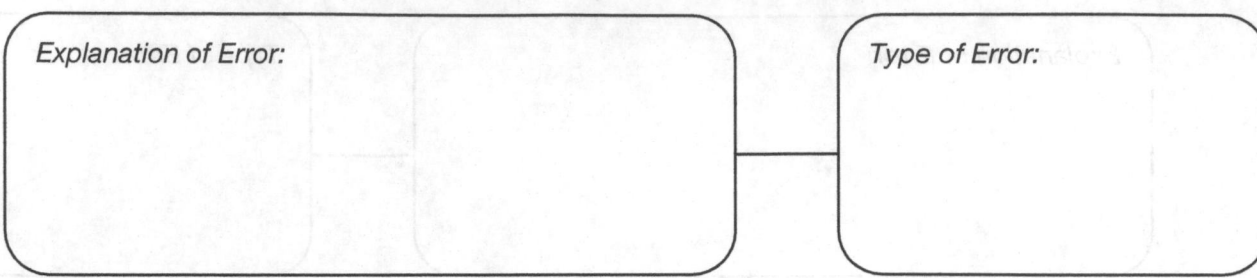

Prefix:

Definition:

Root:

circumlocution

Worksheet 157

Suffix:

What it Looks Like:

Analogous Exercise:

directness : circumlocution   _____ : superfluity

Why? Nature of the Relationship:	*Original Analogy Using the Vocabulary Word:*

Ungrammatical Sentence:

In addition to synchronized effervescent laughter, the twin sisters also expressed profusely <u>sympathetic</u> feelings for the stray kitten as well.

Explanation of Error:

Type of Error:

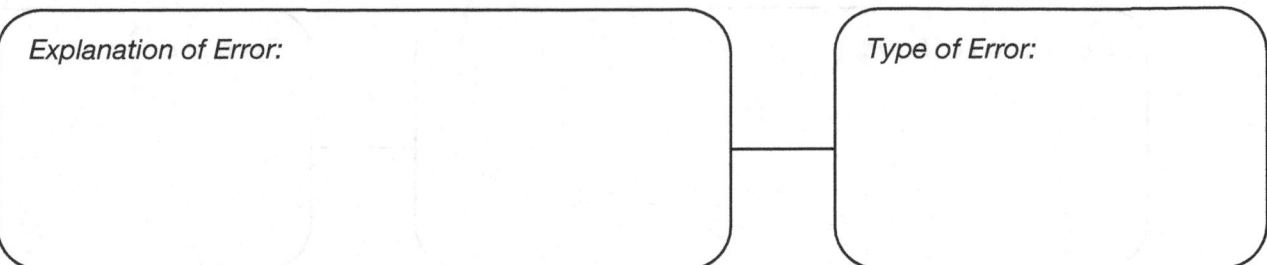

Prefix:

Definition:

Root:

sympathetic

Worksheet 158

Suffix:

What it Looks Like:

Analogous Exercise:

condolence : sympathetic

_____ : incredulous

Why? Nature of the Relationship:

Original Analogy Using the Vocabulary Word:

Ungrammatical Sentence:

Although The Chief Justice of the United States valued contemplation, quiet, and wisdom, she actually had no time for sedentary <u>indolence</u>.

Explanation of Error:	Type of Error:

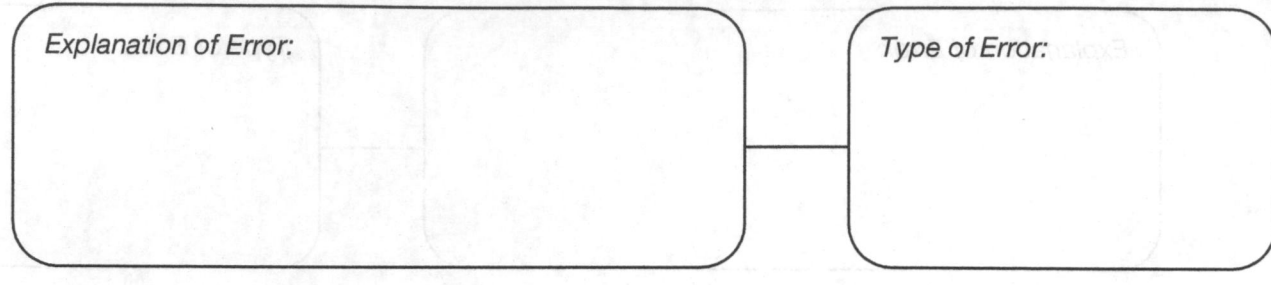

Prefix:

Definition:

Root:

indolence
Worksheet 159

Suffix:

What it Looks Like:

Analogous Exercise:

indolence : effervescence   _____ : circumvention

Why? Nature of the Relationship:	Original Analogy Using the Vocabulary Word:

Name:_____ Date:_____

Ungrammatical Sentence:

The architectural diagram was far to <u>abstruse</u> to comprehend,
so the crew of builders completed the office building erroneously.

Explanation of Error:

Type of Error:

Prefix:

Definition:

Root:

abstruse

Worksheet 160

Suffix:

What it Looks Like:

Analogous Exercise:

abstruse : obfuscate   _____ : elucidate

Why? Nature of the Relationship:

Original Analogy Using the Vocabulary Word:

Name:_____ Date:_____

Ungrammatical Sentence:

Other than fear and lowered self-esteem, it is unknown whether the witch's <u>malediction</u> had any real affect on the fairy tale's protagonist.

> **Explanation of Error:**
>
> **Type of Error:**

Prefix:

Definition:

Root:

malediction

Worksheet 161

Suffix:

What it Looks Like:

Analogous Exercise:

disparage : malediction   _____ : gratuity

> **Why? Nature of the Relationship:**
>
> **Original Analogy Using the Vocabulary Word:**

Name:______________________________ Date:____________

Ungrammatical Sentence:

Impressionist painter Claude Monet might of been <u>enamored</u> of light, as evidenced by his famous series of 250 paintings of water lilies.

Explanation of Error:

Type of Error:

Prefix:

Definition:

Root:

enamored

Worksheet 162

Suffix:

What it Looks Like:

Analogous Exercise:

enamored : sentient ______________ : indolent

Why? Nature of the Relationship:

Original Analogy Using the Vocabulary Word:

Worksheet 162

Chapter 4

Students' and Teachers' Guide to Daily Worksheets

The following daily entries summarize how their respective worksheets should be completed successfully. For further explanation and elaboration in all cases, please refer to the Glossary of Morphemes (pages 259–268) and the Glossary of Grammatical Terms and Errors (pages 269–275) found in this book.

Explanations of Daily Worksheets

Worksheet 1

- *Required Correction*: an additional "s" is required following the apostrophe in "Casey Jones' "
- *Explanation of Error*: plural nouns ending in "s" are made possessive by the simple addition of an apostrophe, while singular nouns ending in "s" are made possessive by adding both an apostrophe and an additional "s"
- *Type of Error*: possession
- *Prefix*: "a-" meaning "without" or "not"
- *Root*: "morph" meaning "form" or "shape"
- *Suffix*: "-ous" meaning "full of" or "having"
- *Definition*: not having form or shape (i.e., formless)
- *Analogy*: air can be described as amorphous, so the relationship is that the adjective on the left describes the noun on the right; as such, words like "tangible" and "hard" could accurately fill in the blank

Worksheet 2

- *Required Correction*: "implied" should be replaced with the word "inferred"
- *Explanation of Error*: to imply something is to hint or suggest it indirectly, while to infer something is to assume or understand a suggestion (i.e., to "get the hint"); in this case, the pedagogue lectured, while the speaker/student inferred while listening to the lecture
- *Type of Error*: diction
- *Prefix*: this word has no prefix
- *Root*: "pedo" meaning child or children

- *Suffix*: "-agogue" meaning "leader"
- *Definition*: a leader of children (i.e., a teacher)
- *Analogy*: books are the stereotypical materials of a pedagogue, so "paint," the material of a painter, is the logical choice to fill in the blank

Worksheet 3

- *Required Correction*: the word "were" should be replaced by "are"
- *Explanation of Error*: because events in literary works occur anew every time that those works are read, all events in literature should be referred to in the present tense
- *Type of Error*: literary present tense
- *Prefix*: this word has no prefix
- *Root*: "culp" meaning "blame"
- *Suffix*: "-able" meaning "able to be"
- *Definition*: able to be blamed (i.e., blameworthy or guilty)
- *Analogy*: someone who makes a mistake is culpable, so the adjective on the left describes a person who enacts the noun on the right; as such, "accomplished" and "victorious" would be fine ways to fill in the blank

Worksheet 4

- *Required Correction*: a comma must follow the word "ago"
- *Explanation of Error*: "Many centuries ago" is an introductory phrase describing when the barbarians in question were belligerent
- *Type of Error*: punctuation
- *Prefix*: "belli-" or "bellum" meaning "war"

- *Root*: "gerere" meaning "to bear" or "to carry"
- *Suffix*: "-ent" meaning "performing" or "being in a particular state"
- *Definition*: carrying war or inclined to fight (e.g., a bully or someone who picks many fights)
- *Analogy*: the adjective on the right does not apply to the noun on the left—a pacifist is quite the opposite of belligerent—so a noun such as "optimist" would accurately fill in the blank

Worksheet 5

- *Required Correction*: the word "or" must be replaced by "nor"
- *Explanation of Error*: "neither" and "nor" denote negativity, and thus accompany each other, while "either" and "or" do likewise because they convey positivism
- *Type of Error*: correlative conjunction *or* seesaw conjunction
- *Prefix*: this word has no prefix
- *Root*: "dign" meaning "worth" or "value"
- *Suffix*: "-ity" meaning "a state or quality of"
- *Definition*: a state of being worthy (i.e., honored or perhaps noble)
- *Analogy*: an individual's dignity can be lessened by falling down, so the verb on the right negatively impacts or is conversely related to the noun on the left, meaning that "worthlessness" or "failure" could accurately fill in the blank

Worksheet 6

- *Required Correction*: commas are required after the word "professor" and the word "passion"
- *Explanation of Error*: the phrase "a man of great knowledge and passion" is an appositive, falling under the larger umbrella of "extra information," and thus should be surrounded by commas
- *Type of Error*: punctuation
- *Prefix*: "in- " meaning "not"
- *Root*: "dubit" meaning "doubt"

- *Suffix*: "-able" meaning "able to be"
- *Definition*: not able to be doubted (i.e., completely truthful)
- *Analogy*: the adjective on the left describes the noun on the right, so the word "theoretical" or "inferred" would accurately fill in the blank

Worksheet 7

- *Required Correction*: the phrase "he also enjoyed spending time with" should be eliminated entirely from the sentence
- *Explanation of Error*: elements of a list must be formatted in uniform, parallel ways; in this case, all elements of this list are nouns of whom the convivial student was fond—his friends, his teachers, and his parents
- *Type of Error*: parallel construction *or* parallel structure
- *Prefix*: "con-" meaning "with" or "together"
- *Root*: "viv" meaning "alive" or "life"
- *Suffix*: "-al" meaning "relating to" or "having the character of"
- *Definition*: characterized by communal liveliness (e.g., a party or partygoer)
- *Analogy*: hermits are generally not portrayed as or thought to be convivial, so the adjective on the left does not describe the noun on the right; thus, "shy" and "stoic" are fine ways to fill in the blank

Worksheet 8

- *Required Correction*: the adverb "quickly" must be moved outside of the verb "to abduct," either prior to the word "tried" or after the word "abduct"
- *Explanation of Error*: "to abduct" is an infinitive verb, although technically composed of two different words, and it should not be separated by an adverb of any kind
- *Type of Error*: split infinitive
- *Prefix*: "ab-" meaning "apart" or "away from"

- *Root*: "duct" meaning "to lead"
- *Suffix*: this word has no suffix
- *Definition*: to lead away from (i.e., to take something from its rightful place)
- *Analogy*: the two verbs are synonyms for each other, as "snatch" and "abduct" mean essentially the same thing; therefore, words such as "bestow" and "provide" fill in the blank well

Worksheet 9

- *Required Correction*: the phrase "gray suited" must be hyphenated
- *Explanation of Error*: compound adjectives are composed of multiple words, yet function as singular adjectives; in this case, "gray suited" functions as an adjective to modify the noun "politician," and thus should be hyphenated, as compound adjectives must be
- *Type of Error*: compound adjective
- *Prefix*: "eu-" meaning "good" or "well"
- *Root*: "log" meaning "word" or "speech"
- *Suffix*: "-y" meaning "characterized by" or "inclined to"
- *Definition*: speech inclined to speak well of others (e.g., an honorary speech delivered at someone's funeral)
- *Analogy*: eulogies are often delivered by funereal mourners, so the noun on the right is produced by the noun on the left; in this sense, "valedictorian" or "honored guest" would be an accurate way to fill in the blank

Worksheet 10

- *Required Correction*: either the word "Though" or the word "yet" should be eliminated from the sentence
- *Explanation of Error*: the words "though" and "yet," like "but" and "however," imply negation or contrariness, and thus are redundant if doubled up in a single sentence in this way

- *Type of Error*: redundancy
- *Prefix*: "in-" meaning "within" or "inside of"
- *Root*: "carn" meaning "flesh"
- *Suffix*: "-ate" meaning "to act in such a manner"
- *Definition*: to make flesh inside of something (i.e., to make something real by giving it a bodily form)
- *Analogy*: to incarnate something is to make it solid, so the verb on the left leads to the physical state on the right; in terms of states of matter, therefore, the words "melt" and "evaporate" would both fill in the blank accurately

Worksheet 11

- *Required Correction*: the word "then" must be rewritten as "than"
- *Explanation of Error*: the word "then" is used when describing either time (e.g., "then it rained") or causation (e.g., "if you go to sleep, then you will feel rested"), while "than" is comparative (e.g., "I am taller than my friend")
- *Type of Error*: diction
- *Prefix*: "auto-" meaning "self"
- *Root*: "nom" meaning "name"
- *Suffix*: "-y" meaning "characterized by" or "inclined to"
- *Definition*: characterized by having one's own name (i.e., independent and able to make one's own decisions)
- *Analogy*: a toddler has no autonomy, so the noun on the left and the adjective on the right are negatively related; therefore, a person who has little dignity, such as a playground bully or a sore loser, would accurately fill in the blank

Worksheet 12

- *Required Correction*: the pronoun "he" must be replaced by either "Paul Bunyan" or "the latter"
- *Explanation of Error*: the pronoun "he" is

ambiguous, as it might refer either to John or to Paul, and it thus needs to be clarified

- *Type of Error*: unclear referent
- *Prefix*: this word has no prefix
- *Root*: "doc" meaning "teach"
- *Suffix*: "-ile" meaning "capable of" or "suited to"
- *Definition*: suited to or capable of being taught (e.g., sitting quietly and attentively)
- *Analogy*: depending upon one's point of view, a kitten either can be described as docile (i.e., a cute, cuddly kitten) or cannot be described as such (i.e., a playful, yarn-assailing kitten); per the former relationship, a person who can be described as belligerent, such as Alexander the Great, should fill in the blank, while in the latter case, someone who is or was not belligerent, such as Mother Teresa, accurately fills it in

Worksheet 13

- *Required Correction*: the pronoun "whom" should be replaced by "who"
- *Explanation of Error*: in the clause beginning with "he was actually," the pronoun "he" serves as the subject rather than as a direct object—if it were a direct object, it would require the usage of "whom"
- *Type of Error*: pronoun agreement
- *Prefix*: "ex-" meaning "to intensify"
- *Root*: "acri" meaning "bitter"
- *Suffix*: "-ate" meaning "to act in such a manner"
- *Definition*: to intensify the bitterness of something (i.e., to make it worse)
- *Analogy*: a water leak is often exacerbated if left unattended, so the verb on the right describes or is accomplished by the noun on the left; in this way, a noun such as "thief" would adequately fill in the blank

Worksheet 14

- *Required Correction*: the possessive pronoun "Its" must be replaced by the contraction "It's"
- *Explanation of Error*: the phrase "It is" would effectively begin this sentence, and its contraction "It's" is a substitute, while the possessive pronoun "Its" makes no sense grammatically here
- *Type of Error*: while one may assume that the insertion of an apostrophe means that this is a punctuation error, "its" and "it's" are technically two different words with two different meanings, so this error is more accurately labeled a problem with diction
- *Prefix*: "magn-" meaning "large"
- *Root*: "anim" meaning "life" or "spirit"
- *Suffix*: "-ous" meaning "full of" or "having"
- *Definition*: having a large or grand spirit (e.g., a chivalrous knight or benefactor)
- *Analogy*: Mother Teresa can be described as magnanimous, so the adjective on the left describes the noun on the right; thus, "curious" or "mischievous" would certainly fill in the blank and describe Goldilocks

Worksheet 15

- *Required Correction*: either the word "did" or the word "allowed" must be inserted after the word "team" at the end of the sentence
- *Explanation of Error*: the amount of goals allowed by the first hockey goalie is in this sentence being compared to the second hockey goalie himself, *not* to the amount of goals allowed by that second goalie; the words "did" and "allowed" would fix this discrepancy by returning, like a coda, to the sentence's initial verb
- *Type of Error*: faulty comparison
- *Prefix*: "pro-" meaning "forth" or "forward"
- *Root*: "fus" meaning "to pour"

- *Suffix*: this word has no suffix
- *Definition*: poured forth (i.e., excessive)
- *Analogy*: the contents of a dictionary are profuse, so the contents of the noun on the left can be described by the adjective on the right; a noun such as "list of world's records" or "true facts" would thus fill in the blank accurately

Worksheet 16

- *Required Correction*: "eloquent" should be rewritten as "eloquently," and "full" should be replaced with "fully"
- *Explanation of Error*: both "eloquent" and "full" are adjectives, while this sentence requires two adverbs to modify the verb "wrote"
- *Type of Error*: because this error has less to do with the meanings of the two offending words than with their part of speech, this error is better labeled "grammar" than "diction"
- *Prefix*: "in-" meaning "within" or "inside of"
- *Root*: "her" meaning "to stick"
- *Suffix*: "-ent" meaning "performing" or "being in a particular state"
- *Definition*: being what is stuck within one's self (i.e., naturally characteristic of)
- *Analogy*: one's eye color is inherent, so the adjective on the left describes the noun on the right; as such, adjectives such as "learned" and "observed" would finely fill in the blank

Worksheet 17

- *Required Correction*: "Irregardless" must be replaced by either the word "Regardless" or the word "Irrespective"
- *Explanation of Error*: this very common error—"irregardless" is in fact not a true English word, yet is often used—occurs because people conflate the synonyms "irrespective" and "regardless," conjoining the two into a double negative
- *Type of Error*: diction

- *Prefix*: this word has no prefix
- *Root*: "nov" meaning "new"
- *Suffix*: "-ice" meaning "the condition or quality of"
- *Definition*: the quality of newness (e.g., a rookie)
- *Analogy*: an expert in any field is generally considered indubitable, so the adjective on the left describes the noun on the right; therefore, "inexperienced" or "doubtable" would work to fill in the blank

Worksheet 18

- *Required Correction*: the plural verb "demonstrate" must be replaced with the singular verb "demonstrates"
- *Explanation of Error*: the presence of two cooperative subjects—the car dealership and the circus—leads many people to use a plural verb, albeit incorrectly, in a sentence such as this one; the key here is the seesaw conjunction "neither–nor," which effectively does the opposite of "and," separating the two cooperative subjects and keeping them both singular, rather than conjoining them into a plurality, and thereby requiring accompaniment by a singular verb
- *Type of Error*: subject-verb agreement
- *Prefix*: this word has no prefix
- *Root*: "par" meaning "equal"
- *Suffix*: "-ity" meaning "a state or quality of"
- *Definition*: a state of being equal (i.e., equality and fairness)
- *Analogy*: the two words are synonyms, so "partiality" or "favoritism," both synonyms for "bias," can be used to fill in the blank

Worksheet 19

- *Required Correction*: a comma must be inserted before the conjunction "but"
- *Explanation of Error*: commas work alongside

words implying contrariness or contradiction, such as "but" or "although," to signal tonal reversals in sentences

- *Type of Error*: punctuation
- *Prefix*: "bene-" meaning "good" or "favorable"
- *Root*: "vol" meaning "to wish" or "to will"
- *Suffix*: "-ent" meaning "performing" or "being in a particular state"
- *Definition*: feeling or willing good circumstances for others (i.e., kind and helpful to other people)
- *Analogy*: a ruthless dictator cannot be described accurately as benevolent, so the adjective on the right does not describe the noun on the left; thus, any kind of person who is not magnanimous, such as a scam artist, correctly fills in the blank

Worksheet 20

- *Required Correction*: the semicolon following "novel" should be replaced by a comma
- *Explanation of Error*: semicolons join two independent clauses, yet the conjunction "but" makes the second clause dependent; a comma can accompany "but," however, to indicate the sentence's reversal
- *Type of Error*: punctuation
- *Prefix*: this word has no prefix
- *Root*: "dole" meaning "sadness" or "suffering"
- *Suffix*: "-ful" meaning "full of" or "having"
- *Definition*: full of sadness (i.e., depressed)
- *Analogy*: because eulogies are often doleful, the adjective on the right describes the noun on the left; a greeting card might therefore fill in the blank appropriately

Worksheet 21

- *Required Correction*: the word "too" is used incorrectly here, and it should be replaced by "to"
- *Explanation of Error*: "too" is used either as a synonym for "also" or to convey extremism

(e.g., too hungry, too tired, etc.), while "to" can function either as a preposition, thus indicating direction, or as part of an infinitive verb, which is the case in this sentence

- *Type of Error*: diction
- *Prefix*: this word has no prefix
- *Root*: "frag-" meaning "to break"
- *Suffix*: "-ment" meaning "the state or result of" *and* "-ary" meaning "relating to" or "of"
- *Definition*: relating to having been broken (i.e., incomplete and shattered)
- *Analogy*: fragmentary things are by nature incomplete, so the two adjectives are antonyms; the word "scarce" could therefore be used to fill in the blank

Worksheet 22

- *Required Correction*: either the comma following "city" should be replaced by a semicolon or, if the comma is retained, a conjunction indicating reversal (e.g., "yet") should follow it
- *Explanation of Error*: the comma is here used to conjoin two independent clauses, which is a task for which is it unsuited by itself
- *Type of Error*: punctuation
- *Prefix*: this word has no prefix
- *Root*: "capit" meaning "head"
- *Suffix*: "-al" meaning "relating to" or "having the character of"
- *Definition*: relating to the head (i.e., the most important or chief)
- *Analogy*: the capital position is the head of any hierarchy, just as one's "destination" is at the end of any road

Worksheet 23

- *Required Correction*: the word "less" should be replaced by "fewer"
- *Explanation of Error*: "less" is only used correctly

to modify singular nouns, while "fewer" modifies plural nouns, such as "assignments" in this case

- *Type of Error*: diction
- *Prefix*: "ag-" meaning "to lead" or "to force"
- *Root*: "greg" meaning "herd" or "group"
- *Suffix*: "-ate" meaning "characterized by" or "resembling"
- *Definition*: characterized by having been led into a group (i.e., herded together into a mass)
- *Analogy*: considering its common separation into social groups and its stratification into different grades and classes, high school can be described as fragmentary; as the adjective on the right in this way modifies the noun on the left, a word such as "taxes" or "population" can adequately fill in the blank

Worksheet 24

- *Required Correction*: a noun, such as "poets" or "works," must follow the pronoun "those"
- *Explanation of Error*: "this," "that," "those," and "these" are demonstrative pronouns—otherwise known as pointing pronouns—that must direct attention (i.e., point) to particular nouns; it is ambiguous and grammatically incorrect to allow pointing pronouns to stand alone
- *Type of Error*: unattributed pointing pronoun
- *Prefix*: "dif-" meaning "away from" or "apart," or otherwise indicating a reversal
- *Root*: "fid" meaning "faith" or "trust"
- *Suffix*: "-ent" meaning "performing" or "being in a particular state"
- *Definition*: being away from faith in others (i.e., shy and reserved, perhaps distrustfully so)
- *Analogy*: diffident persons are quite the opposite of lively, so a word conveying the opposite of "convivial," such as "cold" or "inhospitable," would finely fill in the blank

Worksheet 25

- *Required Correction*: the possessive pronoun "their" must be replaced by the phrase "his or her"
- *Explanation of Error*: the subject of the sentence, "a given teacher," is singular, therefore requiring a singular possessive pronoun with which to agree, but "their" is plural
- *Type of Error*: pronoun agreement
- *Prefix*: "re-" meaning "again" or "back"
- *Root*: "mit" meaning "to send"
- *Suffix*: this word has no suffix
- *Definition*: to send back (e.g., a telephone bill)
- *Analogy*: to remit is to send something back to its place of origin (i.e., to send it a second time), so the words "send" or "mail" would finely fill in the blank

Worksheet 26

- *Required Correction*: the word "but" should be inserted prior to "it," and the word "also" should be inserted before the word "may"
- *Explanation of Error*: the phrase "not only" accompanies "but also," the latter of which may be separated and still adequately complete the seesaw conjunction
- *Type of Error*: correlative conjunction *or* seesaw conjunction
- *Prefix*: "ex-" meaning "to intensify"
- *Root*: "ped" meaning "foot"
- *Suffix*: "-ite," a variant of "-ate" meaning "to act in such a manner"
- *Definition*: to act to intensify the foot speed of (i.e., to speed something up)
- *Analogy*: a traffic jam delays motorists, so the verb on the right is the effect of the noun on the left; in this way, something concerning speed, such as "full throttle" or "acceleration," accurately fills in the blank

Worksheet 27

- *Required Correction*: the phrase "on television" should be moved, probably to after the word "coalesced"
- *Explanation of Error*: the prepositional phrase "on television" modifies its antecedent, in this case the eyes of the watchers; however, their eyes are not on television at all, but the warring political factions' coalescence is
- *Type of Error*: misplaced modifier
- *Prefix*: "co-" meaning "together" or "with"
- *Root*: "al" meaning "toward" or "near"
- *Suffix*: "-esce" meaning "to do" or "to act"
- *Definition*: to act or move toward togetherness (i.e., to unify)
- *Analogy*: something described by the adjective "aggregate" has coalesced into some kind of a collection, so the verb on the right essentially leads to the adjectival state on the left; thus, something that is separate, such as varsity vs. junior varsity athletes, should fill in the blank

Worksheet 28

- *Required Correction*: either the word "Each" should be replaced by the word "All" or the plural verb "have" should be replaced by "has"
- *Explanation of Error*: "each" is a singular pronoun, requiring a singular verb to accompany the ambulatory creatures that are thereby counted out or identified singly, while "all" is a plural pronoun, lumping all ambulatory creatures into a plurality and thus requiring a plural verb
- *Type of Error*: subject/verb agreement
- *Prefix*: this word has no prefix
- *Root*: "ambul" meaning "walk"
- *Suffix*: "-ate" meaning "characterized by" or "resembling" *and* "-ory" meaning "of" or "relating to"
- *Definition*: relating to the characteristic of walking (i.e., capable of walking or occurring during a walk)
- *Analogy*: by definition, anything ambulatory must have feet, so the adjective on the left requires or is associated with the noun on the right; in this way, an adjective associated with the usage of hands, such as "manipulatory," will fill in the blank well

Worksheet 29

- *Required Correction*: the word "with" should be replaced with the word "to"
- *Explanation of Error*: the definition of "correspond with" is communicative (i.e., writing letters or e-mails to an absent person), while "correspond to" is used to express correlation or relationship (e.g., my choice of a heavy coat corresponded to the snowy weather)
- *Type of Error*: diction
- *Prefix*: "in- " meaning "not"
- *Root*: "fab" meaning "speak"
- *Suffix*: "-able" meaning "able to be"
- *Definition*: not able to be spoken (i.e., indescribable or taboo)
- *Analogy*: per definition, ineffable things cannot be put into words, so the noun on the left can potentially be described by the adjective on the right; "ideas" or "theories," therefore, would adequately fill in the blank

Worksheet 30

- *Required Correction*: the word "persons" should be replaced with "people"
- *Explanation of Error*: "persons" refers to a group of individually identifiable humans, while "people" describes a homogeneous group; because the desire for omniscience is the singular way in which the group being described is identified, the members of that group qualify as homogeneous in this way

- *Type of Error*: diction
- *Prefix*: "omni-" meaning "all"
- *Root*: "sci" meaning "to know"
- *Suffix*: "-ence" meaning "the state or quality of"
- *Definition*: the state of knowing everything (i.e., all-knowing)
- *Analogy*: humans can not possess omniscience, so the two nouns are negatively correlated; what should fill in the blank, therefore, is a noun that countries cannot possess, such as "omnipotence" or "total world domination"

Worksheet 31

- *Required Correction*: the word "because" should be replaced with "that"
- *Explanation of Error*: the phrase "the reason why" essentially serves the same purpose that the word "because" serves, so to include them both in one explanatory sentence is redundant
- *Type of Error*: redundancy
- *Prefix*: "mis-" meaning "bad" or "wrong"
- *Root*: "anthrop" meaning "man" or "human"
- *Suffix*: this word has no suffix
- *Definition*: a wrong human (e.g., a person who does not like other people in general)
- *Analogy*: a misanthrope has social autonomy, so the noun on the right possesses the noun on the left; the blank can thus be filled in simply with the word "movies"

Worksheet 32

- *Required Correction*: the word "eminent" should be replaced with "imminent"
- *Explanation of Error*: someone eminent is famously successful and admired, while something imminent is forthcoming or soon to arrive; the latter word simply makes sense in this sentence
- *Type of Error*: diction
- *Prefix*: "se-" meaning "apart"

- *Root*: "ques" meaning "to seek" *and* "tra" meaning "to draw or pull"
- *Suffix*: "-ate" meaning "to act in such a manner" *and* "-ion" meaning "the act or condition of"
- *Definition*: the act of seeking to pull someone or something apart from its place (e.g., lawful repossession of someone's property or isolation of an individual)
- *Analogy*: sequestration is an act of law, and largely requires legal support, so the noun on the right is a precondition for the noun on the left; therefore, a word such as "foresight" or "prudence" would accurately fill in the blank

Worksheet 33

- *Required Correction*: the pronoun "me" should be replaced with "I"
- *Explanation of Error*: the pronoun "I" is used as the subject of a sentence or clause, while "me" is used as a direct object; a simple trick to tell which pronoun works is to eliminate the other parties involved—"My friends," in this case—in order to identify the correct pronoun (e.g., it would be accurate to say "I am intelligent," not "me am intelligent")
- *Type of Error*: pronoun agreement
- *Prefix*: this word has no prefix
- *Root*: "cred" meaning "to believe" or "to trust"
- *Suffix*: "-ible" meaning "able to be" *and* "-ity" meaning "a state or quality of"
- *Definition*: the quality of being able to be believed (i.e., one can trust it)
- *Analogy*: an expert at any activity has authoritative credibility; thus, as the noun on the right possesses the noun on the left, a word such as "naivety" or "inexperience" would accurately fill in the blank

Worksheet 34

- *Required Correction*: the colon should be eliminated
- *Explanation of Error*: colons correctly follow independent clauses, which "The political analyst's prognosis of our country's imminent condition was" is not
- *Type of Error*: punctuation
- *Prefix*: "pro-" meaning "before"
- *Root*: "gno" meaning "know"
- *Suffix*: "-osis" meaning "the state of"
- *Definition*: the state of knowing something beforehand (i.e., a prediction)
- *Analogy*: one's prognosis is his or her vision of the future, so the noun on the left concerns the noun on the right; thus, "observation" is a fine way to fill in the blank

Worksheet 35

- *Required Correction*: the word "farther" should be replaced with "further"
- *Explanation of Error*: "farther" is used adverbially to describe things that can be measured in quantifiable increments, such as temperature or distance, while "further" simply means "more" or "to a greater extent"; in this sentence, the mayor's disparagement of his opponent's ideas can not be quantified and tracked numerically, at least not without inventing a somewhat arbitrary system for doing so
- *Type of Error*: diction
- *Prefix*: "dis-" meaning "not," "away," or "apart"
- *Root*: "par" *or* "peer" meaning "equal"
- *Suffix*: "-age" meaning "the act or result of"
- *Definition*: the act of making something or someone not equal (i.e., to cause the lowering of something or someone below its, his, or her peers)
- *Analogy*: a misanthrope disparages other people, so the verb on the right is enacted by the noun on the left; a cheerleader or proponent is the kind of person, therefore, who would acceptably fill in the blank

Worksheet 36

- *Required Correction*: the word "then" must be inserted after the comma
- *Explanation of Error*: the traditional "if-then statement" is called such for a reason; the word "then" must accompany the word "if"
- *Type of Error*: correlative conjunction *or* seesaw conjunction
- *Prefix*: "pug-" meaning "to fight"
- *Root*: "nat" meaning "to be born" or "to spring from"
- *Suffix*: "-ious" meaning "full of" or "having"
- *Definition*: having been born to fight (i.e., naturally aggressive and hostile)
- *Analogy*: a pugnacious person is also belligerent, so the two adjectives are related, if not approximate synonyms; in this way, the words "kind" or "compassionate" can fill in the blank well

Worksheet 37

- *Required Correction*: the word "which" should be replaced with "that"
- *Explanation of Error*: following and modifying any noun, "which" concerns the entire group of its antecedent, in this case implying that all stories, essentially worldwide, involve spaceships and alien visitors; the word "that," by contrast, limits the focus on the antecedent, concerning only a subgroup of the preceding noun, such as only those stories involving spaceships and aliens, which in this case are the stories considered apocryphal
- *Type of Error*: diction
- *Prefix*: "apo-" meaning "away"
- *Root*: "cryp" meaning "hidden"

- *Suffix*: "-al" meaning "relating to" or "having the character of"
- *Definition*: relating to being hidden away (i.e., not necessarily authentic or true)
- *Analogy*: something apocryphal engenders doubt, so the adjective on the right and the noun on the left are related; thus, the words "truth" and "fact" would adequately fill in the blank

Worksheet 38

- *Required Correction*: the word "Between" should be replaced with "Among"
- *Explanation of Error*: "between" is used correctly only relative to two choices, partners, or parts, whereas "among" is used in relation to three or more, such as the 12 members of the jury mentioned in this sentence
- *Type of Error*: diction
- *Prefix*: "ex-" meaning "out of" or "from"
- *Root*: "oner," variant of "onus" meaning "burden"
- *Suffix*: "-ate" meaning "to act in such a manner"
- *Definition*: to relieve one from a burden (i.e., to remove someone's responsibility for something)
- *Analogy*: to exonerate someone is to demonstrate that he or she is innocent, so the verb on the left applies to or leads to the adjective on the right; per this relationship, the word "convict" or "blame" should fill in the blank

Worksheet 39

- *Required Correction*: the verb "affect" should be replaced with "effect"
- *Explanation of Error*: these two words are commonly misunderstood and often taught incorrectly to students, largely owing to the fact that they each can function as both a noun and a verb; the verb "affect" means to change something that previously existed, while the noun "affect" concerns emotion and atmospheric feel,

as in a classroom; the noun "effect," by contrast, is the result of an action or circumstance, while the verb "effect" means to instigate or engender the creation of something that was previously nonexistent; it is the latter usage that is correct in this sentence, as the mentioned upswing in sales does not previously exist, but occurs as a result of the fervid advertising campaign

- *Type of Error*: diction
- *Prefix*: this word has no prefix
- *Root*: "ferv" meaning "to boil, bubble, or burn"
- *Suffix*: "-id" meaning "resembling" or "similar to"
- *Definition*: resembling a bubbling or burning substance (i.e., hotly passionate)
- *Analogy*: someone docile is rarely fervid about anything, so the two adjectives are inversely related; thus, the words "stationary" and "inactive" provide appropriate ways to fill in the blank

Worksheet 40

- *Required Correction*: the word "incredulous" should be replaced with "incredible"
- *Explanation of Error*: "incredible" describes things that are difficult or impossible to believe, such as the rumor concerning taxation, while "incredulous" describes people who do not believe something in particular
- *Type of Error*: diction
- *Prefix*: "inter-" meaning "between"
- *Root*: "mit" meaning "to send"
- *Suffix*: "-ent" meaning "performing" or "being in a particular state"
- *Definition*: being in the state of sending between (i.e., not constant, but alternating or sporadic)
- *Analogy*: the rotation of the Earth is constant, so the movement of the noun on the left can be described by the adjective on the right; thus,

cars in traffic or elevators can finely fill in the blank

Worksheet 41

- *Required Correction*: the phrase "obstruction of justice" should be surrounded by quotation marks
- *Explanation of Error*: whenever a writer refers to particular letters, words, or phrases, rather than to their signified objects (e.g., the word "cat" rather than the feline animal that the word represents) he or she should place quotation marks around that letter, word, or phrase in order to distinguish it as a strictly linguistic subject
- *Type of Error*: punctuation
- *Prefix*: "ob-" meaning "against"
- *Root*: "struct" meaning "to build"
- *Suffix*: "-ion" meaning "the act or condition of"
- *Definition*: the condition of having been built against (i.e., a blockage hampering movement)
- *Analogy*: an obstruction delays people or things, so the noun on the left enacts the verb on the right; the words "problems" and "lies" fill in the blank well

Worksheet 42

- *Required Correction*: the preposition "of" should be replaced with "have"
- *Explanation of Error*: even though phonetic spelling perhaps suggests that "might of" is correct, the word "have" is used alongside "should," "might," "could," and "would" to signify hypothetical possibility
- *Type of Error*: diction
- *Prefix*: this word has no prefix
- *Root*: "ver" meaning "truth"
- *Suffix*: "-ity" meaning "a state or quality of"
- *Definition*: a quality of truth (e.g., a truthful fact)

- *Analogy*: the verity of something apocryphal is questionable, so the two words are inversely related; in this way, the word "smallness" can be used to fill in the blank

Worksheet 43

- *Required Correction*: the word "practical" should be replaced with "practicable"
- *Explanation of Error*: something practical is purposeful or useful, yet this sentence contradicts itself in stating that the teacher's plan had little usefulness, yet was practical; instead, the word "practicable" means possible or plausible, and the corrected sentence states that even though the plan was technically possible to enact, it had little purpose, which makes much more sense
- *Type of Error*: diction
- *Prefix*: "ad-" meaning "toward" or "near"
- *Root*: "voc" meaning "to call"
- *Suffix*: "-ate" meaning "to act in such a manner"
- *Definition*: acting to call toward someone or something (i.e., to speak on behalf of another)
- *Analogy*: a person or cause's ally advocates for that person or cause, so the noun on the left engages in the verb on the right; thus, tabloid newspapers, as periodicals that disparage individuals, can accurately fill in the blank

Worksheet 44

- *Required Correction*: the word "that" must be inserted before "Albert Einstein"
- *Explanation of Error*: the speaker of this sentence does not personally know Albert Einstein, but the fact *that* Einstein utilized perfunctory preparation at times; as a rule of thumb, when two combinations of nouns and verbs are situated in close proximity (e.g., "I know" and "Einstein must have delivered") they should be

separated by the word "that" in order to avoid miscommunication

- *Type of Error*: grammar
- *Prefix*: "per-" meaning "through," thus "completely"
- *Root*: "funct" meaning "performance" or "function"
- *Suffix*: "-ory" meaning "of" or "relating to"
- *Definition*: related completely to the function or performance of something (i.e., routine and expected, thus lacking enthusiasm)
- *Analogy*: brushing one's teeth is a perfunctory activity, so the action on the left is accomplished in the manner on the right; in this way, something exciting, such as stock car driving or playing basketball, can fill in the blank

Worksheet 45

- *Required Correction*: "70's" should be rewritten " '70s," with the apostrophe preceding the number 7
- *Explanation of Error*: just as in a linguistic contraction (e.g., "can't" and "wouldn't"), the apostrophe in a numerical contraction replaces what is eliminated, in this case the century number 19; an apostrophe is incorrect if used prior to the "s," since the '70s were not possessive, just plural
- *Type of Error*: punctuation
- *Prefix*: "ab-" meaning "apart" or "away from"
- *Root*: "dict" meaning "to tell" or "to use words"
- *Suffix*: "-ate" meaning "to act in such a manner"
- *Definition*: to act by using words away from something (i.e., to renounce or discard something formally)
- *Analogy*: one abdicates authority, so the verb on the right is done relative to the noun on the left; thus, "payment" and "a bill" are fine ways to fill in the blank

Worksheet 46

- *Required Correction*: the comma following the word "that" should be eliminated
- *Explanation of Error*: many students believe incorrectly that commas must always be used to introduce quotations; actually, if quotations are worked fluidly into writers' own syntactic language, as accomplished in this sentence by the usage of the word "that," then they need not be introduced using the traditional comma
- *Type of Error*: comma splice
- *Prefix*: "con-" meaning "with" or "together"
- *Root*: "junct" meaning "to meet" or "to join"
- *Suffix*: "-al" meaning "relating to" or "having the character of"
- *Definition*: characterized by being joined together (i.e., pertaining to marriage)
- *Analogy*: conjugal relationships require that people be together, emotionally if not physically, so the two words are related components; as such, "apart" is a counterpart to "fragmentary" and a logical way to fill in the blank

Worksheet 47

- *Required Correction*: the word "respectfully" should be replaced with "respectively"
- *Explanation of Error*: the adverb "respectfully" means accomplished with respect, describing perhaps the way in which one might speak to a hierarchical superior; the word "respectively," however, refers to things being correlated in a particular order, so eulogists in this sentence are explained to be doleful, and comedians are described as loquacious
- *Type of Error*: diction
- *Prefix*: this word has no prefix
- *Root*: "loq" meaning "word" or "speak"
- *Suffix*: "-ate" meaning "to act in such a manner" *and* "-ous" meaning "full of" or "having"

- *Definition*: full of the action of speaking (i.e., talkative and wordy)
- *Analogy*: loquacious people stereotypically do not find many things ineffable, so the two words are approximate opposites; in this way, "creative" and "imaginative" are appropriate words with which to fill in the blank

Worksheet 48

- *Required Correction*: the word "disinterested" should be replaced with "uninterested"
- *Explanation of Error*: someone described as uninterested is bored, not taken with a particular subject or activity, while a person who is disinterested is unbiased and impartial, such as a judge or a referee, and has no particular rooting interest in one side over another; the sleepy student in this sentence is clearly uninterested in the lecture
- *Type of Error*: diction
- *Prefix*: "de-" meaning "away" or "down"
- *Root*: "rog" meaning "to ask"
- *Suffix*: "-ate" meaning "to act in such a manner" *and* "-ory" meaning "of" or "relating to"
- *Definition*: related to the action of talking down to someone or something; something belittling or a put-down
- *Analogy*: derogatory remarks disparage the person(s) about whom they are uttered or written, so the adjective on the left enacts the verb on the right; the word "supportive" thus sensibly fills in the blank

Worksheet 49

- *Required Correction*: this sentence should not end with the preposition "from," but should instead have its conclusion rewritten, "to be that from which most American citizens died"
- *Explanation of Error*: prepositions are "relationship words" and thus should never end

sentences, because in that position, they signify incomplete relationships; as I explain it to my own students, a relationship takes a partner on each side
- *Type of Error*: syntax
- *Prefix*: "pan-" meaning "everywhere"
- *Root*: "dem" meaning "people"
- *Suffix*: "-ic" meaning "relating to" or "characterized by"
- *Definition*: related to people everywhere (i.e., affecting a great number of people in a great number of places)
- *Analogy*: anything pandemic affects all aspects of a particular society, just as something local—that word could appropriately fill in this blank—affects some aspects of a society or its people

Worksheet 50

- *Required Correction*: the word "his," within the quotation, should be surrounded by square brackets
- *Explanation of Error*: the speaker's grandfather would not have referred to himself in the third person, but would have instead said "my"; although students are under the common impression that direct quotations cannot and should never be altered, it is actually quite legitimate and common to edit their syntactical aspects to improve flow, as in this case, by placing brackets around whatever is changed within the quotations
- *Type of Error*: punctuation
- *Prefix*: "ab-" meaning "apart" or "away from"
- *Root*: "err" meaning "to wander"
- *Suffix*: "-ant" meaning "performing" or "being in a particular state"
- *Definition*: having wandered away from (i.e., not usual or typical)
- *Analogy*: something aberrant is not routine,

so the two adjectives are antonyms; as such, "failed" and "fallible" can accurately fill in the blank

Worksheet 51

- *Required Correction*: the conjunction "For" should be removed from the sentence
- *Explanation of Error*: most students have been taught correctly that sentences should not begin with conjunctions, but sometimes students fail to understand the technical reason why: clauses beginning with conjunctions are dependent clauses, which simply cannot stand alone as sentences
- *Type of Error*: grammar
- *Prefix*: this word has no prefix
- *Root*: "bibl" meaning "book"
- *Suffix*: "-phile" meaning "lover of"
- *Definition*: a lover of books (e.g., a book collector)
- *Analogy*: bibliophiles probably appreciate or are enamored of libraries, so the noun on the left is a place associated with the noun on the right; per this relationship, either "school" or "classroom" would correctly fill in the blank

Worksheet 52

- *Required Correction*: the singular word "conclusion" should be pluralized as "conclusions"
- *Explanation of Error*: Shakespeare wrote many different tragedies, of course, and they all have individual conclusions, rather than a singular shared one
- *Type of Error*: grammar
- *Prefix*: "apo-" meaning "away"
- *Root*: "plex" meaning "to tangle or bend"
- *Suffix*: "-y" meaning "characterized by" or "inclined to"
- *Definition*: characterized by tangling something away (e.g., a seizure or spasmodic outburst)
- *Analogy*: an apoplexy is a sudden, violent outburst, while pugnacious individuals are prone to violence, so the two words share a common characteristic; in this way, a word that somewhat resembles benevolence, such as "generosity" or "aid," would finely fill in the blank

Worksheet 53

- *Required Correction*: the word "The" should be lowercased
- *Explanation of Error*: articles preceding proper nouns should not be capitalized unless they are part of a published title, as in *A Tale of Two Cities*
- *Type of Error*: capitalization
- *Prefix*: this word has no prefix
- *Root*: "vi" meaning "alive" or "life"
- *Suffix*: "-able" meaning "able to be" *and* "-ity" meaning "a state or quality of"
- *Definition*: the quality of being potentially alive (i.e., realistically possible)
- *Analogy*: something's viability can be prevented or lessened by an obstruction, so an accomplishment or quality that can be prevented by a miscalculation, such as success or accuracy, should fill in the blank

Worksheet 54

- *Required Correction*: the second clause should be rewritten, "countless musicians have played those pieces millions of times"
- *Explanation of Error*: the second clause is written in the passive voice, whereby the verb "is done to" the subject, rather than the subject "doing" the verb
- *Type of Error*: passive voice
- *Prefix*: "amb-" meaning "both" or "more than one"
- *Root*: "val," a variant of "vol" meaning "to wish" or "to will"
- *Suffix*: "-ent" meaning "performing" or "being in a particular state"

- *Definition*: in the state of wishing for more than one thing (i.e., having mixed emotions concerning a topic)
- *Analogy*: ambivalent people feel confusion, so the noun on the left contributes to the adjective on the right; "sorrow" or "unhappiness" would therefore fill in the blank correctly

Worksheet 55

- *Required Correction*: the verb "imply" should be changed to "infer"
- *Explanation of Error*: the sentence's speaker inferred pruning dates from the almanac, which implied the timeline to its reader
- *Type of Error*: diction
- *Prefix*: "pre-" meaning "before"
- *Root*: "dict" meaning "to tell" or "to use words"
- *Suffix*: "-ive" meaning "performing" or "tending to"
- *Definition*: intending to tell something before it occurs (e.g., a prediction of the future)
- *Analogy*: by its nature, a prognosis is predictive, so the adjective on the left describes the noun on the right; thus, a word such as "wistful" or "retrospective" would adequately fill in the blank

Worksheet 56

- *Required Correction*: the word "it's" should be replaced with "its," minus the apostrophe
- *Explanation of Error*: the word "it's" is a contraction for "it is," while the "its" *sans* apostrophe is possessive
- *Type of Error*: some students might be tempted to label this a punctuation error, but because the two are technically two different words with two different uses, it is more appropriately labeled a diction error
- *Prefix*: this word has no prefix
- *Root*: "dubit" meaning "doubt"
- *Suffix*: "-ous" meaning "full of" or "having"

- *Definition*: including doubt (i.e., perhaps or probably untrue, and thus doubtful)
- *Analogy*: people are ambivalent about dubious things or issues, so the adjective on the right describes people's relationship to the noun on the left; as such, a word requiring many skills, such as "decathlon," appropriately fills in the blank

Worksheet 57

- *Required Correction*: The word "And" should be eliminated, and "furthermore" should be capitalized
- *Explanation of Error*: beginning a sentence with a conjunction automatically makes it a dependent clause, which technically cannot stand alone as a sentence
- *Type of Error*: grammar
- *Prefix*: "in-" meaning "within" or "inside of"
- *Root*: "fer" meaning "to bring or carry"
- *Suffix*: "-ence" meaning "the state or quality of"
- *Definition*: the state of carrying forward the meaning inside of something (e.g., an educated guess or assumption based on evidence)
- *Analogy*: viability is a critical component of inference, so the noun on the left is strongly related to the noun on the right; in this way, "definiteness" is an appropriate way to fill in the blank

Worksheet 58

- *Required Correction*: a comma must be inserted before the word "yet"
- *Explanation of Error*: commas accompany contradiction or negation in a sentence
- *Type of Error*: punctuation
- *Prefix*: "re-" meaning "again" or "back"
- *Root*: "frac" meaning "to break"
- *Suffix*: "-ory" meaning "characterized by"
- *Definition*: characterized by breaking back (i.e.,

resistant to or otherwise unaffected by outside influence)

- *Analogy*: a conjugal relationship relies on togetherness, so the adjective on the right requires the noun on the left; refractory relationships and refractory people similarly require "difference" or "separation"

Worksheet 59

- *Required Correction*: the word "that" must be inserted between "recognize" and "the"
- *Explanation of Error*: the "You" to whom this sentence is addressed must not recognize the eminent architect himself, but rather the fact that his theory regarding building materials is a good one; as a rule of thumb, two combinations of nouns and verbs in close proximity (e.g., "You must recognize" and "the eminent architect's . . . theory . . . is") should be separated by the word "that" in order to avoid confusion
- *Type of Error*: grammar
- *Prefix*: "homo-" meaning "the same as"
- *Root*: "gen" meaning "creation" or "race or kind"
- *Suffix*: "-ous" meaning "full of" or "having" *and* "-ness" meaning "the state of"
- *Definition*: the state of having the same kind (i.e., of uniform composition, all parts being the same)
- *Analogy*: homogeneousness describes characteristic singularity, so the noun on the right demonstrates the number on the left; because amorphousness is without form, the number zero or the word "none" would correctly fill in the blank

Worksheet 60

- *Required Correction*: following the comma, the sentence should read, "but they also won"
- *Explanation of Error*: "not only" must be accompanied by "but also"

- *Type of Error*: correlative conjunction *or* seesaw conjunction
- *Prefix*: this word has no prefix
- *Root*: "capit" meaning "head"
- *Suffix*: "-ul" meaning "tending or inclined to" *and* "-ate" meaning "to act in such a manner"
- *Definition*: to incline to the head (i.e., to succumb to the influence of a superior)
- *Analogy*: to capitulate is to surrender, so the two words are effective synonyms; as such, a word like "fit" or "outburst" fills in the blank well

Worksheet 61

- *Required Correction*: the word "imminent" should be replaced with "eminent"
- *Explanation of Error*: an eminent attorney is a famous attorney, but as the word "imminent" means soon to arrive, the phrase "imminent attorney" makes little sense in this sentence
- *Type of Error*: diction
- *Prefix*: "du-," variant of "di-" meaning "two"
- *Root*: "plic," variant of "plex" meaning "to tangle or bend"
- *Suffix*: "-ity" meaning "a state or quality of"
- *Definition*: the state of being bended into two (i.e., deceptiveness in speech or behavior)
- *Analogy*: duplicity implies two-facedness, while homogeneousness suggests oneness, so the relationship between the two is that the noun on the left signifies plurality, while the noun on the right signifies singularity; "a gymnastics team" is thus an appropriate way to fill in the blank

Worksheet 62

- *Required Correction* the pronoun "who" must be replaced with "whom"
- *Explanation of Error*: "whom" is used in relation to a direct object, rather than a subject. A

simple trick is to substitute either the word "he" or "him" into the offending phrase; because the phrase more appropriately reads, "many jazz aficionados cite him" rather than, "aficionados cite he," students can easily tell that "whom" is the correct pronoun to use

- *Type of Error*: pronoun agreement
- *Prefix*: "melli-" meaning "honey"
- *Root*: "flu" meaning "to flow"
- *Suffix*: "-ous" meaning "full of" or "having"
- *Definition*: having a flow of honey (i.e., smooth and sweet, especially aurally)
- *Analogy*: a traffic jam is anything but mellifluous, so the adjective on the left is rather opposite of the noun on the right; as such, "fragrant" is an appropriate word with which to fill in the blank

Worksheet 63

- *Required Correction*: the word "because" should be replaced with the word "that"
- *Explanation of Error*: the phrase "the reason why" and the word "because" accomplish the same grammatical purpose, so to include both in one sentence is redundant
- *Type of Error*: redundancy
- *Prefix*: "trans-" meaning "across"
- *Root*: "mut" meaning "change"
- *Suffix*: "-ate" meaning "to act in such a manner" *and* "-ive" meaning "performing" or "tending to"
- *Definition*: tending to change across boundaries (i.e., able to transform from one form or state into another)
- *Analogy*: per the water cycle, water is transmutative, so the adjective on the left describes the noun on the right; in this way, "solid" and "manufactured" would be adequate ways to fill in the blank

Worksheet 64

- *Required Correction*: either the comma in this sentence should be replaced with a semicolon, or a conjunction such as "and" should be added after the comma
- *Explanation of Error*: a comma cannot correctly join two independent clauses by itself, although it works if accompanied by a conjunction, serving the same purpose as a lone semicolon
- *Type of Error*: punctuation
- *Prefix*: "inter-" meaning "between"
- *Root*: "loc" meaning "word" or "speak"
- *Suffix*: "-ute," variant of "ate" meaning "characterized by" or "resembling" *and* "-or" meaning "one who does"
- *Definition*: one who is characterized by speaking between (i.e., a participant in a dialogue or conversation)
- *Analogy*: an interlocutor is probably loquacious—or at least both words have to do with speech—so the adjective on the right is thusly related to the noun on the left; therefore, the word "rebel" is an appropriate way to fill in the blank

Worksheet 65

- *Required Correction*: the phrase "and she thinks that it may also be on" should be removed from the sentence
- *Explanation of Error*: items in lists must be formatted in parallel, uniform ways, as "tonight, tomorrow, and next weekend"
- *Type of Error*: parallel structure *or* parallel construction
- *Prefix*: "pre-" meaning "before"
- *Root*: "sent" meaning "to feel or be aware"
- *Suffix*: "-ment" meaning "the state or result of"
- *Definition*: the result of being aware beforehand (i.e., a sense of something soon to occur or arise)
- *Analogy*: inferences are made based on observations, so the noun on the right requires the

noun on the left; thus, a word such as "fore-thought" fills in the blank finely

Worksheet 66

- *Required Correction*: the pronoun "she" must be replaced with a word or phrase indicating either the philanthropist (the former) or the widow (the latter)
- *Explanation of Error*: we are unsure if the philanthropist is male or female, so the ambiguous pronoun "she" could refer to either subject
- *Type of Error*: unclear referent
- *Prefix*: "philo-" meaning "love"
- *Root*: "anthrop" meaning "man" or "human"
- *Suffix*: "-ist" meaning "a person who practices" or "a person concerned with"
- *Definition*: a person who practices the love of humans (i.e., one who improves the welfare of humankind, often by charitable donations or acts)
- *Analogy*: a philanthropist, by definition, is magnanimous, so the noun on the left can be described by the adjective on the right; any type of successful orator or singer therefore fills in the blank appropriately

Worksheet 67

- *Required Correction*: "20's" must be rewritten " '20s"
- *Explanation of Error*: just as in a contracted word, the apostrophe should replace what is removed from a numerical contraction, in this case the "19"; moreover, to include the apostrophe prior to the "s" implies possession, which is incorrect here
- *Type of Error*: punctuation
- *Prefix*: "equ-" meaning "equal"
- *Root*: "anim" meaning "life" or "spirit"
- *Suffix*: "-ity" meaning "a state or quality of"
- *Definition*: the quality of having an equal spirit (i.e., calm and composed)

- *Analogy*: people demonstrating personal equanimity can be described as emotionally flat, so the adjective on the left is a visualization of the noun on the right; therefore, any word or phrase indicating visual differentness, such as an arrow, a mountainous peak, or a curvy line, fills in the blank well

Worksheet 68

- *Required Correction*: the "s" following the apostrophe should be removed
- *Explanation of Error*: singular nouns ending in "s" are made possessive by an apostrophe and an additional "s," but because "novels" is a plural noun, it is made possessive by the sole addition of an apostrophe
- *Type of Error*: possession
- *Prefix*: this word has no prefix
- *Root*: "tent" meaning "to stretch" or "to thin"
- *Suffix*: "-ate" meaning "characterized by" or "resembling" *and* "-ive" meaning "performing" or "tending to"
- *Definition*: tending to be characterized by thinness (i.e., uncertain and open rather than solid and definite)
- *Analogy*: to a degree, anything tentative also is predictive, so the two adjectives are not synonyms, but positively related; as such, a word like "sure" or "solid" would adequately fill in the blank

Worksheet 69

- *Required Correction*: the word "between" should be replaced with "among"
- *Explanation of Error*: "between" is useable only for situations involving two parties or options; as there are many more instruments than two in a pit, the word "among" is appropriate
- *Type of Error*: diction
- *Prefix*: "dis-" meaning "not," "away," or "apart"

- *Root*: "cord," variant of "cors" meaning "heart"
- *Suffix*: "-ant" meaning "performing" or "being in a particular state"
- *Definition*: not being hearty or healthy (i.e., conflicting or disagreeable)
- *Analogy*: things that are discordant do not coalesce, so the verb on the left does not describe or apply to the adjective on the right; thus, a verb such as "break up" or "fracture" appropriately fills in the blank

Worksheet 70

- *Required Correction*: a noun, such as "things" or "beings," should follow the pronoun "those"
- *Explanation of Error*: "this," "that," "those," and "these" are pointing (a.k.a. demonstrative) pronouns because they effectively point at particular objects or things; as such, pointing pronouns always should be followed by specific nouns at which to point
- *Type of Error*: unattributed pointing pronoun
- *Prefix*: "poly-" meaning "many"
- *Root*: "morph" meaning "form" or "shape"
- *Suffix*: "-ous" meaning "full of" or "having"
- *Definition*: having many forms (e.g., the butterfly and its transformative cycle)
- *Analogy*: "duplicity" and "polymorphous" are both words concerning plurality or multiples, so a noun implying or based on sameness, such as "unification," fills in the blank well

Worksheet 71

- *Required Correction*: the word "less" should be replaced by "fewer"
- *Explanation of Error*: "less" modifies singular nouns, while "fewer" modifies plural nouns, such as "hours"
- *Type of Error*: diction
- *Prefix*: "in-" meaning "within" or "inside of"
- *Root*: "cli" meaning "to lean toward"

- *Suffix*: "-ate" meaning "characterized by" or "resembling" *and* "-ion" meaning "the act or condition of"
- *Definition*: the act of being characterized by a leaning toward something within one's self (i.e., a personal or institutional preference or tendency)
- *Analogy*: per the technical definition of the word "inclination," a triangle has one, so the noun on the right contains, establishes, or demonstrates the noun on the left; in this way, a word such as "equidistance" or "uniformity" appropriately fills in the blank

Worksheet 72

- *Required Correction*: the sentence's conclusion should be rewritten, "the nurse to whom she was assigned"
- *Explanation of Error*: prepositions should not conclude sentences
- *Type of Error*: syntax
- *Prefix*: this word has no prefix
- *Root*: "qui" meaning "quiet"
- *Suffix*: "-esce" meaning "to do" or "to act" *and* "-ent" meaning "performing" or "being in a particular state"
- *Definition*: being in a state of quiet (i.e., inactive or still)
- *Analogy*: bibliophiles can probably be described in most cases as quiescent, so the adjective on the right describes the noun on the left; in this way, a person such as a race walker or sprinter correctly fills in the blank

Worksheet 73

- *Required Correction*: the phrase "my dog and I" should be replaced with either "me and my dog" or "my dog and me"
- *Explanation of Error*: "I" is used as a subject pronoun, but "my dog" and "me" here function

as direct objects; an easy trick to teach students is that omitting "my dog and" clarifies the fact that "me" is correct, rather than "I"

- *Type of Error*: pronoun agreement
- *Prefix*: "co-" meaning "together" or "with"
- *Root*: "gnos" meaning "know"
- *Suffix*: "-ant" meaning "performing" or "being in a particular state"
- *Definition*: being with knowledge (i.e., knowledgeable of something)
- *Analogy*: cognizance of something lends credibility to one's observation or belief, so the adjective on the left relates to, if not precedes, the noun on the right; in this way, an adjective such as "naivety" or "ignorance" would finely fill in the blank

Worksheet 74

- *Required Correction*: the comma following the word "that" should be removed
- *Explanation of Error*: although students often believe that all quotations must be introduced by commas, quotations that are worked into the flow of authors' sentences—such fluidity is achieved in this case by the inclusion of the word "that"—can be introduced without commas
- *Type of Error*: comma splice
- *Prefix*: "hetero-" meaning "different"
- *Root*: "dox" meaning "opinion"
- *Suffix*: this word has no suffix
- *Definition*: of a different opinion (i.e., different than the norm/orthodox)
- *Analogy*: groupings of things that are heterodox can by their nature be described as discordant, so the two adjectives are related, albeit not synonymous; as such, an adjective like "cohesive" or "similar" would fill in the blank acceptably

Worksheet 75

- *Required Correction*: the word "too" must be replaced with "to"
- *Explanation of Error*: "too" is used either as a substitute for "also" or to indicate extremism (e.g., too tall, too small), while "to" is used either as part of an infinitive verb or as a preposition, which is the case here
- *Type of Error*: diction
- *Prefix*: "im- " meaning "not"
- *Root*: "ped" meaning "foot"
- *Suffix*: "-ment" meaning "the state or result of"
- *Definition*: the state of not walking on foot (i.e., a roadblock or obstacle)
- *Analogy*: the two nouns are synonyms, as an obstruction to something is also an impediment; thus, a shade of purple, like violet, fills in the blank well

Worksheet 76

- *Required Correction*: the article "The" must be lowercased prior to the phrase "Revolutionary War"
- *Explanation of Error*: articles introducing proper nouns should not be capitalized unless they are actually parts of the titles of published works
- *Type of Error*: capitalization
- *Prefix*: "e-" meaning "out of" or "beyond"
- *Root*: "greg" meaning "herd" or "group"
- *Suffix*: "-ious" meaning "full of" or "having"
- *Definition*: of something beyond the group (i.e., extremely out of the accepted ordinary, remarkably extreme)
- *Analogy*: someone or something egregious is against the proverbial grain, acting or existing contrary to the flock from which the word is derived, while someone who capitulates falls in line with that flock, and in this way the adjective on the left and the verb on the right are

connotative opposites; thus, an adjective such as "solo" or "inharmonic" is an appropriate way to fill in the blank

Worksheet 77

- *Required Correction*: commas should be inserted surrounding the phrase "at least for her"
- *Explanation of Error*: not exactly a descriptive appositive, but an elaborative phrase, "at least for her" falls under the larger umbrella of extra information that can be removed from a sentence without altering its essential meaning; such information, like an appositive or an address, should be surrounded by commas
- *Type of Error*: punctuation
- *Prefix*: "a-" meaning "without" or "not"
- *Root*: "nom" meaning "name"
- *Suffix*: "-al" meaning "relating to" or "having the character of" *and* "-y" meaning "characterized by" or "inclined to"
- *Definition*: having the characteristic of something without a name (i.e., the state of being out of a normal and expected place or position)
- *Analogy*: heterodoxy requires difference, just as an anomaly does, so the two words share this characteristic; thus, the adjective "orthodox" fills in the blank perfectly

Worksheet 78

- *Required Correction*: a comma should be inserted after the word "match"
- *Explanation of Error*: "Watching the tennis match" is an introductory phrase
- *Type of Error*: punctuation
- *Prefix*: "re-" meaning "again" or "back"
- *Root*: "ced" meaning "to go" or "to yield"
- *Suffix*: this word has no suffix
- *Definition*: to go back (e.g., lowering floodwaters or tide)

- *Analogy*: tides recede, so the noun on the right enacts the verb on the left; therefore, a verb such as "set" or "arc" should fill in the blank

Worksheet 79

- *Required Correction*: the sentence should be reordered so that it reads, "The impressively talented student completed concurrently the essay for English class and the scientific experiment"
- *Explanation of Error*: the original sentence is written using the passive, rather than the active, voice
- *Type of Error*: passive voice
- *Prefix*: "con-" meaning "with" or "together"
- *Root*: "cur" meaning "a course that is run"
- *Suffix*: "-ent" meaning "performing" or "being in a particular state" *and* "-ly" meaning "accomplished in such a manner"
- *Definition*: done by running a course together (i.e., accomplished at the same time as and parallel to something else)
- *Analogy*: cars on an interstate highway travel concurrently, so the adverb on the right is central to the functioning of the noun on the left; thus, a noun like "coffeemaker," which denotes something used intermittently, should fill in the blank

Worksheet 80

- *Required Correction*: the adjective "easy" should be replaced by the adverb "easily"
- *Explanation of Error*: an adverb is required to modify the exoneration of the tabloids
- *Type of Error*: grammar
- *Prefix*: "de-" meaning "away" or "down"
- *Root*: "fam" meaning "fame or renown," variant of "fab"
- *Suffix*: "-ate" meaning "to act in such a manner" *and* "-ion" meaning "the act or condition of"

- *Definition*: the act of lowering someone's renown (i.e., attacking someone's reputation, particularly through speech)
- *Analogy*: something ineffable is unspeakable (i.e., impossible to communicate linguistically), while defamation requires such communication in a negative way; in this way, the adjective on the left has a contrary central quality than the noun on the right, so a word such as "untouchable" should fill in the blank

Worksheet 81

- *Required Correction*: quotation marks should surround the underlined word "Providence"
- *Explanation of Error*: quotation marks must surround words and phrases that act solely as themselves, as linguistic objects, rather than as the objects that they signify
- *Type of Error*: punctuation
- *Prefix*: "pro-" meaning "before"
- *Root*: "vid" meaning "to see"
- *Suffix*: "-ence" meaning "the state or quality of"
- *Definition*: the state of seeing beforehand (i.e., foresight and prudence)
- *Analogy*: per the etymological definition of "providence," that phenomenon requires thought, so the noun on the left is a precursor or necessary part of the noun on the right; in this way, a noun such as "chance" or "randomness" would fill in the blank finely

Worksheet 82

- *Required Correction*: either the phrase "Even though" should be removed, in which case the word "fears" should be capitalized, or the conjunction "but" should be omitted
- *Explanation of Error*: "even though" and "but" serve the same grammatical purpose, implying contradiction (i.e., a negative pivot), so to include them both in this sentence is redundant

- *Type of Error*: redundancy
- *Prefix*: "in- " meaning "not"
- *Root*: "noc" meaning "harm" or "death"
- *Suffix*: "-ous" meaning "full of" or "having"
- *Definition*: not having harm (i.e., harmless)
- *Analogy*: tea is medically innocuous—it is greatly healthful in many ways, actually—so the adjective on the left describes the noun on the right; thus, an adjective such as "detrimental" or "fattening" should fill in the blank

Worksheet 83

- *Required Correction*: the word "then" should be replaced with "than"
- *Explanation of Error*: "then" is used either temporally or causally, while "than" is comparative, as is this sentence
- *Type of Error*: diction
- *Prefix*: "contra-" meaning "against"
- *Root*: "ven" meaning "to come" or "to move forward"
- *Suffix*: this word has no suffix
- *Definition*: to move against (i.e., to confront, dispute, or oppose)
- *Analogy*: to contravene is by definition to be somewhat discordant, so the adjective on the left describes the verb on the right; as such, an adjective such as "agreeable" or "accepting" fills in the blank well

Worksheet 84

- *Required Correction*: following the word "institution," either the verb "employs" or the verb "does" should be inserted
- *Explanation of Error*: this sentence is written as if to compare the number of colonial tradesmen employed by Colonial Williamsburg to another educational institution itself, rather than to a number of tradesmen employed by said institution, as is numerically proper

- *Type of Error*: faulty comparison
- *Prefix*: "ana-," variant of "anti-" meaning "against"
- *Root*: "chron" meaning "time"
- *Suffix*: "-ism" meaning "the condition or action of being"
- *Definition*: the condition of being against time (i.e., something that exists out of its appropriate time period)
- *Analogy*: an anachronism is definable in terms of a temporal relationship (i.e., because of time), and 1990 is a temporal date, so the two parts of the analogy share the common characteristic of time; in this way, a noun concerning differences in physical space or place, such as "teleportation," should fill in the blank

Worksheet 85

- *Required Correction*: the phrase "well known" should be hyphenated
- *Explanation of Error*: "well known" is a compound adjective modifying the noun "theorist," and compound adjectives should always be hyphenated
- *Type of Error*: compound adjective
- *Prefix*: this word has no prefix
- *Root*: "her" meaning "to stick"
- *Suffix*: "-ity" meaning "a state or quality of" *and* "-ary" meaning "relating to" or "of"
- *Definition*: relating to the quality of sticking (i.e., something that is natural and inherited within one's family)
- *Analogy*: while a presentiment is supported by thought in some way, a wild guess is not, so the two nouns are opposites in this way; as such, a word or phrase suggesting the opposite of hereditary inheritance, such as "gifted" or "unpredictably talented," should fill in the blank

Worksheet 86

- *Required Correction*: the phrase "to confidently

converse" should be rewritten "to converse confidently"
- *Explanation of Error*: "to converse" is an infinitive verb, split here by the adverb "confidently"
- *Type of Error*: split infinitive
- *Prefix*: "magn-" meaning "large"
- *Root*: "loq" meaning "word" or "speech"
- *Suffix*: "-ent" meaning "performing" or "being in a particular state"
- *Definition*: being large of speech (i.e., high-flown and perhaps ostentatious in speaking)
- *Analogy*: the speech of someone magniloquent can probably be described as mellifluous, so the two adjectives, while not synonyms, are certainly related; in this way, a word such as "perfumed" should fill in the blank

Worksheet 87

- *Required Correction*: the word "persons" should be replaced with "people"
- *Explanation of Error*: "persons" is used to describe a group of plural, but individually identifiable, humans, while "people" is used to describe a group of undifferentiated humans, as the thousands in Saint Peter's Square are in this case
- *Type of Error*: diction
- *Prefix*: "bene-" meaning "good" or "favorable"
- *Root*: "dict" meaning "to tell" or "to use words"
- *Suffix*: "-ion" meaning "the act or condition of"
- *Definition*: the condition of telling favorable words (e.g., a blessing or honorary toast)
- *Analogy*: gossip tabloids engage commonly in defamation, so the noun on the right is the product of the noun on the left; therefore, a noun related to religion, such as "priests" or "nuns," would fill in the blank appropriately

Worksheet 88

- *Required Correction*: inside of the quotation,

the word "his" should be encased within square brackets

- *Explanation of Error*: the newscaster in this sentence would probably not speak of himself using the third person point of view, yet we can assume that the editor/writer of this sentence has altered the quote so that it flows with the rest of the sentence; thus, the word that was altered for the sake of flow must be indicated with square brackets
- *Type of Error*: punctuation
- *Prefix*: "amb-" meaning "both" or "more than one"
- *Root*: "ag" meaning "to drive or lead"
- *Suffix*: "-ous" meaning "full of" or "having"
- *Definition*: having the potential to drive in more than one direction (i.e., interpretable in multiple ways)
- *Analogy*: most poetry is ambiguous, to say the least, so the adjective on the left describes the noun on the right; thus, an adjective like "complicated" fills in the blank finely

Worksheet 89

- *Required Correction*: the possessive pronoun "their" should be replaced with the gender-neutral phrase "his or her"
- *Explanation of Error*: "No aberrant student" acts as the singular subject of the sentence, but the pronoun "their" is plural and should be replaced with the singular "his or her"
- *Type of Error*: pronoun agreement
- *Prefix*: "lit-," variant of "liter" meaning "letter"
- *Root*: "ag" meaning "to drive or lead"
- *Suffix*: "-ate" meaning "to act in such a manner"
- *Definition*: to act to drive by letter (i.e., to use the law to compel someone's behavior)
- *Analogy*: in court, a judge presides over people who litigate, so the noun on the right oversees

the verb on the left; thus, a verb like "compete" is an appropriate way to fill in the blank

Worksheet 90

- *Required Correction*: the phrase "corresponds with" should be replaced with "corresponds to"
- *Explanation of Error*: to correspond *with* someone is to communicate over distance (e.g., via letters or e-mails), while to correspond *to* something is to be in agreement or conjunction with it
- *Type of Error*: diction
- *Prefix*: "cryp-" meaning "hidden"
- *Root*: "graph" meaning "to write"
- *Suffix*: "-y" meaning "characterized by" or "inclined to"
- *Definition*: characterized by hidden writing (i.e., the practice of writing indecipherably or symbolically, as in code)
- *Analogy*: multiplication is generally introduced to students in elementary school, while cryptography is almost certainly taught at higher educational levels, such as high school, college, and graduate school, any of which would finely fill in the blank

Worksheet 91

- *Required Correction*: the word "incredible" should be replaced with "incredulous"
- *Explanation of Error*: something that is not believable is incredible, while a person who does not believe something, such as the stunned snowboarder of this sentence, is described as incredulous
- *Type of Error*: diction
- *Prefix*: "de-" meaning "away" or "down"
- *Root*: "ject" meaning "to throw"
- *Suffix*: "-ed" meaning "resembling," as an adjective

- *Definition*: resembling someone thrown down (i.e., depressed)
- *Analogy*: someone dejected is probably quiescent as a result, so the adjective on the left "causes" the adjective on the right; thus, an adjective like "inspired" fills in this blank well

Worksheet 92

- *Required Correction*: the colon must be removed from this sentence
- *Explanation of Error*: colons must follow independent clauses, and the colon in this sentence does not
- *Type of Error*: punctuation
- *Prefix*: this word has no prefix
- *Root*: "lumin" meaning "light"
- *Suffix*: "-ous" meaning "full of" or "having"
- *Definition*: full of or having light (e.g., a lightbulb)
- *Analogy*: stars are luminous, so the adjective on the left describes the noun on the right; an adjective such as "vast" or "powerful" thus appropriately fills in the blank

Worksheet 93

- *Required Correction*: "respectfully" should be replaced with "respectively"
- *Explanation of Error*: the adverb "respectfully" means "with respect," a usage that makes no sense in this sentence, though "respectively" means "in that particular order," thereby lining up the ambiguous painting and the reductive song
- *Type of Error*: diction
- *Prefix*: "re-" meaning "again" or "back"
- *Root*: "duct" meaning "to lead"
- *Suffix*: "-ive" meaning "performing" or "tending to"
- *Definition*: tending to lead back (i.e., excessively simple)

- *Analogy*: an encyclopedia is thorough, so the adjective on the right describes the noun on the left; thus, something overly simplistic, like the rough draft of an essay, should fill in the blank

Worksheet 94

- *Required Correction*: the comma and the word "although" should be removed from the sentence
- *Explanation of Error*: concluding the sentence in this way makes it a dependent clause, requiring further elaboration or expansion after "although"; dependent clauses by definition can not stand alone as sentences
- *Type of Error*: grammar
- *Prefix*: "in-" meaning "within" or "inside of"
- *Root*: "doc" meaning "teach" *or* "doc," variant of "dox" meaning "opinion"
- *Suffix*: "-ine" meaning "the nature or quality of" *and* "-ate" meaning "to act in such a manner"
- *Definition*: to act to teach one the nature of what is within (i.e., to educate someone in a particular train of thought or knowledge)
- *Analogy*: the purpose or action of a pedagogue is to indoctrinate students, so the noun on the left enacts the verb on the right; therefore, a student or an apprentice is an appropriate person to fill in the blank

Worksheet 95

- *Required Correction*: the word "or" should be replaced with "nor"
- *Explanation of Error*: "neither" and "nor" collectively constitute a correlative conjunction, with both parts equally required
- *Type of Error*: correlative conjunction *or* seesaw conjunction
- *Prefix*: "de-" meaning "away" or "down"
- *Root*: "grad" meaning "to step"

- *Suffix*: "-ate" meaning "to act in such a manner" *and* "-ion" meaning "the act or condition of"
- *Definition*: the condition of stepping down (i.e., the lowering of one's position or stature)
- *Analogy*: degradation causes a person to become doleful, so the noun on the right is a precursor to the adjective on the left; in this way, a word such as "fortunate" or "elated" fills in the blank well

Worksheet 96

- *Required Correction*: the semicolon should be replaced with a comma
- *Explanation of Error*: semicolons conjoin two independent clauses, but the second clause in this sentence is dependent; it is more sensible to consider "to say the least" as an elaborative phrase (i.e., extra information), which should be surrounded by commas
- *Type of Error*: punctuation
- *Prefix*: "eu-" meaning "good" or "well"
- *Root*: "gen" meaning "creation" or "race or kind"
- *Suffix*: "-ic" meaning "relating to" or "characterized by"
- *Definition*: characterized by good racial creation (i.e., the science of improving genetic characteristics by way of particularized breeding)
- *Analogy*: the science or practice of eugenics depends upon hereditary properties and principles, so the noun on the left "requires" the adjective on the right; thus, a noun such as "invention" or "innovator" fills in the blank acceptably

Worksheet 97

- *Required Correction*: the word "irregardless" should be replaced either with "regardless" or with "irrespective"
- *Explanation of Error*: the word "irregardless" is not actually an English word, but a double-negative conflation of "irrespective" and "regardless"

- *Type of Error*: diction
- *Prefix*: this word has no prefix
- *Root*: "fid" meaning "faith" or "trust"
- *Suffix*: "-ity" meaning "a state or quality of"
- *Definition*: a quality of faith (i.e., faithfulness and loyalty)
- *Analogy*: a conjugal relationship usually relies upon or assumes fidelity, so the two adjectives are related positively; therefore, an adjective such as "self-serving" or "misleading" appropriately fills in the blank

Worksheet 98

- *Required Correction*: the past tense verb "was" should be replaced with "is"
- *Explanation of Error*: literary works, and events described therein, should be referred to always in the present tense, because they are constantly "alive" for all readers
- *Type of Error*: literary present tense
- *Prefix*: "e-" meaning "thoroughly or completely"
- *Root*: "luc," variant of "lum" meaning "light"
- *Suffix*: "-id" meaning "resembling" or "similar to" *and* "-ate" meaning "to act in such a manner"
- *Definition*: to make something similar to being completely lit (i.e., to clarify understanding and eliminate confusion)
- *Analogy*: something ambiguous can be elucidated for clarification, so the verb on the left is a remedy for the adjective on the right; as such, a verb such as "elaborate" or "build upon" fills in the blank well

Worksheet 99

- *Required Correction*: the word "uninterested" should be replaced with "disinterested"
- *Explanation of Error*: someone uninterested does not care about and is bored by a topic—the judge who is fleeing for his or her life is obviously not bored, in this case—while a

disinterested person is impartial, holding no bias or interest in an outcome
- *Type of Error*: diction
- *Prefix*: "pan-" meaning "everywhere"
- *Root*: "demon," an evil and malicious variant of "dem" meaning "people"
- *Suffix*: "-ium" meaning "a compound of"
- *Definition*: a compound of demons everywhere (e.g., a violent riot)
- *Analogy*: by definition, pandemonium implies a physical, geographical spread (i.e., distance), so the noun on the right is the defining quality of the noun on the left; in this way, a noun like "millennium" or "anachronism" would appropriately fill in the blank

Worksheet 100

- *Required Correction*: either the word "each" should be replaced with "all" or the verb "demonstrate" needs to be replaced with the singular "demonstrates"
- *Explanation of Error*: "each" is a singular pronoun, identifying or separating the students singly, while "all" is a plural pronoun, lumping the students together into a collective; the verb in each case must agree with its subject
- *Type of Error*: subject/verb agreement
- *Prefix*: "im- " meaning "not"
- *Root*: "pas," variant of "path" meaning "feeling" or "suffering"
- *Suffix*: "-ive" meaning "performing" or "tending to" *and* "-ity" meaning "a state or quality of"
- *Definition*: the quality of tending not to feel (i.e., the quality of being unemotional and unexpressive)
- *Analogy*: impassivity is the condition of being outwardly emotionless (i.e., emotionally recessive), so the adjective on the left is related to the verb on the right; in this way, an adjective like "hot-tempered" or "excited" should fill in the blank

Worksheet 101

- *Required Correction*: the word "effected" should be replaced with "affected"
- *Explanation of Error*: the Battle of the Alamo took place in the midst of and altered the Texas Revolution, but the usage of "effected" in this sentence would imply that the Battle of the Alamo kick-started the Texas Revolution, which would be historically inaccurate; the phrase "adding acrimonious fire to an already hot political issue" suggests this inaccuracy
- *Type of Error*: diction
- *Prefix*: "acri-" meaning "bitter"
- *Root*: "mon" meaning "to warn" or "to remind"
- *Suffix*: "-ious," a variant of "-ous" meaning "full of" or "having"
- *Definition*: having the characteristic of warning someone bitterly (i.e., biting and bitter in language and/or manner)
- *Analogy*: an apoplexy cannot be described as quiescent, so the noun on the left and the noun on the right are, if not antonyms, inversely related; as such, a word such as "helpful" or "friendly" should fill in the blank

Worksheet 102

- *Required Correction*: the phrase "are appropriate responses" should be replaced with "is an appropriate response"
- *Explanation of Error*: the correlative conjunction of "neither" and "nor" implies singularity, separating condolence and quiescence into dual singular subjects rather than conjoining them into a plurality, as "and" would do; thus, the subjects require a singular verb
- *Type of Error*: subject/verb agreement
- *Prefix*: "con-" meaning "with" or "together"
- *Root*: "dole" meaning "sadness" or "suffering"
- *Suffix*: "-ence" meaning "the state or quality of"

- *Definition*: the quality of sadness with others (i.e., an expression of empathy or sympathy)
- *Analogy*: part of the purpose of a eulogy is to offer condolence at a funeral, so the noun on the right is the goal, or at least a component, of the noun on the left; thus, something describable as a goal of litigation, like recompense or damages, should fill in the blank

Worksheet 103

- *Required Correction*: the word "farther" must be replaced with "further"
- *Explanation of Error*: "farther" is used to compare incrementally quantifiable measurements (e.g., physical distance, time, and temperature) while "further" is used essentially as a synonym for "more" or "to a greater extent"; in the case of this sentence, the potential for Vietnamese rebellion is not numerically quantifiable
- *Type of Error*: diction
- *Prefix*: "in-" meaning "within" or "inside of"
- *Root*: "grat" meaning "favor" or "pleasing"
- *Suffix*: "-ate" meaning "to act in such a manner"
- *Definition*: to act to please others inside and thus gain favor (i.e., to make someone or something agreeable to others)
- *Analogy*: magniloquence is a useful tool for someone attempting ingratiation, so the noun on the left aids the verb on the right; thus, a word such as "meanness" or "cynicism" fills in the blank well

Worksheet 104

- *Required Correction*: the phrase "to the audience in the theater" should be moved, most appropriately to the space between the words "presented" and "his"
- *Explanation of Error*: the prepositional phrase "to the audience in the theater" modifies its antecedent, which in this case is mistakenly the noun "extinction," implying that the blue

whale needs to be saved from extinction in the minds of the particular audience in the theater; in reality, what really occurs "to the audience" is the scientist's presentation, which should be the phrase's antecedent

- *Type of Error*: misplaced modifier
- *Prefix*: this word has no prefix
- *Root*: "tenu" meaning "to stretch" or "to thin"
- *Suffix*: "-ous" meaning "full of" or "having"; "-ness" meaning "the state of"
- *Definition*: full of thinness (i.e., fragile and weak rather than strong)
- *Analogy*: something tenuous can be visualized or described as thin, so the noun on the left can be described by the adjective on the right; therefore, a noun such as "solidness" would fill in the blank

Worksheet 105

- *Required Correction*: the word "which" should be replaced with the word "that"
- *Explanation of Error*: the pronoun "which" implies that its accompanying modifying phrase applies to the entire group of its antecedents, making this sentence mean that all computer-generated effects appear in blockbuster movies, which is untrue; the pronoun "that," however, implies that only a subgroup or small part of its antecedent, "computer-generated special effects," appear in blockbuster films, which is accurate
- *Type of Error*: diction
- *Prefix*: "ver-" meaning "truth"
- *Root*: "simil" meaning "resembling"
- *Suffix*: "-tude" meaning "the condition or quality of"
- *Definition*: the condition of resembling truth (i.e., the appearance of reality)
- *Analogy*: the adjectives "complete" and "reductive" are antonyms, so an antonym of "verisimilitude," such as the word "truthfulness" or "integrity," should fill in the blank

Worksheet 106

- *Required Correction*: the preposition "of" should be replaced with "have"
- *Explanation of Error*: "should have," "could have," "might have," and "would have" are conditional (i.e., hypothetical) propositions—appropriate in the case of this sentence—whereas "of" is a preposition, which simply does not work here
- *Type of Error*: diction
- *Prefix*: "se-" meaning "apart"
- *Root*: "cess" meaning "to go" or "to yield"
- *Suffix*: "-ion" meaning "the act or condition of"
- *Definition*: the act of going apart (i.e., the removal of one's self from a larger group)
- *Analogy*: secession requires movement, be it political, geographical, or otherwise, so the verb on the left describes or at least relates to the noun on the right; an appropriate counterpoint with which to fill in the blank, therefore, might be a verb such as "stay"

Worksheet 107

- *Required Correction*: the word "then" should be inserted after the comma
- *Explanation of Error*: "if" and "then" constitute a correlative (a.k.a. seesaw) conjunction, so both words are necessary to complete this if-then statement
- *Type of Error*: correlative conjunction *or* seesaw conjunction
- *Prefix*: "ne-" meaning "not"
- *Root*: "sci" meaning "to know"
- *Suffix*: "-ent" meaning "performing" or "being in a particular state"
- *Definition*: not being knowledgeable (i.e., ignorant)
- *Analogy*: a newborn is close to, if not fully, nescient, so the adjective on the right describes the noun on the left; as such, a noun such as "deity" should fill in the blank

Worksheet 108

- *Required Correction*: the word "practical" should be replaced with "practicable"
- *Explanation of Error*: the word "practical" describes or defines a good idea, so the phrase "was both a good idea and totally practical" is redundant; on the other hand, "practicable" means "able to be practiced or accomplished" (i.e., physically possible), so that substitution makes the sentence sensible
- *Type of Error*: diction *or* redundancy
- *Prefix*: "pre-" meaning "before"
- *Root*: "ambul" meaning "walk"
- *Suffix*: this word has no suffix
- *Definition*: a walk beforehand (i.e., an introductory consideration of a topic, as in a speech or document)
- *Analogy*: by definition, the preamble to anything occurs early, so the adjective on the right describes the noun on the left; a word such as "epilogue" or "conclusion" should fill in the blank

Worksheet 109

- *Required Correction*: the verb "were" should be replaced with "was"
- *Explanation of Error*: the singular subject "insurance company" is here described by the plural verb "were," which is incorrect; instead, the singular verb "was" correlates with the singular subject
- *Type of Error*: subject-verb agreement
- *Prefix*: "ex-" meaning "out of" or "from"
- *Root*: "culp" meaning "blame" or "guilt"
- *Suffix*: "-ate" meaning "to act in such a manner"
- *Definition*: to free one from blame or guilt (e.g., to acquit)
- *Analogy*: to exculpate someone is to free him or her from culpability, so the verb on the right countermines or undoes the noun on the left; thus, the noun "ignorance" fills in the blank perfectly

Worksheet 110

- *Required Correction*: commas should be inserted after the words "professor" and "manner"
- *Explanation of Error*: the phrase "demonstrating an indignant manner" is an appositive, further describing the eminent professor; it falls under the larger syntactical umbrella of "extra information" (i.e., phrases and words that can be extracted from sentences without changing the basic meaning), and such extra information should always be surrounded by commas
- *Type of Error*: punctuation
- *Prefix*: "in- " meaning "not"
- *Root*: "dign" meaning "worth" or "value"
- *Suffix*: "-ant" meaning "performing" or "being in a particular state"
- *Definition*: being in a state lacking worth (i.e., not dignified, but ostensibly resentful or angry)
- *Analogy*: acrimonious people can often be described as indignant, and vice-versa, so the two adjectives, while not full synonyms, are closely related; thus, an adjective like "downtrodden" or "disappointed" should fill in the blank

Worksheet 111

- *Required Correction*: either the colon should be removed from the sentence or the comma and the word "including" should be removed
- *Explanation of Error*: colons must follow independent clauses; the inclusion of "including" makes the central clause dependent
- *Type of Error*: punctuation
- *Prefix*: "flam-" meaning "to burn"
- *Root*: "amb" meaning "around"
- *Suffix*: "-ance" meaning "the state or quality of"
- *Definition*: the state of burning around one's self (i.e., ornate, showy, and colorfully unrestrained)
- *Analogy*: impassivity and flamboyance are

opposites, so an antonym of "color," such as "plainness," should fill in the blank

Worksheet 112

- *Required Correction*: the possessive pronoun "his" should be replaced with "the General's," with "his own," or with "the former's"
- *Explanation of Error*: the possessive pronoun "his" could refer either to the Major General or to the Lieutenant Colonel, so it is unclear whose ceremony was missed here; it should thus be clarified
- *Type of Error*: unclear referent
- *Prefix*: "ig-," variant of "in" meaning "not"
- *Root*: "nomin" meaning "name"
- *Suffix*: "-y" meaning "characterized by" or "inclined to"
- *Definition*: characterized by not being named (i.e., dishonorable disgrace and humiliation)
- *Analogy*: defamation causes ignominy, so the noun on the left precedes or leads to the noun on the right; in this way, a noun such as "bravery" or "worth" should fill in the blank

Worksheet 113

- *Required Correction*: the contraction "it's" should be replaced with the possessive pronoun "its"
- *Explanation of Error*: the possessive pronoun "its," referring to the antecedent "any algebraic equation," is here appropriate, while the contraction for "it is" makes no sense in this sentence
- *Type of Error*: although students might initially assume this to be a punctuation error, the words "it's" and "its" are two separate words, so this error is better labeled one concerning diction
- *Prefix*: "per-" meaning "completely"
- *Root*: "plex" meaning "to tangle or bend"

- *Suffix*: "-ity" meaning "a state or quality of"
- *Definition*: the state of being completely tangled (i.e., utter confusion)
- *Analogy*: elucidation clears up or aids perplexity, so the verb on the left counteracts or remedies the noun on the right; therefore, the verbs "invent" and "circumnavigate" fill in the blank well

Worksheet 114

- *Required Correction*: the possessive pronoun "their" should be replaced with the singular and gender-neutral phrase "his or her"
- *Explanation of Error*: the subject "a . . . real estate agent" is singular, yet "their" is a plural possessive pronoun; the singular subject must correlate with a singular possessive pronoun, and because the real estate agent in question might be either male or female, the phrase "his or her" is most appropriate
- *Type of Error*: pronoun agreement
- *Prefix*: "circu-" meaning "around or on all sides"
- *Root*: "spec" meaning "to look" or "to see"
- *Suffix*: this word has no suffix
- *Definition*: seeing or looking on all sides (i.e., careful to consider all elements and consequences of a situation)
- *Analogy*: someone who can be described as circumspect is, or at least has attempted to be, fully cognizant of a situation, so the adjective on the left is related to the adjective on the right; therefore, an adjective such as "nescient" or "ignorant" fills in the blank finely here

Worksheet 115

- *Required Correction*: the noun "persons" should be replaced with "people"
- *Explanation of Error*: while "persons" is used to describe a group of individually identifiable humans (i.e., a group in which people can be

picked out one by one), "people" describes members of a homogeneous group; in this sentence, because all of the humans in question share the common characteristics of eating at French restaurants and ordering similarly to one another, they can be described with the generalized "people"
- *Type of Error*: diction
- *Prefix*: "pre-" meaning "before" *and* "di," variant of "dict" meaning "to tell" or "to use words"
- *Root*: "lect" meaning "to select" or "to choose"
- *Suffix*: "-ion" meaning "the act or condition of"
- *Definition*: the condition of verbalizing a choice beforehand (i.e., an established tendency or preference for something)
- *Analogy*: prognoses and predilections share the common trait of earliness (i.e., being determined by or dependent upon something occurring beforehand), so the two nouns share a common relationship to time or in time; a preamble shares that same sense of earliness, so a fourth such word, possibly "prologue," should fill in the blank

Worksheet 116

- *Required Correction*: an apostrophe should be inserted prior to the number 65
- *Explanation of Error*: apostrophes serve the same purpose in contracted dates as they do in contracted phrases, as substitutes for whatever is contracted *out*; in the case of 1865, the apostrophe stands in for the "18"
- *Type of Error*: punctuation
- *Prefix*: "re-" meaning "again" or "back"
- *Root*: "mon" meaning "to warn" or "to remind"
- *Suffix*: "-ance" meaning "the state or quality of"
- *Definition*: the state of warning someone again (i.e., a firm statement of opposition or grievance)
- *Analogy*: fidelity and secession are opposites,

if not outright antonyms, so a word such as "agreement" or "praise" should fill in the blank

Worksheet 117

- *Required Correction*: the word "less" should be replaced with "fewer"
- *Explanation of Error*: "less" modifies singular nouns, while "fewer" modifies plural nouns, such as the stage directions mentioned in this sentence
- *Type of Error*: diction
- *Prefix*: "ob-" meaning "against"
- *Root*: "fus" meaning "to pour"
- *Suffix*: "-ate" meaning "to act in such a manner"
- *Definition*: acting to pour against (i.e., to confuse, mystify, or obscure something)
- *Analogy*: obfuscation requires the muddying of facts, understandings, and principles, so the two verbs are synonyms, although the one on the left is more physical, *per sé*, than the one on the right; as such, the verbs "clear up" and "illuminate" fill in the blank well

Worksheet 118

- *Required Correction*: the phrase "not quite awake" must be hyphenated
- *Explanation of Error*: compound adjectives—multiple words acting in concert to modify single nouns—must be hyphenated; in this case, the compound adjective "not-quite-awake" modifies "brother" independently of "little," which is a separate adjective
- *Type of Error*: compound adjective
- *Prefix*: "syn-" meaning "together" or "with"
- *Root*: "chron" meaning "time"
- *Suffix*: "-ize" meaning "to become" or "to treat as"
- *Definition*: to come together in time (i.e., to arrange events or schedules to coincide)
- *Analogy*: things that are synchronized run or

operate concurrently, so the adverb on the right describes things affected by the verb on the left; in this way, a verb such as "stagger" should fill in the blank

Worksheet 119

- *Required Correction*: the words "Introspection" and "hypnosis" should each be placed within quotation marks
- *Explanation of Error*: quotation marks are used to indicate, among other things, words that act as themselves—as words or collections of letters—rather than as the actual objects or principles that they signify; because this sentence concerns the words "introspection" and "hypnosis," rather than the phenomena themselves, both words should be encapsulated by quotation marks
- *Type of Error*: punctuation
- *Prefix*: "intro-," variant of "intra" meaning "within"
- *Root*: "spec" meaning "to look" or "to see"
- *Suffix*: "-ion" meaning "the act or condition of"
- *Definition*: the act of looking within (i.e., a reflective examination of one's own thoughts and feelings)
- *Analogy*: circumspection is an examination *around* something, while introspection is an investigation *within* one's self, so while both words concern investigation, their prepositional focuses differ; thus, a word such as "other" or "area" fills in the blank finely

Worksheet 120

- *Required Correction*: the word "that" should be inserted between "knew" and "Yauncey Hill"
- *Explanation of Error*: what the speaker of this sentence knew was not Yauncey Hill Preparatory School itself, but the *fact* that the school had a particular reputation, so the word

"that" should be inserted for clarification; as a rule of thumb, rather than a hard-and-fast rule, two combinations of nouns and verbs in close proximity to one another should be separated by the word "that" in order to avoid this confusion

- *Type of Error*: grammar
- *Prefix*: this word has no prefix
- *Root*: "matrix" meaning "list"
- *Suffix*: "-ul" meaning "tending or inclined to" *and* "-ate" meaning "to act in such a manner"
- *Definition*: to act as inclined to a list (i.e., to sign up or enroll, as in a college or university)
- *Analogy*: to ignite something and to matriculate somewhere both have to do with beginnings, in a general sense, so the two words are related in terms of temporal process; indoctrination is not so immediate a beginning as the other two words are, but connotatively a more gradual process, so an alteration or expansion that takes time, such as "weight gain," would fill in the blank

Worksheet 121

- *Required Correction*: a plural noun referring to rocks, such as "minerals" or "stones," should be inserted after the word "those"
- *Explanation of Error*: the words "this," "that," "those," and "these" are demonstrative (a.k.a. pointing) pronouns and thus, for clarity, they need to be followed by nouns, lest they *point at* nothing in particular
- *Type of Error*: unattributed pointing pronoun
- *Prefix*: "im- " meaning "not"
- *Root*: "mut" meaning "change"
- *Suffix*: "-able" meaning "able to be"
- *Definition*: not able to be changed (i.e., permanent and fixed)
- *Analogy*: something immutable is not transmutative, so the two adjectives are antonyms; mutative, so the two adjectives are antonyms;

therefore, a noun such as "boisterousness" or "excitement" should fill in the blank

Worksheet 122

- *Required Correction*: a comma must be inserted after the word "argument"
- *Explanation of Error*: the phrase "Trying hard to make a successfully discursive argument" is an introductory phrase explaining how the debater used evidence
- *Type of Error*: punctuation
- *Prefix*: "dis-" meaning "not," "away," or "apart"
- *Root*: "cur" meaning "a course that is run"
- *Suffix*: "-ive" meaning "performing" or "tending to"
- *Definition*: tending away from a set course (i.e., moving from topic to topic as if wandering)
- *Analogy*: while the Equator is straight, most coastlines meander or are at least irregular, so the two words are opposites in terms of their directness or straightness; as such, an adjective like "direct" should fill in the blank

Worksheet 123

- *Required Correction*: the word "respectfully" should be replaced with "respectively"
- *Explanation of Error*: "respectfully" is an adverb modifying verbs accomplished with respect, while "respectively" lines things up in a particular order, as in this sentence
- *Type of Error*: diction
- *Prefix*: "ab-" meaning "apart" or "away from"
- *Root*: "ject" meaning "to throw"
- *Suffix*: this word has no suffix
- *Definition*: thrown away (i.e., in a low state of hopelessness or spiritless resignation)
- *Analogy*: both "inject" and "abject" etymologically come from "to throw," but their prepositional prefixes differ, the former being "inside" and the latter "outside," so they are

opposites in this way; therefore, as the morpheme "nomin" means "name," a noun such as "anonymity" or "synonym" should fill in the blank

Worksheet 124

- *Required Correction*: the word "irregardless" should be replaced either with "irrespective" or with "regardless"
- *Explanation of Error*: "irregardless," though commonly used, is actually not a real English word, but rather an invented double negative
- *Type of Error*: diction
- *Prefix*: "neo-" meaning "new"
- *Root*: "log" meaning "word" or "speech"
- *Suffix*: "-ism" meaning "the condition or action of being"
- *Definition*: the condition of a new word (i.e., a recently coined word or expression)
- *Analogy*: both "anomaly" and "neologism" are etymologically related to words meaning "name," so the two words are similar in terms of their central meanings; thus, a word related to speech, such as "contradict," should fill in the blank

Worksheet 125

- *Required Correction*: the phrase "A demographic study was conducted by" should be removed and instead rewritten at the end of the sentence as, "wealthy, anonymous philanthropist, conducted a demographic study."
- *Explanation of Error*: this sentence is written in the passive voice, which is far weaker than the active voice
- *Type of Error*: passive voice
- *Prefix*: "dem-" meaning "people"
- *Root*: "graph" meaning "to write"
- *Suffix*: "-ic" meaning "relating to" or "characterized by"
- *Definition*: relating to writing about people (i.e.,

concerning the human population of a given area or body)
- *Analogy*: while cryptography concerns signs, symbols, and code, demography concerns people and their societal groups, so the focus or purpose of the two adjectives differs in this way; thus, "code" or "symbols" should fill in the blank

Worksheet 126

- *Required Correction*: an additional "s" should be inserted after "class'" so that the phrase reads "the class's nescient comprehension"
- *Explanation of Error*: singular nouns ending in "s" are made possessive by the addition of both an apostrophe and an additional "s," while plural nouns ending in "s" require only an apostrophe to become possessive
- *Type of Error*: possession
- *Prefix*: "ex-" meaning "out of" or "from"
- *Root*: "ferv" meaning "to boil, bubble, or burn"
- *Suffix*: "-esce" meaning "to do" or "to act" *and* "-ence" meaning "the state or quality of"
- *Definition*: the quality of bubbling or boiling out of something (i.e., liveliness or exhilaration, as in a carbonated beverage)
- *Analogy*: flamboyance and effervescence both demonstrate much outward movement, action, or color, so they are, if not outright synonyms, meaningfully related; thus, a word such as "independence" or "aloneness" should fill in the blank

Worksheet 127

- *Required Correction*: the word "then" should be replaced with "than"
- *Explanation of Error*: the temporal-causal word "then" is out of place in this sentence, but the comparative "than" is appropriate
- *Type of Error*: diction
- *Prefix*: "con-" meaning "with" or "together"

- *Root*: "flag," variant of "flam" meaning "to burn"
- *Suffix*: "-ate" meaning "characterized by" or "resembling" *and* "-ion" meaning "the act or condition of"
- *Definition*: a condition resembling things burning together (i.e., a large and disastrous fire)
- *Analogy*: both pandemonium and conflagrations are widespread and etymologically "everywhere," so the two words share that common scope; in contrast, a fire is presumably small, so a correlate such as "argument" or "fistfight" would appropriately fill in the blank

Worksheet 128

- *Required Correction*: the plural verb "are" should be replaced with the singular "is"
- *Explanation of Error*: although "definitions" *is* a plural noun, "neither" establishes antecedent singularity, effectively doing the opposite of the conjunction "and," which combines disparate things into a plurality; thus, the inclusion of "neither," like "either," necessitates a singular verb
- *Type of Error*: subject-verb agreement
- *Prefix*: "homo-" meaning "the same as"
- *Root*: "nym" meaning "name"
- *Suffix*: this word has no suffix
- *Definition*: a name that is the same as another (i.e., one of several words that are spelled and pronounced alike, but have distinct meanings)
- *Analogy*: verisimilitude is by definition an imitation of verity, so the noun on the right mimics, but does not equal, the noun on the left; because homonyms sound alike, yet are different, the word "synonym" is perhaps the perfect way to fill in the blank

Worksheet 129

- *Required Correction*: the word "which" should be replaced with "that"

- *Explanation of Error*: the pronoun "which" implies that what follows applies to all members of the antecedent group, so it would here mean that all European countries attempted to subjugate foreign nations; "that" implies only a subgroup of the preceding noun, which in this case is correct
- *Type of Error*: diction
- *Prefix*: "sub-" meaning "below"
- *Root*: "junct" meaning "to meet" or "to join"
- *Suffix*: "-ate" meaning "to act in such a manner"
- *Definition*: to act to join things below (i.e., to conquer and make others submissive)
- *Analogy*: to advocate for someone, something, or a group is effectively the opposite of subjugating it/them, so the two verbs are antonyms; thus, the adjective "above" is the logical choice to fill in the blank

Worksheet 130

- *Required Correction*: the pronoun "I" should be replaced with "me"
- *Explanation of Error*: "I" is used as a subject, while "me" functions as a direct object; the simple trick to teach students is that if the other people are removed from the sentence (e.g., if "my classmates and" is deleted), then reading the sentence without them makes clear which pronoun, "I" or "me," is correct
- *Type of Error*: pronoun agreement
- *Prefix*: this word has no prefix
- *Root*: "am" meaning "love"
- *Suffix*: "-ic" meaning "having characteristics of" *and* "-able" meaning "able to be"
- *Definition*: characteristically able to be loved (i.e., friendly and peaceable)
- *Analogy*: pugnacious people are generally not amicable, so the two adjectives, while not literal antonyms, describe opposite characteristics; in this way, an adjective such as "happy"

or "welcoming" is an appropriate way to fill in the blank

Worksheet 131

- *Required Correction*: the opening conjunction "For" should be removed, and "perniciousness" should thus be capitalized as the sentence's first word
- *Explanation of Error*: beginning sentences with conjunctions technically makes them dependent clauses, which cannot stand alone as sentences
- *Type of Error*: grammar
- *Prefix*: "per-" meaning "completely"
- *Root*: "nic" meaning "harm" or "death"
- *Suffix*: "-ous" meaning "full of" or "having" *and* "-ness" meaning "the state of"
- *Definition*: the state of having been conceived completely of harm or death (i.e., deadly and destructive)
- *Analogy*: to exonerate another person can be described as an act of benevolence, so the noun on the right is thus related to the verb on the left; therefore, a verb such as "accuse" or "curse" would be an adequate way in which to fill in the blank here

Worksheet 132

- *Required Correction*: the word "incredulous" should be replaced with "incredible"
- *Explanation of Error*: the adjective "incredible" describes things that are hard or impossible to believe (e.g., Ptolemy's efforts), while "incredulous" is used to describe people who do not believe things; in this sentence, the latter word is simply incorrect
- *Type of Error*: diction
- *Prefix*: this word has no prefix
- *Root*: "err" meaning "to wander"
- *Suffix*: "-ous" meaning "full of" or "having"

- *Definition*: having wandered or full of wandering (i.e., containing an error or mistake)
- *Analogy*: people whose knowledge bases can be described by the noun "nescience" are probably erroneous in most respects, so the adjective on the right is the effect of the quality on the left; in this way, the correlate noun "omniscience," or at least "experience," is a fine way to fill in the blank

Worksheet 133

- *Required Correction*: the concluding phrase should be rewritten, "of which there are many"
- *Explanation of Error*: sentences should not end with prepositions, of which "of" is an example
- *Type of Error*: syntax
- *Prefix*: "super-" meaning "above"
- *Root*: "flu" meaning "to flow"
- *Suffix*: "-ity" meaning "a state or quality of"
- Definition: a quality of flowing above (i.e., an excessive supply or unnecessary abundance)
- *Analogy*: superfluity by nature can be described as profuse, so the adjective on the right modifies the noun on the left; as such, "shortfall" or "scarcity" can fill in the blank well

Worksheet 134

- *Required Correction*: the word "quick" should be replaced with "quickly"
- *Explanation of Error*: adverbs, rather than adjectives, modify verbs (e.g., "think")
- *Type of Error*: grammar
- *Prefix*: "syn-" meaning "together" or "with"
- *Root*: "nym" meaning "name"
- *Suffix*: this word has no suffix
- *Definition*: a name that is with another (i.e., one of several words that have extremely similar or identical meanings)
- *Analogy*: synonyms are, by definition, words, so the noun on the right is a subset or example of the noun on the left; a subcategory of

synchronization, such as "setting a clock," should in this way fill in the blank

Worksheet 135

- *Required Correction*: either the comma following "tenuous" should be replaced with a semicolon or an appropriate conjunction, such as "for," should be added after that comma
- *Explanation of Error*: "indubitable proof does not exist" is an independent clause, which cannot be combined with another independent clause with a comma alone
- *Type of Error*: punctuation
- *Prefix*: "anti-" meaning "against"
- *Root*: "path" meaning "feeling" or "suffering"
- *Suffix*: "-y" meaning "characterized by" or "inclined to"
- *Definition*: characterized by feeling against another (i.e., dislike or otherwise oppositional feeling)
- *Analogy*: antipathy generally can be defined as acrimonious, so the adjective on the left describes the noun on the right; effervescence can, of course, be described by the adjective "bubbly," which finely fills in the blank here

Worksheet 136

- *Required Correction*: the word "imply" should be replaced with "infer"
- *Explanation of Error*: to imply is to hint or suggest indirectly, which is what the scattered sunflower seeds do, while to infer is to *get* the hint or to assume, which is what this sentence's speaker does
- *Type of Error*: diction
- *Prefix*: "dif-" meaning "away from" or "apart," or otherwise indicating a reversal
- *Root*: "fus" meaning "to pour"
- *Suffix*: "-ness" meaning "the state of"

- *Definition*: the state of being poured apart (i.e., a scattered, rather than consolidated, condition)
- *Analogy*: diffuseness in general is spread out, and circumspection requires a spreading out of one's attention, so the two nouns share the quality of roundness or space; therefore, a noun sharing introspection's inherent central quality, such as "individual" or "loneliness," should fill in the blank

Worksheet 137

- *Required Correction*: either the phrase "All members" should be replaced with "Each member" or the verb "is" should be replaced with "are"
- *Explanation of Error*: "all" is a plural pronoun, grouping the members of the electorate together into a plurality that therefore requires a plural verb, while "each" is a singular pronoun requiring a singular verb
- *Type of Error*: subject-verb agreement
- *Prefix*: "e-" meaning "thoroughly or completely"
- *Root*: "lect" meaning "to select" or "to choose"
- *Suffix*: "-or" meaning "one who performs" or "one who functions as" *and* "-ate" meaning "an institution or formal office"
- *Definition*: the institution of those who choose completely (i.e., a group of people entitled to vote)
- *Analogy*: an electorate of any type is aggregated, so the verb on the right affects or causes the noun on the left; thus, a noun such as "flower seeds" fills in the blank well

Worksheet 138

- *Required Correction*: either the semicolon should be replaced with a comma or the conjunction "and" that follows the semicolon should be removed
- *Explanation of Error*: semicolons join

independent clauses together, and any clause beginning with a conjunction is a dependent clause

- *Type of Error*: punctuation
- *Prefix*: "ante-" meaning "before"
- *Root*: "ced" meaning "to go" or "to yield"
- *Suffix*: "-ent" meaning "performing" or "being in a particular state"
- *Definition*: being that which goes before (i.e., a preceding event, word, cause, or condition)
- *Analogy*: preambles appear in various documents, so the noun on the left is the domain of the noun on the right; as such, the noun "sentence" logically fills in the blank here

Worksheet 139

- *Required Correction*: the word "also" should be inserted after "but"
- *Explanation of Error*: "not only" and "but also" constitute a correlative conjunction, and both of its parts are required
- *Type of Error*: correlative conjunction *or* seesaw conjunction
- *Prefix*: "trans-" meaning "across"
- *Root*: "gress" meaning "to step"
- *Suffix*: this word has no suffix
- *Definition*: to step across (i.e., to violate or cross a limit, law, or boundary)
- *Analogy*: to transgress the law or the directions of a superior is pernicious, so the noun on the left and the verb on the right are inherently related; thus, a noun such as "movement" or "arrival" would adequately fill in the blank here

Worksheet 140

- *Required Correction*: the word "between" should be replaced with "among"
- *Explanation of Error*: "between" is used for two options or elements, while "among" describes three or more options or elements

- *Type of Error*: diction
- *Prefix*: "hetero-" meaning "different"
- *Root*: "gen" meaning "creation" or "race or kind"
- *Suffix*: "-ous" meaning "full of" or "having"
- *Definition*: full of different kinds (i.e., composed of a diversity)
- *Analogy*: the adjectives "heterogeneous" and "homogeneous" are antonyms; ironically, it is the word "antonym" itself that should fill in the blank

Worksheet 141

- *Required Correction*: the word "imminent" should be replaced with "eminent"
- *Explanation of Error*: imminent events or things are soon to arrive or pending, while eminent individuals, like Cleopatra, are famous and well-respected
- *Type of Error*: diction
- *Prefix*: "matr-" meaning "woman" or "mother"
- *Root*: "-arch" meaning "chief or ruler"
- *Suffix*: "-al" meaning "relating to" or "having the character of"
- *Definition*: related to the character of a female ruler (e.g., the reign of Queen Elizabeth I)
- *Analogy*: a mother is, or at least has the potential to be, matriarchal, so the adjective on the right describes the noun on the left; therefore, a person who can be described as misanthropic, such as a grumpy sourpuss, should fill in the blank

Worksheet 142

- *Required Correction*: the phrase "the taste of" should be replaced with "tasting"
- *Explanation of Error*: all elements or items in a list must be formatted uniformly, so "investigating" and "discovering" must be followed by "tasting" to preserve this uniformity

- *Type of Error*: parallel structure *or* parallel construction
- *Prefix*: "gastr-" meaning "stomach"
- *Root*: "nom" meaning "name"
- *Suffix*: "-ic" meaning "relating to" or "characterized by"
- *Definition*: characterized by names related to one's stomach (i.e., concerning cuisine and cooking)
- *Analogy*: things describable as demographic concern people and culture, while things describable as gastronomic concern food; as "food" fills in the respective right side of the other pair of words, "people" should fill in the blank

Worksheet 143

- *Required Correction*: "further" should be replaced with "farther"
- *Explanation of Error*: the word "farther" is used in conditions that are measurable in numerical increments, while "further" simply means "more" or "to a greater extent" and is used to describe elements or actions that are numerically immeasurable
- *Type of Error*: diction
- *Prefix*: "de-" meaning "away" or "down"
- *Root*: "gen" meaning "creation" or "race or kind"
- *Suffix*: "-ate" meaning "to act in such a manner"
- *Definition*: to act away from one's creation (i.e., to deteriorate or otherwise decline in quality)
- *Analogy*: to improve and to degenerate are essential opposites, so the two verbs are antonyms; thus, "expansion" or "growth" appropriately fill in the blank

Worksheet 144

- *Required Correction*: a comma must be inserted prior to the word "though"
- *Explanation of Error*: commas are used when

contradictory or negative tones arise in sentences in order to signal negation or contradiction
- *Type of Error*: punctuation
- *Prefix*: "ante-" meaning "before"
- *Root*: "bellum" meaning "war"
- *Suffix*: this word has no suffix
- *Definition*: as before war (e.g., the early 19th century American South)
- *Analogy*: in American history, as referred to in this worksheet's sentence, Southern secession effectively ended the antebellum period, so the noun on the right concludes the adjective on the left; thus, either an adjective like "dark" or a noun like "nighttime" should fill in the blank

Worksheet 145

- *Required Correction*: the pronoun "whom" should be replaced with "who"
- *Explanation of Error*: "who" is used in the subject position, while "whom" is used in place of a direct object; a simple trick to teach students is that "he," "she," and "they" correlate with "who," while "him," "her," and "them" correspond to "whom," so because the clause in question would read, "they were no longer able to trust him," it is clear that "who" is correctly substituted
- *Type of Error*: pronoun agreement
- *Prefix*: "ex-" meaning "to intensify"
- *Root*: "tenu" meaning "to stretch" or "to thin"
- *Suffix*: "-ate" meaning "to act in such a manner" *and* "-ion" meaning "the act or condition of"
- *Definition*: the condition of intensifying something's thinness (i.e., to lessen the seriousness and strength of a condition or action)
- *Analogy*: this analogy is perhaps a difficult one to decipher. One possible interpretation considers extenuation, as of criminal circumstances, to be an aftereffect of transgression, so an effect of good grades, such as college admissions,

appropriately completes the analogy; a second interpretation considers transgression as the complete crossing of a line, while extenuation as the thinning of a line, in which case something like "earning 'C' grades" should fill in the blank.

Worksheet 146

- *Required Correction*: the word "then" must be inserted after the comma and before the word "why"
- *Explanation of Error*: "if" and "then" constitute a correlative (a.k.a. seesaw) conjunction, requiring both parts in order to function correctly
- *Type of Error*: correlative conjunction *or* seesaw conjunction
- *Prefix*: "pre-" meaning "before"
- *Root*: "mon" meaning "to warn" or "to remind"
- *Suffix*: "-tion" meaning "the act or condition of"
- *Definition*: the condition of warning beforehand (i.e., anticipation or early knowledge of an event)
- *Analogy*: both premonitions and antecedents share the common characteristic of earliness, so the two nouns are related in terms of their defining quality; thus, a word that shares the excessive characteristic of superfluity, such as "overkill" or "extremism," should fill in the blank

Worksheet 147

- *Required Correction*: the word "because" should be replaced with "that"
- *Explanation of Error*: the phrase "the reason why" and the conjunction "because" serve the same grammatical purpose, so to include both in one sentence is technically redundant
- *Type of Error*: redundancy
- *Prefix*: "re-" meaning "again" or "back"
- *Root*: "pug" meaning "to fight"
- *Suffix*: "-ant" meaning "performing" or "being in a particular state"

- *Definition*: being in a state of fighting back (i.e., causing distaste, disgust, or aversion)
- *Analogy*: to find something repugnant is to shy away from it in some way, while an antipathy is effectively an opposition of some sort, so the adjective on the left and the noun on the right share the common quality of avoidance or contradiction; in this way, an adjective basically similar to amicability, such as "helpful" or "friendly," should fill in the blank

Worksheet 148

- *Required Correction*: the phrase "to simply capitulate" should be rewritten "to capitulate simply," or the adverb "simply" should be moved to the position between "incredulity" and "made"
- *Explanation of Error*: "to capitulate" is an infinitive verb, which, being a single verb that happens to consist of two separate words, should never be split by an adverb such as "simply"
- *Type of Error*: split infinitive
- *Prefix*: "in-" meaning "not"
- *Root*: "cred" meaning "to believe" or "to trust"
- *Suffix*: "-ul" meaning "tending or inclined to" *and* "-ity" meaning "a state or quality of"
- *Definition*: the state of tending not to believe or trust (i.e., skepticism or disbelief)
- *Analogy*: incredulity is often the response to statements that are erroneous, so the adjective on the left incites the noun on the right; therefore, an adjective like "clumsy" or "silly" fills in the blank well as a precursor to indignity

Worksheet 149

- *Required Correction*: the phrase "under the microscope" must be moved so that it follows either the verb "multiply" or the word "observed"
- *Explanation of Error*: the prepositional phrase

"under the microscope" modifies its antecedent, in this case making it seem as if the scientist himself or herself was under the microscope; either the nonmultiplying amoebae or the observation of those amoebae should thusly be the correct antecedent

- *Type of Error*: misplaced modifier
- *Prefix*: "con-" meaning "with" or "together"
- *Root*: "cord," variant of "cors" meaning "heart"
- *Suffix*: "-ance" meaning "the state or quality of"
- *Definition*: the state of being together in heart (i.e., agreement)
- *Analogy*: things that are either concordant or synchronized are perfectly aligned (i.e., in agreement), so they share this inherent quality; in this way, a word sharing the central characteristic of diffusion, such as "spread" or "scattering," fills in the blank finely

Worksheet 150

- *Required Correction*: the preposition "with" should be replaced with "to"
- *Explanation of Error*: to correspond *with* someone is to communicate over distance (e.g., via e-mail or posted letters), while corresponding *to* someone or something is a demonstration of agreement; in this sentence, the latter usage is correct
- *Type of Error*: diction
- *Prefix*: "pre-" meaning "before"
- *Root*: "rog" meaning "to ask"
- *Suffix*: "-ate" meaning "characterized by" or "resembling" *and* "-ive" meaning "performing" or "tending to"
- *Definition*: resembling an asking beforehand (i.e., a privilege or power accompanying one's position in a particular office or condition)
- *Analogy*: a matriarch has many prerogatives, being in a position of authority and power, so the noun on the right is held or experienced by

the noun on the left; in this way, a noun such as "servant" or "feudal peasant" should fill in the blank

Worksheet 151

- *Required Correction*: the verb "demonstrated" should be changed from its past tense form to the present "demonstrates"
- *Explanation of Error*: events occurring in works of literature, being essentially frozen in time, should always be referred to in the present tense
- *Type of Error*: literary present tense
- *Prefix*: "pro-" meaning "before"
- *Root*: "cli" meaning "to lean toward"
- *Suffix*: "-ity" meaning "a state or quality of"
- *Definition*: the quality of leaning toward something beforehand (i.e., an inherent tendency or strong inclination toward a particular course)
- *Analogy*: "proclivity" and "predilection" are, if not outright synonyms, very closely related; as such, the word "bright" would finely fill in the blank alongside "luminous"

Worksheet 152

- *Required Correction*: a verb such as "do," "display," or "demonstrate" must be inserted following the word "rocks"
- *Explanation of Error*: this sentence, as written, weighs the number of sentient characteristics displayed by robots against rocks themselves, whereas it should weigh two different numbers of sentient characteristics, the number displayed by robots and the number displayed by rocks
- *Type of Error*: faulty comparison
- *Prefix*: this word has no prefix
- *Root*: "sent" meaning "to feel or be aware"
- *Suffix*: "-ent" meaning "performing" or "being in a particular state"

- *Definition*: being aware and able to feel (i.e., responsive to sensory and emotional impressions)
- *Analogy*: a mountain is not sentient, so the adjective on the right does not describe the noun on the left; thus, a noun such as "theory" or "daydream" should fill in the blank

Worksheet 153

- *Required Correction*: the phrase "Even though" should be removed from the sentence, and the word "anarchic" should be capitalized as the sentence's opening word
- *Explanation of Error*: the transitional phrase "even though" is out of place opening this sentence, as it never joins to or transitions from anything at all, thereby making the sentence a dependent clause
- *Type of Error*: grammar
- *Prefix*: "a-" meaning "without" or "not"
- *Root*: "-arch" meaning "chief or ruler"
- *Suffix*: "-ic" meaning "relating to" or "characterized by"
- *Definition*: characterized by having no ruler (i.e., chaotically lawless)
- *Analogy*: pandemonium is naturally anarchic, so the adjective on the right describes the noun on the left; therefore, a word describable as gastronomic, such as "cuisine," should fill in the blank

Worksheet 154

- *Required Correction*: the word "uninterested" should be replaced with "disinterested"
- *Explanation of Error*: "uninterested" describes people who are not interested in or bored by topics—obviously not the case of this vociferous referee—while "disinterested" describes people who are unbiased, or who do not hold an interest in the outcome of a contest or debate, such as a judge or referee

- *Type of Error*: diction
- *Prefix*: "voc-" meaning "to call"
- *Root*: "fer" meaning "to bring or carry"
- *Suffix*: "-ous" meaning "full of" or "having"
- *Definition*: having brought a call (i.e., marked by a strongly insistent outcry)
- *Analogy*: while "mellifluous" and "vociferous" are not complete antonyms, they are probably exclusive of one another in most cases; thus, an adjective such as "happy" or "effervescent" fills in the blank well

Worksheet 155

- *Required Correction*: the word "practicable" should be replaced with "practical"
- *Explanation of Error*: things that are practicable are technically possible (i.e., able to be practiced), which is how the secondary clause in this sentence describes the practice in question, while practical things are purposeful; obviously, the latter usage is suitable here in order to avoid redundancy
- *Type of Error*: diction
- *Prefix*: this word has no prefix
- *Root*: "grat" meaning "favor" or "pleasing," and related to "freely"
- *Suffix*: "-ity" meaning "a state or quality of"
- *Definition*: having a quality of pleasing or showing favor (i.e., something given to others voluntarily and beyond obligation in order to demonstrate approval)
- *Analogy*: an apoplexy is anything but docile, so the adjective on the left does not describe the noun on the right; therefore, an adjective such as "necessary" adequately fills in the blank

Worksheet 156

- *Required Correction*: the word "or" should be replaced with "nor"
- *Explanation of Error*: the negatives "neither"

and "nor" constitute a correlative (a.k.a., see-saw) conjunction, as do the positives "either" and "or"; the pairs should not be mixed

- *Type of Error*: correlative conjunction *or* seesaw conjunction
- *Prefix*: "circu-" meaning "around or on all sides"
- *Root*: "vent" meaning "to come" or "to move forward"
- *Suffix*: this word has no suffix
- *Definition*: to move around something (i.e., to bypass an obstacle)
- *Analogy*: in order to pass by an obstruction, one can circumvent it, so the verb on the right counteracts or overcomes the noun on the left; in this way, a word describing something that can be overcome by extenuation, such as "evidence" or "culpability," should fill in the blank

Worksheet 157

- *Required Correction*: within the quotation, the word "his" should be placed within square brackets
- *Explanation of Error*: the mayor would not describe himself using the third person point of view, so although it can be assumed that his quote initially read, "might delay *my* political agenda," the author of this sentence has altered the possessive pronoun for the sake of flow, which should be indicated through the usage of square brackets
- *Type of Error*: punctuation
- *Prefix*: "circu-" meaning "around or on all sides"
- *Root*: "loc" meaning "word" or "speak"
- *Suffix*: "-tion" meaning "the act or condition of"
- *Definition*: the act of speaking around something (i.e., evasive speech), usually through the use of unnecessarily large or confusing words or techniques
- *Analogy*: circumlocution is the opposite of directness in speech, so the two nouns are

antonyms; thus, a noun such as "shortage" fills in the blank appropriately

Worksheet 158

- *Required Correction*: both the word "also" and the phrase "as well" should be removed from the sentence
- *Explanation of Error*: "also" and "as well" accomplish the same purpose as "In addition to," so to include them is redundant
- *Type of Error*: redundancy
- *Prefix*: "sym-," variant of "syn-" meaning "together" or "with"
- *Root*: "path" meaning "feeling" or "suffering"
- *Suffix*: "-ic" meaning "relating to" or "characterized by"
- *Definition*: characterized by feeling with others (i.e., approving of, in agreement with, or demonstrating compassion for something or someone)
- *Analogy*: someone expressing condolence is sympathetic, so the adjective on the right describes the noun, or at least someone conveying the noun, on the left; thus, a noun such as "skepticism" should fill in the blank

Worksheet 159

- *Required Correction*: the article "The" should be lowercased
- *Explanation of Error*: articles introducing proper nouns, unless a part of the title of a published work, should not be capitalized
- *Type of Error*: capitalization
- *Prefix*: "in-" meaning "not"
- *Root*: "dole" meaning "sadness" or "suffering"
- *Suffix*: "-ence" meaning "the state or quality of"
- *Definition*: the quality of having no pain or suffering (i.e., painlessness, often from habitual inactivity or laziness)
- *Analogy*: indolence and effervescence are, if not outright antonyms, quite contrasting; thus,

a noun such as "prevention" fills in the blank finely

Worksheet 160

- *Required Correction*: the preposition "to" prior to "abstruse" should be replaced with "too"
- *Explanation of Error*: "to" is used either as part of an infinitive verb or as a preposition, while "too" is used either as a synonym for "also" or to indicate extremism; the latter usage is appropriate in this phrase
- *Type of Error*: diction
- *Prefix*: "ab-" meaning "apart" or "away from"
- *Root*: "stru" meaning "to build"
- *Suffix*: this word has no suffix
- *Definition*: built apart from (i.e., difficult to understand or comprehend)
- *Analogy*: to obfuscate is to make something abstruse, so the verb on the right causes or leads to the adjective on the left; in this way, an adjective such as "clear" should fill in the blank

Worksheet 161

- *Required Correction*: the word "affect" should be replaced with "effect"
- *Explanation of Error*: as a noun, "affect" means "feeling and temperament," while "effect" describes the outcome or impact of some action or event; clearly, the latter word is appropriate in this sentence
- *Type of Error*: diction

- *Prefix*: "mal-" meaning "bad" or "wrong"
- *Root*: "dict" meaning "to tell" or "to use words"
- *Suffix*: "-ion" meaning "the act or condition of"
- *Definition*: the condition of telling something bad (i.e., a curse or slanderous statement)
- *Analogy*: malediction is a way to disparage someone or something, so the noun on the right enacts the verb on the left; thus, a verb such as "praise" or "reward" should fill in the blank

Worksheet 162

- *Required Correction*: the first occurrence of word "of," following "might," should be replaced with "have"
- *Explanation of Error*: while the preposition "of" makes no sense in this case, the conditional or hypothetical "have" accompanies "might" to describe a situation with potentiality
- *Type of Error*: diction
- *Prefix*: "en-" meaning "to cause it to be"
- *Root*: "am" meaning "love"
- *Suffix*: "-ed" meaning "resembling," as an adjective
- *Definition*: caused to be in love (i.e., captivated or inspired by love)
- *Analogy*: only sentient creatures have the potential to be enamored of beings or things, so the adjective on the right is a precondition of the adjective on the left; as such, an adjective such as "slothful" appropriately fills in the blank

Chapter 5

Practice Quizzes

These quizzes should be taken or administered to students following 18 days of sequential worksheet completion. For example, the first multiple choice quiz assesses students' understanding and retention of the information learned from Worksheets 1–18, while the second quiz assesses their mastery of Worksheets 19–36. An answer key follows at the end of this chapter.

Practice Quiz
for Worksheets 1–18

Read carefully the directions preceding each section, then choose the best answer to each question.

Section 1: Fill in the Blank

Each sentence below contains one or two blanks. Following all sentences are five individual words or pairs of words. Select the best word or pair of words to complete the sentence according to its meaning.

1. When I was in the first grade, my teacher assumed my _____ when cookies went missing from the cookie jar.

   (a) belligerence
   (b) autonomy
   (c) culpability
   (d) parity
   (e) profusion

2. The _____ politician refused reporters who wished to cover his large donation to the struggling orphanage; this refusal only _____ the tension that already existed between City Hall and the press.

   (a) inherent . . . abducted
   (b) amorphous . . . dignified
   (c) indubitable . . . eulogized
   (d) magnanimous . . . exacerbated
   (e) convivial . . . incarnated

3. _____ in the United States, even _____ fresh out of college, must be licensed by their respective states' Departments of Education in order to maintain employment.

   (a) pedagogues . . . novices
   (b) autonomies . . . parity
   (c) dignities . . . docile
   (d) abductions . . . indubitably
   (e) incarnations . . . profusions

4. A _____ amount of saturated fat is never good for one's overall health, but it is especially bad for cholesterol levels.

   (a) novice
   (b) culpable
   (c) convivial
   (d) profuse
   (e) docile

Section 2: Revision

Each sentence below contains an underlined portion. Following all sentences are five ways of writing that underlined portion. Select the choice that, if substituted for the underlined portion, results in the clearest, most grammatically effective sentence.

5. I was <u>able to quickly infer from the smoke</u> on the horizon that a fire had somehow started in the valley.

   (a) as written
   (b) able to quickly imply from the smoke
   (c) able to imply from the smoke quickly
   (d) quickly able to infer from the smoke
   (e) able quickly to imply from the smoke

6. April is usually a beautiful month, <u>irregardless of its total</u> amount of rainfall.

   (a) as written
   (b) irregardless of it's total
   (c) irrespective of its total
   (d) regardless of it's total
   (e) irregardless of it's total

7. <u>Next week I have to write an essay for Mrs. James's class.</u>

   (a) as written
   (b) Next week, I have to write an essay for Mrs. James' class.
   (c) Next week I have to write an essay for Mrs. James' class.
   (d) Next week, I have to write an essay for Mrs. James's class.
   (e) Next week I have to write an essay, for Mrs. James's class.

8. I am unaware of any <u>person who enjoys spicy food more than my brother</u> Hank does.

   (a) as written
   (b) person whom enjoys spicy food more then my brother
   (c) person whom enjoys spicy food more than my brother
   (d) person enjoying spicy food more then my brother
   (e) person who enjoys spicy food my brother

Section 3: Error Recognition

Each sentence below either is correct or contains one error. No sentence contains multiple errors. The error in each sentence, if it exists, is underlined. Select the underlined portion of each sentence that must be corrected, but select choice (e) if the sentence is correctly written.

9. The student read *A Tale of Two Cities* so quick
   (a)

   that she did not remember all of the events that
   (b)

   its pages contain.
   (c)   (d)

   (e) there is no error

10. Tomorrow, neither my math teacher nor my
    (a)   (b)

    history teacher are going to assign homework.
    (c)   (d)

    (e) there is no error

11. My hamster sheds more fur than my cat, my
    (a)

    guinea pig, and even more than my dog do,
    (b)   (c)

    which dirties the carpet.
    (d)

    (e) there is no error

12. Texas' size is extremely large, as one can infer
    (a)   (b)   (c)

    from a map, yet people who enjoy driving long
    (d)

    distances perhaps enjoy traveling there.

    (e) there is no error

13. Trying to drive while talking on a cellular phone
    (a)

    is neither safe nor wise, but its a common practice
    (b)   (c)

    among in-a-rush commuters.
    (d)

    (e) there is no error

Section 4: Reading Comprehension

The following paragraphs are excerpted from a letter that Karl Marx sent to Abraham Lincoln in 1865. Read the passage and select the best answer to each question.

We congratulate the American people upon your re-election by a large majority. If resistance to the Slave Power was the reserved watchword of your first election, the triumphant war cry of your re-election is Death to Slavery.

From the commencement of the titanic American strife the workingmen of Europe felt instinctively that the star-spangled banner carried the destiny of their class.

... the working classes of Europe understood at once, even before the fanatic partisanship of the upper classes for the Confederate gentry had given its dismal warning, that the slaveholders' rebellion was to sound the tocsin for a general holy crusade of property against labor, and that for the men of labor, with their hopes for the future, even their past conquests were at stake in that tremendous conflict on the other side of the Atlantic. Everywhere they bore therefore patiently the hardships imposed upon them by the cotton crisis, opposed enthusiastically the proslavery intervention of their betters—and, from most parts of Europe, contributed their quota of blood to the good cause...

The workingmen of Europe feel sure that, as the American War of Independence initiated a new era of ascendancy for the middle class, so the American Antislavery War will do for the working classes. They consider it an earnest of the epoch to come that it fell to the lot of Abraham Lincoln, the single-minded son of the working class, to lead his country through the matchless struggle for the rescue of an enchained race and the reconstruction of a social world.

Signed on behalf of the International Workingmen's Association, the Central Council

14. The tone of this letter can best be described as

    (a) docile   (d) dignified
    (b) pedagoguish   (e) eulogistic
    (c) belligerent

15. It can be inferred from this letter that the International Workingmen's Association supported Abraham Lincoln's dedication to human

    (a) abduction   (d) conviviality
    (b) culpability   (e) profusion
    (c) parity

16. This letter's statement that for European men of labor, "even their past conquests were at stake" in the American Civil War indicates that the International Workingmen's Association recognized its own apparent lack of

    (a) exacerbation   (d) inherence
    (b) magnanimity   (e) amorphousness
    (c) autonomy

Practice Quiz
for Worksheets 19–36

Read carefully the directions preceding each section, then choose the best answer to each question.

Section 1: Fill in the Blank

Each sentence below contains one or two blanks. Following all sentences are five individual words or pairs of words. Select the best word or pair of words to complete the sentence according to its meaning.

1. The _____ physician offered to the patient a _____ of the illness's probable duration.

   (a) aggregate . . . diffidence
   (b) credible . . . sequestration
   (c) benevolent . . . prognosis
   (d) omniscient . . . remission
   (e) doleful . . . diffidence

2. Geoffrey Chaucer's *The Canterbury Tales* is a _____ work, since only select portions of it have ever been found intact.

   (a) capital
   (b) fragmentary
   (c) benevolent
   (d) misanthropic
   (e) pugnacious

3. Income tax is always calculated based on a person's _____ income.

   (a) expedited
   (b) ambulatory
   (c) diffident
   (d) disparaged
   (e) aggregate

4. The _____ frustration felt by the _____ refugees is clearly visible in the award-winning photograph.

   (a) remitted . . . pugnacious
   (b) diffident . . . capital
   (c) doleful . . . omniscient
   (d) ineffable . . . ambulatory
   (e) sequestrated . . . coalescent

Section 2: Revision

Each sentence below contains an underlined portion. Following all sentences are five ways of writing that underlined portion. Select the choice that, if substituted for the underlined portion, results in the clearest, most grammatically effective sentence.

5. The reason why our city has become unsafe in recent years <u>is that fewer young men and women</u> have joined the police force.

   (a) as written
   (b) is because fewer young men and women
   (c) is because less young men and women
   (d) is that less young men and women
   (e) is that less young people

6. Not only has your classmate's grade <u>fallen farther in class, but he is</u> in danger of failing the course completely.

   (a) as written
   (b) fallen farther in class, but he also is
   (c) fallen further in class, but he is also
   (d) fallen further in class, but he is
   (e) fallen farther in class, he is

7. I <u>only correspond with two people:</u> my girlfriend and my aunt Hilda.

   (a) as written
   (b) only correspond with two persons:
   (c) only correspond with two persons,
   (d) only correspond to two people:
   (e) only correspond to two persons,

8. The film critics seemed to love the new movie, but <u>my friends and I could not stand that</u>.

   (a) as written
   (b) me and my friends could not stand that
   (c) my friends and I could not stand that film
   (d) me and my friends could not stand that
   (e) me and my friends could not stand it

Section 3: Error Recognition

Each sentence below either is correct or contains one error. No sentence contains multiple errors. The error in each sentence, if it exists, is underlined. Select the underlined portion of each sentence that must be corrected, but select choice (e) if the sentence is correctly written.

9. Mohandas Gandhi was actually an attorney

   before he was an <u>imminent international figure,</u>
                                    (a)

   but he <u>is obviously</u> most famous for trying <u>to help</u>
          (b)   (c)

   India gain <u>its independence.</u>
              (d)

   (e) <u>there is no error</u>

10. If you do not leave the cookies <u>in the oven for</u>
                                     (a)

    a sufficient amount of time<u>, not only</u> will <u>they</u> not
                           (b)   (c)

    cook <u>well, but</u> they also might be dangerous to eat.
         (d)

    (e) <u>there is no error</u>

11. I craved cheddar <u>cheese; but</u> the only types
                    (a)

    available at the store <u>were</u> mozzarella and pepper
                     (b)

    <u>jack, the</u> latter of which is <u>too spicy</u>.
     (c)   (d)

    (e) <u>there is no error</u>

12. <u>It may have</u> been <u>illegal, but</u> Martha decided
      (a)   (b)

    <u>to park</u> her car near the abandoned <u>house in the</u>
     (c)   (d)

    <u>middle of the street</u>.

    (e) <u>there is no error</u>

13. Many <u>cities are</u> <u>farther away</u> from Boston <u>than</u>
        (a)   (b)   (c)

    New York is, <u>including:</u> Tokyo, London, and
             (d)

    Sacramento.

    (e) <u>there is no error</u>

Section 4: Reading Comprehension

The following paragraphs are excerpted from a floral encyclopedia. Read the passage and select the best answer to each question.

The narcissus is among the most popular of flowers. Wordsworth wrote poems about it, untold numbers of its variants have been planted in gardens from Maine to Florida, and generations of Americans have loved its early bloom and sweet scent.

Debate exists about the origin and correctness of the name "narcissus." While linguists and gardeners alike still contend that the flower took its name from the Narcissus of Greek mythology, it is probable that the flower's narcotic quality initially inspired its name. Moreover, in 1629, Charles I's royal botanist, John Parkinson, set down in print that "Narcissus is the Latin name [of this flower], and Daffodil the English of one and the same things." Nevertheless, much confusion remains as to what one should properly call this popular plant. Regina Mathilde, in *Flora for a Summer Ever*, solved the dilemma succinctly: "Just call it perfect."

There are eleven taxonomical categories of narcissi, related by their common—and commonly beloved—qualities, yet separable for various botanical reasons. The true Southern jonquil is an especially beloved variety of narcissus, "old as honey and just as sweet," in the words of poet Isaac Friend. This particular floral strain is classified as an heirloom plant, passed down through familial generations and prized like a piece of jewelry. Since the jonquil, like all narcissi, naturally multiplies each year, the proliferation of this treasure will undoubtedly only be limited by gardeners themselves.

14. In the second paragraph, the author probably quotes John Parkinson because of his

    (a) diffidence   (d) benevolence
    (b) credibility   (e) omniscience
    (c) ineffability

15. The "eleven taxonomical varieties of narcissi" mentioned in the third paragraph can collectively be described as

    (a) ambulatory   (d) aggregated
    (b) misanthropic   (e) doleful
    (c) pugnacious

16. The excerpt's conclusion offers readers a

    (a) sequestration   (d) prognosis
    (b) remission   (e) capital
    (c) coalescence

Practice Quiz
for Worksheets 37–54

Read carefully the directions preceding each section, then choose the best answer to each question.

Section 1: Fill in the Blank

Each sentence below contains one or two blanks. Following all sentences are five individual words or pairs of words. Select the best word or pair of words to complete the sentence according to its meaning.

1. My _____ attendance had to do less with my being a _____ than with my desire to graduate from school.

    (a) derogatory . . . pandemic
    (b) fervid . . . viability
    (c) aberrant . . . fervid
    (d) perfunctory . . . bibliophile
    (e) intermittent . . . verity

2. An _____ camper might spend more time deciding where to pitch his or her tent than fishing or cooking.

    (a) apocryphal
    (b) ambivalent
    (c) exonerated
    (d) abdicated
    (e) apoplectic

3. We were delayed by a massive _____ on the highway, which, according to _____ reports on the radio, was caused by a locomotive accident.

    (a) pandemic . . . conjugal
    (b) bibliophile . . . loquacious
    (c) apoplexy . . . fervid
    (d) exoneration . . . viable
    (e) obstruction . . . apocryphal

4. Although I _____ for the purchase of a new television set, my parents ultimately refused my pleas.

    (a) advocated
    (b) abdicated
    (c) conjugated
    (d) derogated
    (e) obstructed

Section 2: Revision

Each sentence below contains an underlined portion. Following all sentences are five ways of writing that underlined portion. Select the choice that, if substituted for the underlined portion, results in the clearest, most grammatically effective sentence.

5. While I recognize the practicability of requiring students to write 20-page essays in August, I am not sure that it is such a good idea.

    (a) as written
    (b) I recognize the practicality of requiring
    (c) I recognize that the practicality of requiring
    (d) I recognize that the practicability of requiring
    (e) I recognize the practicability that of requiring

6. Our experience of watching the film would of been less incredulous if the plot were more realistic.

    (a) as written
    (b) would of been less incredible if
    (c) would have been less incredible if
    (d) would have been less incredulous if
    (e) would have been less incredible if that

7. Although World War II did not actually commence until the 1940s, its initial momentum can be traced to the late '10s, when The Treaty of Versailles followed the conclusion of World War I.

    (a) as written
    (b) the late '10's, when The Treaty of Versailles
    (c) the late '10s, when the Treaty of Versailles
    (d) the late '10's, when the Treaty of Versailles
    (e) the late 10's, when the Treaty of Versailles

8. I am bored by sailboat racing; I find, to quote Norman R. Chadholm, that "[I am] utterly uninterested in it, the most soporific of sports."

    (a) as written
    (b) that, "[I am] utterly uninterested in it,
    (c) that, "[I am] utterly [disinterested] in it,
    (d) that "[I am] utterly [disinterested] in it,
    (e) that I am utterly disinterested, "in it,

Section 3: Error Recognition

Each sentence below either is correct or contains one error. No sentence contains multiple errors. The error in each sentence, if it exists, is underlined. Select the underlined portion of each sentence that must be corrected, but select choice (e) if the sentence is correctly written.

9. My younger brother <u>believes that dragons</u> are
   (a)

   real, but he, like <u>his friends, remain</u> fairly
   (b)

   <u>uninterested</u> in the study <u>of dinosaurs</u>.
   (c)   (d)

   (e) <u>there is no error</u>

10. <u>Canvases were painted by the students</u>, and
    (a)

    soon the art hallway and main hallway were

    decorated with myriad landscapes and portraits,

    <u>respectively</u>, <u>among all</u> of <u>which</u> the art teacher
    (b)   (c)   (d)

    proudly glanced.

    (e) <u>there is no error</u>

11. The phrase <u>"sayonara homerun"</u> is popular <u>in</u>
    (a)   (b)

    Japan; it describes a homerun hit to end a

    baseball game, a beloved pastime in this country

    <u>which</u> the sport long ago <u>emigrated to</u>.
    (c)   (d)

    (e) <u>there is no error</u>

12. The <u>effect of the</u> Wright Brothers' <u>incredible</u>
    (a)   (b)

    invention <u>is still growing</u>, more than a century
    (c)

    past the first successful flight of an airplane in

    <u>the early 1900s</u>.
    (d)

    (e) <u>there is no error</u>

Section 4: Reading Comprehension

The following paragraph is excerpted from Lady Florence Dixie's 1881 travelogue Across Patagonia. *Read the passage and select the best answer to each question.*

I could not repress a pang of regret as we steamed slowly out of Rio Harbour. There may be scenes more impressively sublime; there are, without doubt, landscapes fashioned on a more gigantic scale; by the side of the Himalayas or the Alps, the mountains around Rio are insignificant enough, and one need not go out of England in search for charming and romantic scenery. But nowhere have the rugged and the tender, the wild and the soft, been blended into such exquisite union as at Rio, and it is this quality of unrivalled contrasts, that, to my mind, gives to that scenery its charm of unsurpassed loveliness. Nowhere else is there such audacity, such fierceness even of outline, coupled with such multiform splendour of colour, such fairy-like delicacy of detail. As a precious Jewel is encrusted by the coarse rock, the smiling bay lies encircled by frowning mountains of colossal proportions and the most capricious shapes. In the production of this work the most opposite powers of nature have been laid under contribution. The awful work of the volcano; the immense boulders of rock which lie piled up to the clouds in irregular masses, have been clothed in a brilliant web of tropical vegetation, spun from sunshine and mist. Here nature revels in manifold creation, life multiplies itself a million fold, the soil bursts with exuberance of fertility, and the profusion of vegetable and animal life beggars description. Every tree is clothed with a thousand luxuriant creepers, purple and scarlet-blossomed; they in their turn support myriads of lichens and other verdant parasites. The plants shoot up with marvellous rapidity, and glitter with flowers of the rarest hues and shapes, or bear quantities of luscious fruit, pleasant to the eye and sweet to the taste. The air resounds with the hum of insect life; through the bright green leaves of the banana skim the sparkling humming-birds, and gorgeous butterflies of enormous size float, glowing with every colour of the rainbow on the flower-scented breezes.

13. The tone of this description can best be labeled

    (a) perfunctory   (d) aberrant
    (b) fervid   (e) conjugal
    (c) derogatory

14. One can infer that the author's purpose in writing this selection is to describe Rio's beauty with

    (a) exoneration   (d) apoplexy
    (b) intermittence   (e) verity
    (c) abdication

15. The author of this passage can best be described as

    (a) apocryphal   (d) loquacious
    (b) obstructed   (e) ambivalent
    (c) pandemic

Practice Quiz
for Worksheets 55–72

Read carefully the directions preceding each section, then choose the best answer to each question.

Section 1: Fill in the Blank

Each sentence below contains one or two blanks. Following all sentences are five individual words or pairs of words. Select the best word or pair of words to complete the sentence according to its meaning.

1. The _____ final exam consisted of many parts, one of which required students to draw _____ from a primary source document.

   (a) dubious . . . equanimity
   (b) polymorphous . . . inferences
   (c) tentative . . . inclinations
   (d) discordant . . . homogeneousness
   (e) duplicitous . . . quiescence

2. As a young girl, I greatly enjoyed my grandfather's _____ speaking voice, the lilting, gentle cadences of which always transported me into a state of _____.

   (a) transmutative . . . capitulation
   (b) refractory . . . presentiment
   (c) mellifluous . . . quiescence
   (d) predictive . . . interlocution
   (e) philanthropic . . . duplicity

3. The fire chief demanded utter _____ from his volunteers, lest disorder and disagreement cause a tragedy at some point in the future.

   (a) capitulation
   (b) philanthropy
   (c) inference
   (d) equanimity
   (e) inclination

4. The analyst's _____ conclusions were _____, as she based them on data that were at least three years old.

   (a) refractory . . . mellifluous
   (b) quiescent . . . transmutative
   (c) duplicitous . . . presentiments
   (d) tentative . . . homogeneous
   (e) predictive . . . dubious

Section 2: Revision

Each sentence below contains an underlined portion. Following all sentences are five ways of writing that underlined portion. Select the choice that, if substituted for the underlined portion, results in the clearest, most grammatically effective sentence.

5. The eminent author, who produced one outstanding masterpiece, is speaking tomorrow at the regional library.

   (a) as written
   (b) imminent author, who produced one outstanding
   (c) imminent author, whom produced one outstanding
   (d) eminent author produced one outstanding
   (e) eminent author, whom produced one outstanding

6. In the '90s, less train crashes occurred in the United States than in Europe.

   (a) as written
   (b) In the 90s, less train crashes occurred
   (c) In the '90s, fewer train crashes occurred
   (d) In the 90's, fewer train crashes occurred
   (e) In the 90's, less train crashes occurred

7. The reason why I spend less time watching television these days is because I cannot find many decent shows among which to choose.

   (a) as written
   (b) that I cannot find many decent shows between
   (c) because I cannot find many decent shows between
   (d) that I cannot find many decent shows among
   (e) that I cannot find among many decent shows

8. The movie star disclosed in her interview what kinds of films she enjoys making, who the most professional directors in Hollywood are, and she aspires to achievements in her career.

   (a) as written
   (b) and achievements in her career that she aspires to
   (c) and in her career achievements that she aspires to
   (d) and achievements in her career to which she aspires
   (e) and which achievements in her career she aspires to

Section 3: Error Recognition

Each sentence below either is correct or contains one error. No sentence contains multiple errors. The error in each sentence, if it exists, is underlined. Select the underlined portion of each sentence that must be corrected, but select choice (e) if the sentence is correctly written.

9. Not only was Led Zeppelin an eminent rock and
   (a)

   roll band; but they also wrote some of the most
   (b)   (c)

   memorable song lyrics of the 1970s.
   (d)

   (e) there is no error

10. I once read China has a larger population within
   (a)

   its northern half than most countries in Europe
   (b)   (c)

   share among themselves.
   (d)

   (e) there is no error

11. Your recipe for fettuccine perhaps does not
   (a)

   include basil, but it is very important nonetheless.
   (b)   (c)   (d)

   (e) there is no error

12. Fewer teachers complained about students'
   (a)   (b)

   behavior at the football game than worried about
   (c)

   conduct in the halls, during the pep rally, and on
   (d)

   the last day of school.

   (e) there is no error

13. I watched several movies this weekend, yet I only
   (a)

   recall three actors who implied in those any kind
   (b)   (c)

   of professional skill; the films were not very
   (d)

   entertaining.

   (e) there is no error

Section 4: Reading Comprehension

The following paragraphs are excerpted from a novel called Under Two Flags, *published by Ouida in 1880. Read the passage and select the best answer to each question.*

With the reveille and the break of morning Cigarette woke, herself again; she gave a little petulant shake to her fairy form when she thought of what folly she had been guilty. "Ah, bah! you deserve to be shot," she said to herself afresh. "One would think you were a Silver Pheasant—you grow such a little fool!"

Love was all very well, so Cigarette's philosophy had always reckoned; a chocolate bonbon, a firework, a bagatelle, a draught of champagne, to flavor an idle moment. "Vin et Venus" she had always been accustomed to see worshiped together, as became their alliterative; it was a bit of fun—that was all. A passion that had pain in it had never touched the Little One; she had disdained it with the lightest, airiest contumely. "If your sweetmeat has a bitter almond in it, eat the sugar and throw the almond away, you goose! That is simple enough, isn't it? Bah? I don't pity the people who eat the bitter almond; not I!" she had said once, when arguing with an officer on the absurdity of a melancholy love that possessed him, and whose sadness she rallied most unmercifully. Now, for once in her young life, the Child of France found that it was remotely possible to meet with almonds so bitter that the taste will remain and taint all things, do what philosophy may to throw its acridity aside.

... she had not had more than an hour's slumber, it is true, with a dull ache at her heart that was very new and bitterly unwelcome to her, but with the buoyant vivacity and the proud carelessness of her nature in arms against it, and with that gayety of childhood inherent to her repelling, and very nearly successfully, the foreign depression that weighted on it.

Her first thought was to take care that he should never learn what she had done for him.

14. The relationship between Cigarette's attitude upon awaking and her past philosophy of love can be described as

    (a) tentative   (d) discordant
    (b) duplicitous   (e) dubious
    (c) homogeneous

15. One can infer from these paragraphs that Cigarette has performed for an unnamed man some act of

    (a) interlocution   (d) presentiment
    (b) equanimity   (e) inclination
    (c) philanthropy

16. The conclusion of this excerpt is implicitly

    (a) polymorphous   (d) predictive
    (b) quiescent   (e) capitulatory
    (c) mellifluous

Practice Quiz
for Worksheets 73–90

Read carefully the directions preceding each section, then choose the best answer to each question.

Section 1: Fill in the Blank

Each sentence below contains one or two blanks. Following all sentences are five individual words or pairs of words. Select the best word or pair of words to complete the sentence according to its meaning.

1. With great _____, the investor snatched up shares of the company's stocks just before they escalated in value.

   (a) contravention
   (b) providence
   (c) magniloquence
   (d) impediment
   (e) litigation

2. I studied _____ in college, which was an _____ intellectual pursuit at the time.

   (a) defamation . . . innocuous
   (b) benediction . . . anachronistic
   (c) heterodoxy . . . impedimentary
   (d) cryptography . . . anomalous
   (e) concurrently . . . egregious

3. Reading Shakespeare is quite valuable if one is _____ of the Bard's _____ creative and unorthodox diction.

   (a) cognizant . . . magniloquently
   (b) ambiguous . . . providentially
   (c) hereditary . . . innocuously
   (d) heterodox . . . concurrently
   (e) egregious . . . impedingly

4. While it may be impossible to _____ the spread of certain diseases throughout the Third World, many philanthropic and magnanimous individuals certainly try.

   (a) defame
   (b) contravene
   (c) impede
   (d) recede
   (e) litigate

Section 2: Revision

Each sentence below contains an underlined portion. Following all sentences are five ways of writing that underlined portion. Select the choice that, if substituted for the underlined portion, results in the clearest, most grammatically effective sentence.

5. Margaret and <u>I were to tired to watch</u> the second half of the double feature last night.

   (a) as written
   (b) I was too tired to watch
   (c) I were too tired to watch
   (d) me were to tired too watch
   (e) me were too tired to watch

6. In a 1918 speech, President Woodrow Wilson inspired the creation of <u>the League of Nations, precursor to the United</u> Nations.

   (a) as written
   (b) the League of Nations precursor to the United
   (c) The League of Nations, precursor to The United
   (d) The League of Nations precursor to The United
   (e) the league of Nations, precursor to the united

7. A teacher must be careful not to grade certain <u>of their students more harshly then</u> others.

   (a) as written
   (b) of their students more harshly than
   (c) of his or her students more harshly then
   (d) of his or her students harsher then
   (e) of his or her students more harshly than

8. At the elementary <u>school, juice was consumed by hot and tired students</u>.

   (a) as written
   (b) school juice was consumed by hot and tired students
   (c) school, hot and tired students consumed juice
   (d) school students hot and tired consumed juice
   (e) school, hot students consumed tiredly juice

Section 3: Error Recognition

Each sentence below either is correct or contains one error. No sentence contains multiple errors. The error in each sentence, if it exists, is underlined. Select the underlined portion of each sentence that must be corrected, but select choice (e) if the sentence is correctly written.

9. The philanthropist's <u>self-written</u> will bequeathed
   (a)

   <u>to at least</u> twenty <u>people</u> "an equal share <u>of his</u>
   (b)   (c)   (d)

   fortune."

   (e) <u>there is no error</u>

10. <u>Corresponding with</u> his grandfather over several
    (a)

    <u>years, the</u> boy matured as a writer until he was able
    (b)

    <u>to clearly express</u> even the most <u>heart-wrenching</u>
    (c)   (d)

    emotions with poignancy.

    (e) <u>there is no error</u>

11. <u>"Overseas travel"</u> is a phrase that excites more
    (a)

    young adults <u>than</u> most other collections of
                 (b)

    <u>words do,</u> for <u>it conjures</u> in the mind images of
    (c)   (d)

    romance, adventure, and beauty.

    (e) <u>there is no error</u>

Section 4: Reading Comprehension

The following paragraph is excerpted from an 1892 report of a committee on political reform, taken from the autobiography of Judge Elizur Brace Hinsdale, published in 1901. Read the passage and select the best answer to each question.

At the general election in 1891 the electors of this State elected a Republican Senate. Soon after the election, rumors began to emanate from the executive chamber at Albany that the Democrats would secure a majority of the Senate. So well founded was the belief that, in this State at least, the results of the ballot-box would be accepted as final, and not be questioned or defeated by any party, that no great uneasiness was felt by any honest citizen. The claim of Democratic success was looked upon as only the usual claim of the defeated party for political effect. It was not easy to believe that the chief executive of this great State, David B. Hill, had actually formed, and intended to carry out, a scheme of fraud of unparalleled audacity and wickedness. The sense of security in the foundation of our government

was rudely shaken as the great conspiracy gradually developed and the figure of the governor of the State came into view as the great conspirator in a fraud that ought to have consigned the governor and all those engaged in it to everlasting political infamy. Your committee deemed the matter of so grave import that this club should record its earnest protest against the fraud. Accordingly, your committee submitted, at the March meeting, a report of the leading facts of the case, which report was unanimously adopted, making a record here of the views of this body on the great conspiracy against the ballot-box. As a corollary of this fraud the Democrats in Albany introduced a bill, which they finally passed, destroying the non-partisan character of the Boards of Inspectors of Election in this city. At the April meeting your committee presented a statement of the dangerous character of this proposed legislation, with a resolution protesting against the passage of this bill. This report and resolution were unanimously adopted by the club. Thus the record of this club is complete against these two great crimes against the purity of the ballot-box. It is a fact to cause serious reflections, that the state of public sentiment as to the dangerous tendencies of such political crimes is so low that, instead of the just contempt of an indignant people jealous of their rights following the chief conspirators into that obscurity they so richly deserve, new honors are heaped upon them. The future student of the politics of these times will be puzzled to find out by what logic or under what strange influences the purists and reformers, with high-sounding professions of a desire for the highest ideals of government, could constantly ally themselves with a party with such a record.

12. This report proposed that the outcome of the 1891 election detailed here was far from

    (a) innocuous   (d) anachronistic
    (b) magniloquent   (e) cognizant
    (c) heterodox

13. The bills described by this report proposed and/or enacted political

    (a) heredity   (d) contravention
    (b) benediction   (e) ambiguity
    (c) providence

14. This report's descriptions of 1891 New York Democrats, particularly Governor David B. Hill, are construable as

    (a) concurrent   (d) cryptography
    (b) litigation   (e) anomaly
    (c) defamatory

15. Based on this report's tone, one can infer that the 1891 election detailed here was

    (a) egregious   (d) impeding
    (b) receding   (e) innocuous
    (c) cognizant

Practice Quiz
for Worksheets 91–108

Read carefully the directions preceding each section, then choose the best answer to each question.

Section 1: Fill in the Blank

Each sentence below contains one or two blanks. Following all sentences are five individual words or pairs of words. Select the best word or pair of words to complete the sentence according to its meaning.

1. The police officer and doctor delivered the news to the victim's family with at least the _____ of _____.

    (a) indoctrination . . . acrimony
    (b) nescience . . . impassivity
    (c) degradation . . . elucidation
    (d) luminosity . . . tenuousness
    (e) verisimilitude . . . condolence

2. According to several published scientific reports, any connection between cell phone use and brain cancer is, at the very most, _____.

    (a) pandemonium
    (b) preamble
    (c) tenuous
    (d) fidelity
    (e) dejected

3. A _____ understanding of calculus is not enough to secure for one's self employment as a structural engineer.

    (a) nescient
    (b) secessionist
    (c) luminous
    (d) degrading
    (e) condoling

4. Describing any kind of _____ as _____ is downright self-contradictory.

    (a) verisimilitude . . . acrimonious
    (b) fidelity . . . indoctrination
    (c) pandemonium . . . impassive
    (d) secession . . . eugenics
    (e) dejection . . . reductive

Section 2: Revision

Each sentence below contains an underlined portion. Following all sentences are five ways of writing that underlined portion. Select the choice that, if substituted for the underlined portion, results in the clearest, most grammatically effective sentence.

5. Describing the events portrayed in *The Grapes of Wrath* as lighthearted is neither <u>funny nor insightful; for that novel is</u> powerful, but sad.

    (a) as written
    (b) funny nor insightful; that novel is
    (c) funny or insightful; that novel was
    (d) funny or insightful; for that novel was
    (e) funny nor insightful for that novel is

6. If you undertake a <u>practicable exercise regimen, it should affect</u> your health positively.

    (a) as written
    (b) practicable exercise regimen, then it should effect
    (c) practical exercise regimen, then it should affect
    (d) practical exercise regimen, it should affect
    (e) practicable exercise regimen, it should affect

7. Each step that you take atop the Great Wall of China <u>heightens the incredulous experience of</u> encountering ancient history.

    (a) as written
    (b) heighten the incredible experience of
    (c) heightens the incredulous experience you have
    (d) heighten the incredible experience have
    (e) heightens the incredible experience of

8. Neither Maryland nor Virginia <u>has a larger population than California has, irrespective</u> of their proximity to our nation's capital.

    (a) as written
    (b) have larger populations than California has, irrespective
    (c) has a larger population than California has, irregardless
    (d) have a larger population than California, regardless
    (e) has larger populations than California has, regardless

Section 3: Error Recognition

Each sentence below either is correct or contains one error. No sentence contains multiple errors. The error in each sentence, if it exists, is underlined. Select the underlined portion of each sentence that must be corrected, but select choice (e) if the sentence is correctly written.

9. In America, many foods are associated with
   (a)   (b)

   the traditional Thanksgiving holiday: turkey,
   (c)   (d)

   potatoes, and cranberries.

   (e) there is no error

10. People's choices of clothing and cars usually
    (a)

    correspond to local temperature and the national

    economy, respectively: as each one falls farther,
    (b)   (c)   (d)

    people react in predictable ways.

    (e) there is no error

11. If you have seen neither *Turandot* nor *La Boheme*
    (a)

    because you are uninterested in opera, you are
    (b)   (c)

    surely unaware that neither story takes place in an
    (d)

    English-speaking country.

    (e) there is no error

12. The effect of the new law impacted citizens from
    (a)

    all parts of the city on the road; until it was
    (b)

    repealed, it prevented motorists' ability to pass
    (c)

    by cyclists, pedestrians, and skateboarders.
    (d)

    (e) there is no error

13. So the idea, incredible as it is, is practicable if all
    (a)   (b)   (c)

    students in this school join together.
    (d)

    (e) there is no error

Section 4: Reading Comprehension

The following is a letter written by a soldier in the Vietnam War, sent home to his family in the United States in 1969. Read the passage and select the best answer to each question.

Dear mother and father,

   I write this letter with all sincerity. I also write it with worry, as you are not going to like the topic. It concerns my future and that of the war itself, and you are not going to like the decision which I have reached.

   You know that I am now in my eleventh month of duty. In one more, I could return to Roseville a civilian. I have worried myself sick for what seems forever about what I can do when I get home. Soldiers return here from "the world" with stories of protests at the airports. Many of them could not find jobs, or have trouble sleeping at night.

   Not wanting to subject myself to [illegible], I have decided to reenlist for another tour here. I am not coming back to Minnesota this year.

   I am sorry to cause sadness, but I worry about myself. About my ability to come back home as if it were still last year and I were still in school. Reenlistment I hope will keep me together, at least keep me with my unit. We have grown to be brothers.

   Please try not to worry too much about me. For now at least we are remaining in the city, which is safer these days. I trust you to explain this circumstance to Tim. I love you. Please do not worry.
—Your son

14. The writer's description of the Vietnam War is best described as

    (a) elucidating   (d) reductive
    (b) nescient   (e) pandemonium
    (c) acrimonious

15. The letter's first paragraph can be described as its

    (a) secession   (d) condolence
    (b) verisimilitude   (e) tenuousness
    (c) preamble

16. The tone of the letter's final paragraph is best described as

    (a) dejected   (d) degraded
    (b) impassive   (e) luminous
    (c) ingratiating

Practice Quiz
for Worksheets 109–126

Read carefully the directions preceding each section, then choose the best answer to each question.

Section 1: Fill in the Blank

Each sentence below contains one or two blanks. Following all sentences are five individual words or pairs of words. Select the best word or pair of words to complete the sentence according to its meaning.

1. The jury _____ the thief, citing an _____ oversight on the part of the police force.

   (a) perplexed . . . immutable
   (b) exculpated . . . ignominious
   (c) introspected . . . abject
   (d) matriculated . . . effervescent
   (e) remonstrated . . . obfuscated

2. The student's _____ made him downright _____, as his outrage over the low test grade demonstrated.

   (a) flamboyance . . . introspective
   (b) matriculation . . . discursive
   (c) circumspection . . . demographic
   (d) neologism . . . synchronistic
   (e) perplexity . . . indignant

3. New rules at the office caused silent, yet effective, _____ from most of the workers.

   (a) predilection
   (b) remonstrance
   (c) immutability
   (d) obfuscation
   (e) flamboyance

4. Almost universally, slang terminology evolves through the introductions of _____, the origins of which are varied.

   (a) demographics
   (b) introspections
   (c) neologisms
   (d) synchronisms
   (e) flamboyances

Section 2: Revision

Each sentence below contains an underlined portion. Following all sentences are five ways of writing that underlined portion. Select the choice that, if substituted for the underlined portion, results in the clearest, most grammatically effective sentence.

5. The westernmost portion of Florida, which adjoins Alabama <u>and is known as its "panhandle," can be</u> very humid at times.

   (a) as written
   (b) and is known as it's "panhandle," can be
   (c) and is known as Florida's "panhandle," can be
   (d) and is known as its "panhandle" can be
   (e) and is known as Florida's "panhandle" can be

6. <u>Ireland is spelled with fewer letters than Scotland</u> contains.

   (a) as written
   (b) "Ireland" is spelled with fewer letters than "Scotland"
   (c) "Ireland" is spelled with fewer letters than Scotland
   (d) Ireland is spelled with less letters than Scotland
   (e) "Ireland" is spelled with less letters than "Scotland"

7. The four <u>red capped persons' mission was simple: find</u> out whatever information they could, then report back to headquarters as quickly as possible.

   (a) as written
   (b) red-capped persons' mission was simple, find
   (c) red-capped persons's mission was simple: find
   (d) red capped people's mission was simple, find
   (e) red-capped people's mission was simple: find

8. In <u>the 20s, speakeasies were common, but those sometimes</u> only catered to people with ties to illegal activities.

   (a) as written
   (b) the '20s, speakeasies were common, but those sometimes
   (c) the 20's, speakeasies were common, but those establishments sometimes
   (d) the '20s, speakeasies were common, but those establishments sometimes
   (e) the 1920's, speakeasies were common, but those establishments sometimes

Section 3: Error Recognition

Each sentence below either is correct or contains one error. No sentence contains multiple errors. The error in each sentence, if it exists, is underlined. Select the underlined portion of each sentence that must be corrected, but select choice (e) if the sentence is correctly written.

9. Dante <u>Alighieri, whose</u> most famous literary work is
   (a)

   still read by students today, <u>irregardless</u> of <u>its age,</u>
   (b)   (c)

   was born in Florence <u>in 1265</u>.
   (d)

   (e) <u>there is no error</u>

10. <u>Scientists use cheese to lure</u> mice <u>into their</u>
    (a)   (b)

    experiments, according to a common stereotype,
    <u>but it's</u> improbable that
    (c)

    <u>laboratories around the world actually possess</u>
    (d)

    refrigerators full of dairy products.

    (e) <u>there is no error</u>

11. <u>In 2010,</u> a massive underwater oil leak in
    (a)

    the Gulf of Mexico became so problematic
    that <u>it impacted and involved</u> a great portion of
    (b)

    the <u>nations's</u> population: <u>scientists,</u> mariners,
    (c)   (d)

    engineers, fishermen, merchants, and others.

    (e) <u>there is no error</u>

12. Magicians, mascots, and circus performers
    <u>have various</u> physical objects associated with
    (a)

    <u>their professions, including:</u> decks of cards, fuzzy
    (b)   (c)

    feet, and flaming hoops, <u>respectively</u>.
    (d)

    (e) <u>there is no error</u>

13. I <u>saw the damage</u> was extensive enough
    (a)

    to warrant <u>its status</u> as <u>critical, but</u> the
    (b)   (c)

    <u>local fire department</u> saved the building.
    (d)

    (e) <u>there is no error</u>

Section 4: Reading Comprehension

The following paragraphs are excerpted from Creatures of the Night: A Book of Wildlife in Western Britain, *by Alfred W. Rees. Read the passage and select the best answer to each question.*

One night, while the cubs were rougher than ever in their fun, Lutra slipped off the platform and fell headlong down the pipe into the stream. But almost before she had time to be frightened she discovered that to swim was as easy as to play; and she rose to the surface with a faint, flute-like call. She splashed somewhat wildly, for her stroke was not yet perfected by practice. Hearing the commotion and instantly recognising its meaning, the dam dived quietly and swiftly right beneath the cub, and bore her gently back to the platform, where the rest of the family, having missed their companion, had for the moment ceased to romp and fight.

A few nights after this incident, the mother commenced in earnest to educate her young. Tenderly taking each in turn, she carried the nurslings into the water, and taught them, by a method and in language known only to themselves, how to dive and swim with the least possible exertion and disturbance.

Henceforward, throughout the summer, and till the foliage on the trees near the pool, chilled by the rapid fall of the temperature every evening, became thinner in the breath of the early autumn wind, the otter-cubs fished, and frolicked, and slept, or were suckled by their dam. Sometimes the whole family, together with the old dog-otter, adjourned to the middle of the meadow, and in the tall, dew-drenched grass skipped like kittens, though with comical clumsiness rather than with the agility they displayed in the water. Like kittens, too, the cubs played with their mother, in spite of wholesome chastisement when they nipped her muzzle rather more severely than even long-suffering patience could allow. The dam was at all times loath to correct her offspring, but the sire rarely endured the familiarity of the cubs for long. Directly they became unduly presumptuous, he lumbered off to the river, as if he considered it much more becoming to fish than to join in the sport of his progeny. Perhaps, indeed, he deemed a change of surroundings essential that he might forget the liberties taken with him by his disrespectful youngsters.

14. The young otters engage in behavior describable as

    (a) demographic   (d) indignant
    (b) obfuscated   (e) effervescent
    (c) circumspect

15. The father otter's movement to the river is portrayed as

    (a) introspective   (d) indignant
    (b) perplexed   (e) flamboyant
    (c) discursive

16. The mother otter is portrayed as choosing not to
    (a) remonstrate
    (b) exculpate
    (c) synchronize
    (d) abject
    (e) obfuscate

Practice Quiz
for Worksheets 127–144

Read carefully the directions preceding each section, then choose the best answer to each question.

Section 1: Fill in the Blank

Each sentence below contains one or two blanks. Following all sentences are five individual words or pairs of words. Select the best word or pair of words to complete the sentence according to its meaning.

1. _____ France was a land of great wealth, architecture, and folk art, unaltered as yet by the ravages of warfare.

    (a) Antecedent
    (b) Heterogeneous
    (c) Antebellum
    (d) Amicable
    (e) Degenerate

2. The census worker's assumption that all members of a given family are related turned out to be _____, resulting in a _____ of intact genealogies on the final report.

    (a) degenerate . . . diffuseness
    (b) pernicious . . . heterogeneity
    (c) erroneous . . . superfluity
    (d) electorate . . . subjugation
    (e) homonymous . . . conflagration

3. I have great interest in _____ arts, but I do not have the money to pursue admission to a specialized culinary institute right now.

    (a) amicable
    (b) synonymous
    (c) matriarchal
    (d) pernicious
    (e) gastronomic

4. Realism is the ideological _____ of Romanticism, but several writers actually _____ the boundaries of both philosophies, combining elements of the two in their work.

    (a) antipathy . . . transgress
    (b) synonym . . . subjugate
    (c) heterogeneity . . . antecede
    (d) electorate . . . conflagrate
    (e) antebellum . . . diffuse

Section 2: Revision

Each sentence below contains an underlined portion. Following all sentences are five ways of writing that underlined portion. Select the choice that, if substituted for the underlined portion, results in the clearest, most grammatically effective sentence.

5. My friends and I not only share notes between ourselves, but also help each other to study for major tests.

    (a) as written
    (b) I not only share notes among ourselves, but also help
    (c) I not only share notes between ourselves, but help
    (d) me not only share notes between ourselves, but help
    (e) me not only share notes among ourselves, but also help

6. The reporter found news of the latest scientific discovery to be more incredible than the young student whom it was discovered by.

    (a) as written
    (b) incredulous than the young student whom it was discovered by
    (c) incredible than the young student by whom it was discovered
    (d) incredulous then the young student by whom it was discovered
    (e) incredible then the young student whom it was discovered by

7. The bully did not state his threat, but it was implied clearly.

    (a) as written
    (b) his threat but it was inferred clearly
    (c) his threat but it was implied clearly
    (d) his threat, but it clear was implied
    (e) his threat but it clear was inferred

8. So I was unable to read the sign; I thus turned the wrong way down the street.

    (a) as written
    (b) I was unable to read the sign, I thus
    (c) So I was unable to read the sign, I thus
    (d) I was unable to read the sign; I thus
    (e) I was unable to read the sign; so I thus

Section 3: Error Recognition

Each sentence below either is correct or contains one error. No sentence contains multiple errors. The error in each sentence, if it exists, is underlined. Select the underlined portion of each sentence that must be corrected, but select choice (e) if the sentence is correctly written.

9. Each <u>incredulous</u> observer of the meteor shower
      (a)

   <u>were fully</u> <u>unaware that</u> its conclusion was
      (b)   (c)

   <u>imminent</u>.
      (d)

   (e) <u>there is no error</u>

10. Neither Bombay <u>nor Calcutta is</u> <u>farther away</u> from
                         (a)   (b)

    Sri Lanka <u>than</u> New Delhi <u>is, India</u>, of course, is a
                  (c)   (d)

    very large country.

    (e) <u>there is no error</u>

11. Automobiles <u>which are made</u> in Asia
                      (a)

    <u>sometimes cost</u> American consumers <u>more than</u>
         (b)   (c)

    cars produced in the United States do because

    <u>of tariffs, taxes, and other such</u> fees.
                   (d)

    (e) <u>there is no error</u>

12. When my brother gave his concert tickets to my

    girlfriend <u>and me</u>, I was <u>speechless; after</u> all, it was
                   (a)   (b)

    not that long ago <u>that he and I</u> had fought
                            (c)

    <u>bitterly over</u> the right to buy them.
          (d)

    (e) <u>there is no error</u>

Section 4: Reading Comprehension

The following paragraphs are excerpted from James Fenimore Cooper's novel The Deerslayer. *Read the passage and select the best answer to each question.*

The encampment being temporary, it offered to the eye no more than the rude protection of a bivouac, relieved in some slight degree by the ingenious expedients which suggested themselves to the readiness of those who passed their lives amid similar scenes. One fire, that had been kindled against the roots of a living oak, sufficed for the whole party; the weather being too mild to require it for any purpose but cooking. Scattered around this centre of attraction, were some fifteen or twenty low huts, or perhaps kennels would be a better word, into which their different owners crept at night, and which were also intended to meet the exigencies of a storm.

These little huts were made of the branches of trees, put together with some ingenuity, and they were uniformly topped with bark that had been stripped from fallen trees; of which every virgin forest possesses hundreds, in all stages of decay. Of furniture they had next to none. Cooking utensils of the simplest sort were lying near the fire, a few articles of clothing were to be seen in or around the huts, rifles, horns, and pouches leaned against the trees, or were suspended from the lower branches, and the carcasses of two or three deer were stretched to view on the same natural shambles.

As the encampment was in the midst of a dense wood, the eye could not take in its tout ensemble at a glance, but hut after hut started out of the gloomy picture, as one gazed about him in quest of objects. There was no centre, unless the fire might be so considered, no open area where the possessors of this rude village might congregate, but all was dark, covert and cunning, like its owners. A few children strayed from hut to hut, giving the spot a little of the air of domestic life, and the suppressed laugh and low voices of the women occasionally broke in upon the deep stillness of the somber forest. As for the men, they either ate, slept, or examined their arms. They conversed but little, and then usually apart, or in groups withdrawn from the females, whilst an air of untiring, innate watchfulness and apprehension of danger seemed to be blended even with their slumbers.

13. Cooper implies that the inhabitants of this camp seem particularly concerned with outsiders'

   (a) diffuseness
   (b) perniciousness
   (c) amicability
   (d) matriarchies
   (e) conflagrations

14. The entire collection of physical articles scattered about the camp can be described as

   (a) gastronomic
   (b) homonymous
   (c) antebellum
   (d) heterogeneous
   (e) erroneous

15. Relative to the men, the female inhabitants of this camp appear to be

   (a) degenerate
   (b) superfluous
   (c) antecedent
   (d) amicable
   (e) electoral

Perfect 800: SAT Verbal © Prufrock Press Inc. • Permission is granted to photocopy or reproduce this page for single classroom use only.

Practice Quiz
for Worksheets 145–162

Read carefully the directions preceding each section, then choose the best answer to each question.

Section 1: Fill in the Blank

Each sentence below contains one or two blanks. Following all sentences are five individual words or pairs of words. Select the best word or pair of words to complete the sentence according to its meaning.

1. I found the lecturer's _____ for _____ to be quite upsetting, as it seemed nearly impossible for him to answer a question clearly and succinctly.

    (a) indolence . . . malediction
    (b) prerogative . . . premonition
    (c) extenuation . . . incredulity
    (d) proclivity . . . circumlocution
    (e) gratuity . . . concordance

2. Debate rages as to whether plants are _____ creatures or simply impassive and unfeeling, albeit living, organisms.

    (a) enamored
    (b) sentient
    (c) repugnant
    (d) sympathetic
    (e) vociferous

3. The _____ political structure of barbarian Gaul actually hid a surprising _____ among its great variety of folk cultures.

    (a) repugnant . . . gratuity
    (b) indolent . . . extenuation
    (c) abstruse . . . premonition
    (d) anarchic . . . concordance
    (e) prerogative . . . malediction

4. My _____ cousin never has any problem loudly proclaiming his dislike for cranberries each Thanksgiving.

    (a) vociferous
    (b) gratuitous
    (c) circumlocutory
    (d) sympathetic
    (e) incredulous

Section 2: Revision

Each sentence below contains an underlined portion. Following all sentences are five ways of writing that underlined portion. Select the choice that, if substituted for the underlined portion, results in the clearest, most grammatically effective sentence.

5. The class's <u>uninterested disregard for poetry corresponded to our teacher's worsened affect</u>.

    (a) as written
    (b) uninterested disregard for poetry corresponded with our teacher's worsened affect
    (c) disinterested disregard for poetry corresponded to our teacher's worsened affect
    (d) uninterested disregard for poetry corresponded to our teacher's worsened effect
    (e) disinterested disregard for poetry corresponded with our teacher's worsened effect

6. In addition to identifying the theme of the film, <u>I also was able to list from memory the actors who</u> starred in it.

    (a) as written
    (b) I was able to list from memory the actors who
    (c) I also was able to from memory list the actors whom
    (d) I was able to list from memory as well the actors who
    (e) I was able to list from memory the actors whom

7. The plan is <u>practical if you actually want too lose money</u>.

    (a) as written
    (b) practicable if you want to actually lose money
    (c) practicable if you want too lose money actually
    (d) practical if you actually want to lose money
    (e) practical if you want too actually lose money

8. If you are unaware that the reason why the library is closed <u>is because it is currently past business hours, then you</u> should perhaps purchase a working watch.

    (a) as written
    (b) is because it is currently past business hours, you
    (c) is that it is currently past business hours, then you
    (d) is that it is currently past business hours, you
    (e) is because it is past current business hours, then you

Section 3: Error Recognition

Each sentence below is either correct or contains one error. No sentence contains multiple errors. The error in each sentence, if it exists, is underlined. Select the underlined portion of each sentence that must be corrected, but select choice (e) if the sentence is correctly written.

9. The President of the United States might be

   <u>uninterested</u> in the daily goings-on in Greenland,
   (a)

   but <u>the United</u> States Ambassador <u>to that country</u>
   (b) (c)

   probably cares <u>because</u>.
   (d)

   (e) <u>there is no error</u>

10. I have more coins in my collection

    <u>than my grandmother, who got</u> me started
    (a) (b)

    collecting coins in the first place <u>because</u> she liked
    (c)

    <u>to spend time</u> with me when I was young.
    (d)

    (e) <u>there is no error</u>

11. The Declaration of Independence <u>stated</u> that
    (a)

    "<u>all [human beings] are created</u> equal," which is
    (b)

    probably the most famous portion of any legal

    <u>document in the United States</u>; it was written
    (c)

    <u>neither by George Washington nor by</u> James
    (d)

    Madison, but by Thomas Jefferson.

    (e) <u>there is no error</u>

12. Although the pilot tried <u>to change his course quickly,</u>
    (a)

    he was unable <u>to do so</u> and proceeded on his
    (b)

    original path <u>through the storm cloud</u>, which was
    (c)

    the only <u>practicable</u> approach to the runway.
    (d)

    (e) <u>there is no error</u>

Section 4: Reading Comprehension

The following paragraphs are excerpted from the introduction to Old Cookery Books and Ancient Cuisine, *by William C. Hazlitt. Read the passage and select the best answer to each question.*

Man has been distinguished from other animals in various ways; but perhaps there is no particular in which he exhibits so marked a difference from the rest of creation – not even in the prehensile faculty resident in his hand – as in the objection to raw food, meat, and vegetables. He approximates to his inferior contemporaries only in the matter of fruit, salads, and oysters, not to mention wild-duck....

When we pass from an examination of the state of the question as regarded Cookery in very early times among us, before an even more valuable art – that of Printing – was discovered, we shall find ourselves face to face with a rich and long chronological series of books on the Mystery, the titles and fore-fronts of which are often not without a kind of fragrance and *goût*.

As the space allotted to me is limited, and as the sketch left by Warner of the convivial habits and household arrangements of the Saxons or Normans in this island, as well as of the monastic institutions, is more copious than any which I could offer, it may be best to refer simply to his elaborate preface. But it may be pointed out generally that the establishment of the Norman sway not only purged of some of their Anglo-Danish barbarism the tables of the nobility and the higher classes, but did much to spread among the poor a thriftier manipulation of the articles of food by a resort to broths, messes, and hot-pots. In the poorer districts, in Normandy as well as in Brittany, Duke William would probably find very little alteration in the mode of preparing victuals from that which was in use in his day, eight hundred years ago, if (like another Arthur) he should return among his ancient compatriots; but in his adopted country he would see that there had been a considerable revolt from the common saucepan – not to add from the pseudo-Arthurian bag-pudding; and that the English artisan, if he could get a rump-steak or a leg of mutton once a week, was content to starve on the other six days.

13. The selection's allusions to ancient British history and geography imply the author's scholarly

    (a) malediction   (d) repugnance
    (b) proclivity   (e) extenuation
    (c) circumvention

14. The author's style of describing ancient cuisine and gastronomy resembles

    (a) prerogative   (d) concordance
    (b) premonition   (e) circumlocution
    (c) indolence

Answers for Practice Quiz
for Worksheets 1–18

1. c	5. d	9. a	13. c
2. d	6. c	10. c	14. d
3. a	7. d	11. b	15. c
4. d	8. a	12. a	16. c

Answers for Practice Quiz
for Worksheets 19–36

1. c	5. a	9. a	13. d
2. b	6. b	10. b	14. b
3. e	7. b	11. a	15. d
4. d	8. c	12. d	16. d

Answers for Practice Quiz
for Worksheets 37–54

1. d	5. a	9. b	13. b
2. b	6. c	10. a	14. e
3. e	7. c	11. d	15. d
4. a	8. a	12. e	

Answers for Practice Quiz
for Worksheets 55–72

1. b	5. a	9. b	13. c
2. c	6. c	10. a	14. d
3. a	7. d	11. c	15. c
4. e	8. d	12. e	16. d

Answers for Practice Quiz
for Worksheets 73–90

1. b	5. c	9. d	13. d
2. d	6. a	10. c	14. c
3. a	7. e	11. e	15. a
4. c	8. c	12. a	

Answers for Practice Quiz
for Worksheets 91–108

1. e	5. b	9. e	13. a
2. c	6. c	10. e	14. d
3. a	7. e	11. c	15. c
4. c	8. a	12. b	16. b

Answers for Practice Quiz
for Worksheets 109–126

1. b	5. c	9. b	13. a
2. e	6. b	10. b	14. e
3. b	7. e	11. c	15. d
4. c	8. d	12. c	16. a

Answers for Practice Quiz
for Worksheets 127–144

1. c	5. b	9. b	13. b
2. c	6. c	10. d	14. d
3. e	7. a	11. a	15. d
4. a	8. d	12. e	

Answers for Practice Quiz
for Worksheets 145–162

1. d	5. a	9. d	13. b
2. b	6. b	10. a	14. e
3. d	7. d	11. a	
4. a	8. c	12. e	

Chapter 6

Glossary of Morphemes Found in This Book

a: a common prefix meaning *without* or *not*, as in "amoral" and "atypical"

ab: a prefix derived from Latin meaning *apart* or *away from*, as in "abnormal"

able: a suffix indicating ability, meaning *able to be* in most cases, such as "movable" or "blamable"

acri: a Latin root meaning *bitter*

ad: a prefix derived from Latin meaning *toward* or *near*, as in "advance"

ag: a verbal variant of the Latin prefix "ad-" meaning *to lead*, *to drive*, or *to force*, as in the English verb "agitate"

age: a suffix meaning *the act or result of*, which helps to create cumulative or collective nouns, such as "postage" or "shrinkage"

agogue: a Latin derivative meaning *leader*

al: another variant of "ad-" meaning *toward* or *near*

al: in contrast to the prefix "al-," a Latin suffix meaning *relating to* or *having the character of*, as in "proposal" and "arrival"

am: meaning *love*, this morpheme was derived originally from Latin and adapted to all Romance languages, and hence to English; it is easily recognized because of its commonness of meaning in foreign languages

amb: a Latin derivative meaning *both*, *more than one*, or *around*

ambul: meaning *walk*, this morpheme is another adoption from Latin, easily recognized as the root word of "ambulance"

ana: a variant of "anti-" meaning *against*; anabolic bodily processes or substances, for example, are opposed to or the opposite of catabolic processes

ance: a suffix meaning *the state or quality of*, this morpheme was adopted into English directly from French, which initially derived it from Latin; a word such as "pursuance" explicates its usage as a noun-creating suffix

anim: a Latin root meaning *life* or *spirit*, as in the verb "animate"

ant: this suffix is a French derivative meaning either *performing* or *being in a particular state*; it can be used to create both nouns (e.g., "servant") and adjectives (e.g., "defiant")

ante: meaning *before*, this prefix is derived from a Latin preposition, and is found in the important grammatical word "antecedent"

anthrop: a Greek root meaning *man* or *human*, as in "anthropology"

anti: a prefix meaning *against*, derived from ancient Greek; it denotes opposition when attached to any noun, such as "anti-homework" and "antidote"

apo: a prefix derived from ancient Greek meaning *away*, as in "apology"

arch: a suffix taken from both Latin and ancient Greek meaning *chief or ruler*, as in "monarch"

ary: an adjectival suffix from Latin meaning *relating to* or *of*; it is commonly added to nouns in order to transform them into adjectives, such as "ordinary"

ate: a verbal suffix meaning *to act in such a manner*, as in "abbreviate" and "conjugate"

ate: this suffix has a secondary, nonverbal meaning of *characterized by* or *resembling*, also derived from Latin; this adjectival usage is seen in words such as "Latinate"

auto: a prefix meaning *self* derived from ancient Greek; its meaning is clear in the self-propelled "automobile" and the self-induced "autohypnosis"

belli and **bellum**: meaning *war*, these morphemes have been adopted wholesale from Latin

bene: a Latin adoption meaning *good* or *favorable*, as in "benefit"

bibl: derived from ancient Greek, via Latin, this morpheme means *book*; etymologically, it was born of the Phoenician city of Byblos, which once was a great producer and exporter of paper, and it clearly is the central root of the word "Bible"

capit: a Latin derivative meaning *head*, as in the grisly "decapitation" and the more mundane "capitalization" of letters

carn: taken from Latin and meaning *flesh*, as in the animal designation "carnivore"

ced: a Latin derivative meaning, paradoxically, both *to go* and *to yield*, as in "to accede" and "to cede," respectively

cess: meaning *to go* or *to yield*, this morpheme is a variant of "ced," above

chron: a Greek derivative meaning *time*; related to the Titan Cronus in Greek mythology; it can be found in words pertaining to time, such as "chronology"

circu: meaning *around* or *on all sides*, this morpheme is derived from Latin, and is the root word of the geometric word "circular"

cli: another Latin adoption meaning *to lean toward*, as in the verb "recline"

co and **con**: adopted Latin prefixes meaning *with* or *together*; one of this pair can be conjoined with most nouns to indicate partnership, such as "coauthors"

contra: another prefix adopted wholesale from Latin; meaning *against*, it can precede many nouns to signal opposition, as in "contradiction"

cord and **cors**: these two are puzzling root words, the etymologies of which are apocryphally supposed; in English, they mean and pertain to *heart*, but whether they can be traced strictly to French or to the earlier Latin "*corpus*," meaning *body*, is still debated by linguists

cred: meaning *to believe* or *to trust*, this morpheme is derived from Latin and is the root of such common words as "credit" and "incredible"

cryp: a root that can be traced to both ancient Greek, in which it means *hidden*, and Latin, in which it denotes a vault; the former usage has given us words such as "cryptic"

culp: a Latin derivative meaning *blame*, as in the phrase "*mea culpa*"

cur: from Latin, this morpheme means or indicates *a course that is run*, as in the verbs "recur" and "occur"

de: a prefix adopted from Latin meaning *away* or *down*, as in "descend"

dem: meaning *people*, this morpheme is derived from ancient Greek, in which its linguistic ancestor denoted particularly *the common people*; it is the root of the word "democracy"

di or **dict**: derived from Latin and meaning *to tell* or *to use words*, as in "dictionary" and "dictation"

dif: a prefix meaning *away from* or *apart*, or otherwise indicating a reversal, it is a variant of the Latin prefix "dis-"; its meaning is most clearly seen in the commonplace "different"

dign: a root derived from Latin meaning *worth* or *value*, as in the adjective "dignified"

dis: a Latin prefix meaning *not*, *away*, or *apart*, as in "disperse" and "distract"

doc: a Latin adoption meaning *teach*; all usages of the English word "doctor," especially its academic meaning, are related to this root

dole: a Latin derivative meaning *sadness* or *suffering*, as in "condolence"

dox: a morpheme adopted from ancient Greek meaning *opinion*, as in "ortho-dox," which can be translated as "straight opinion"

du: a variant of "di-" meaning *two*, this prefix is derived from Latin and serves to compose self-explanatory words such as "dual"

dubit: a Latin adoption meaning *doubt*, which is itself a clear English descendent of the original

duct: a Latin adoption meaning *to lead*; an "aqueduct" is called such because it literally leads water from one place to another

e: this prefix comes from Latin and means *out of* or *beyond*, as in "eviction" and "erupt"; its meaning is sometimes extended to mean *thoroughly or completely*

ed: an adjectival suffix meaning *resembling* or *composed by*, added commonly to nouns, as in "painted" and "added"

en: meaning *to cause it to be*, this verbal prefix is derived from Latin via French, and is the prefix found in words such as "enlighten" and "entice"

ence: meaning *the state or quality of*, this suffix is added to words in order to make them nouns, such as "independence"

ent: an adjectival suffix meaning *performing* or *being in a particular state*, as in "dependent"

equ: a Latin adoption meaning *equal*, as in the words "equity" and "equivalent"

err: derived from Latin and meaning *to wander*, the morphological meaning of which adds a polite connotation to the harsh word "error"

esce: meaning *to do* or *to act*, this suffix is derived from the Latin verb meaning *to become or begin*; it is used to create verbs, as in "coalesce" and "phosphoresce"

eu: a prefix adopted from ancient Greek meaning *good* or *well*; the floral designation "eucalyptus," for example, literally means "covered with good" or "well-covered"

ex: a Latin prefix meaning *out of* or *from*, as simplistically shown in "exit"

ex: this prefix can also mean *to intensify*, as in "extend"

fab: meaning *speak*, this morpheme is derived from the Latin "*fari*" and is the root of the English words "fable" and "fabricate"

fam: a Latin derivative meaning *fame or renown*; it is related to "fab," above

fer: derived from a Latin verb meaning *to bring or carry*, as in "differ" and "offer"

ferv: a Latinate root meaning *to boil, bubble, or burn*, as in the adjective "fervent"

fid: meaning *faith* or *trust*, this morpheme is derived from Latin and is the root of such words as "confidence"

flag and **flam**: both mean *to burn*, are derived from Latin, and serve as roots for words such as "unflagging" and "flammable"

flu: derived from Latin and meaning *to flow*, as in "fluid"

frac and **frag**: derived from the Latin verb meaning *to break*, they help to compose such English words as "fraction" and "fragile"

ful: an adjectival suffix meaning *full of* or *having*, or otherwise communicating possession of a particular characteristic, as in "useful" and "beautiful"

funct: a root derived from Latin and meaning *performance* or *function*, as in "dysfunctional"

fus: meaning *to pour*, this morpheme is derived from Latin via Old French and helps to form words such as "infuse"

gastr: a root derived from ancient Greek that means *stomach*, as in "gastronomy"

gen: also derived from ancient Greek, this morpheme means *creation* or *race or kind*, as in "genesis" and "generation"

gerere: derived from the Latin verb meaning *to bear* or *to carry*, as in the syntactical "gerund," denoting a verb bearing the place or purpose of a noun

gno or **gnos**: derived from ancient Greek and meaning *know* or *knowledge*, as in "agnosticism"

grad: meaning *to step*, this morpheme is derived from Latin and is the root of "graduate"

graph: derived from ancient Greek via Latin, this morpheme means *to write* or *writing*; it is related to painting and drawing, as in "photograph" and "graphic"

grat: this morpheme is a Latin derivative meaning *favor* or *pleasing*, as in "gratifying"; it is related to the Latin word for "freely given"

greg: meaning *herd* or *group*, this morpheme is ultimately taken from the Latin word "*Graeco,*" which means "Greek"

gress: a Latin derivative meaning *to step*, as in "digress" and "progress"

her: meaning *to stick*, it is derived from a Latin word that is connotatively translated as *closely connect*; it is central to words such as "coherent" and "adhere"

hetero: a prefix meaning *different*, adopted from ancient Greek and found in English words such as "heterogeneous"

homo: a prefix antonymic to "hetero-," it is also adopted from ancient Greek and means *the same as* (e.g. linguistic "homonyms")

ible: a variant of "-able" meaning *able to be*, used in words such as "edible"

ic: this adjectival suffix means *relating to* or *characterized by* and is derived from ancient Greek; it is usually added to nouns in order to form adjectives, as in "acidic" and "metallic"

ice: a suffix adopted from Latin meaning *the condition or quality of*, as in "cowardice"

id: a suffix derived from ancient Greek meaning *resembling* or *similar to*, as in "horrid" and "candid"

ig: a variant of the prefix "in-" meaning *not*, it makes words such as "ignore"

ile: a Latin suffix meaning *capable of* or *suited to*, as in "servile"

im and **in**: Latin prefixes meaning *not*, they convey negation when appended to adjectives, as in "impossible" and "inaccurate"

in: meaning *within* or *inside of*, this alternately meaningful prefix is adopted from Old English; it is useful in words such as "inbred"

ine: an adjectival suffix meaning *the nature or quality of* that can be traced through Middle English, Old French, Latin, and ultimately ancient Greek; it is used to make adjectives such as "marine"

inter: a prefix meaning *between*, as in "interpersonal" and "interstate highway"

intro: a variant of the more common prefix "intra-" meaning *within*, as in "introvert" and "introduction"

ion: derived from a Latin suffix and meaning *the act or condition of*, as in "consumption" and "preparation"

ious: a variant of "-ous" meaning *full of* or *having*, as in "injurious"

ism: meaning *the condition or action of being*, this suffix is derived from ancient Greek; it is used to create abstract nouns such as "modernism"

ist: meaning *a person who practices* or *a person concerned with*, this suffix is derived from ancient Greek through Latin; it is used to identify people, such as an "artist"

ite: a variant of the suffix "-ate" meaning *to act in such a manner*, as in "invite"

ity: a suffix derived from Latin meaning *a state or quality of*, used to describe often uncountable nouns such as "elasticity" and "popularity"

ium: a Latinate suffix meaning *a compound of*, it is used to form nouns involving complication or large size, such as "auditorium"

ive: an adjectival suffix meaning *performing* or *tending to*, this morpheme is derived from Latin via Anglo-Norman; it is found in adjectives such as "sensitive" and "active"

ize: a verbal suffix derived from ancient Greek meaning *to become* or *to treat as*, as in "pressurize" and "criticize"

ject: a Latin derivative meaning literally *to throw*, as in "eject" and "reject"

junct: a Latinate root meaning *to meet* or *to join*, as in "conjunction"

lect: another derivative of Latin meaning *to select* or *to choose*, as in "elect"

lit: a variant of "liter," this morpheme is derived from ancient Greek via Latin and means *letter*, as in a "liturgy"

loc, **log**, and **loq**: derived from Latin and meaning *word*, *speech*, or *speak*, as in "colloquial" and "dialogue"

luc and **lum**: variants of "lumin," which is derived from Latin and means *light*, as in "illuminate"

ly: an adverbial suffix meaning *accomplished in such a manner*; it transforms adjectives into adverbs, such as "quickly" and "angrily"

magn: derived from Latin and meaning *large*, as in "magnum" and "magnificent"

mal: a morpheme found in many European languages and meaning *bad* or *wrong*; it is derived from Latin and used to compose words such as "maladjusted"

matrix: adopted from Latin and meaning *list*, this morpheme is traceable also to the root "mater," meaning *mother*, as in collegiate *"alma mater"* songs

melli: a Latinate adjectival prefix meaning *honey*, which in Latin is *"mel"*

ment: a suffix meaning *the state or result of*, this morpheme is derived ultimately from Latin via French; it transforms adjectives and verbs into abstract nouns, as in "merriment" and "nourishment"

mis: a Germanic prefix meaning *bad* or *wrong*, as in "mistake"

mit: an adoption from Latin meaning *to send*, as in "transmit" and "submit"

mon: a Latin derivative meaning *to warn* or *to remind*, as in "monitor" and "monument"

morph: adopted from ancient Greek and meaning *form* or *shape*, as in "metamorphosis"

mut: a Latin derivative meaning *change*, as in "mutate"

nat: meaning *to be born* or *to spring from*, this morpheme is another Latin derivative, found in words as common as "natural" and "native"

ne: a prefix traceable to Latin and found in variation among most European languages, it means *not*, connoting negation of whatever it is appended to, as in "never" and "negative"

neo: a prefix adopted from ancient Greek meaning *new*, it is appended to both adjectives and nouns, as in "neoclassical" and "neophyte"

ness: a Germanic suffix meaning *the state of*, it transforms adjectives into nouns, as in "darkness" and "readiness"

nic and **noc**: derived from Latin and meaning *harm* or *death*, as in "obnoxious" and "innocent"

nom and **nomin**: Latin derivatives meaning *name*, as in "nominate"

nov: another root derived from Latin, it means *new* and can be found in words such as "renovate"

nym: a variant of "nom" and "nomin" meaning *name*, as in "synonym"

ob: an adopted Latin prefix meaning *against*, as in "objection"

omni: a prefix derived from Latin and meaning *all*, as in "omnivore" and "omnidirectional"

oner: a variant of the Latin word "*onus*," meaning *burden*, which has been adopted into English

or: a suffix meaning *one who does or performs* or *one who functions*; it is a variant of "-er" and useful for identifying people, such as an "actor"

ory: a suffix derived from Latin and meaning *of*, *relating to*, or *characterized by*; it is appended to both nouns and verbs to create adjectives, such as "sensory" and "mandatory"

osis: a suffix adopted from ancient Greek, meaning *the state of*, as in "hypnosis"

ous: an adjectival suffix derived from Old French and Latin, meaning *full of* or *having*, as in "courageous"

pan: a prefix meaning *everywhere* and adopted from ancient Greek, it is found in words that convey breadth, such as "panacea" and "pantheism"

par and **peer**: meaning *equal* and traceable to Middle English, Old French, and Latin, these morphemes are found in words such as "participant" and "partner"

path: a root derived from ancient Greek meaning *feeling* or *suffering*, it can be varied as "pas" and is found in "passion" and "sympathetic"

ped: meaning *foot*, this morpheme is derived from Latin via French; it is clearly seen in such words as "pedal" and "pedestrian"

pedo: an ancient Greek derivative meaning *child or children*, as in the specialist "pediatrician"

per: a prefix adopted from Latin and meaning *through*, and thus *completely*, as in "perfect"

phile: a personal suffix derived from ancient Greek and meaning *lover of*; it identifies people who care for particular things or topics, such as an "Francophile" or "audiophile"

philo: this morpheme is a variant of the same ancient Greek word "*philos*," meaning *love*; Philadelphia, for example, is nicknamed "the city of brotherly love" because of its combination of "*philo*" and "*adelphos*," meaning "brother"

plex: a Latin derivative meaning *to tangle or bend*, as in "perplexed"; it can be varied as "plic," as in "explicit," which connotes the undoing of tangles

poly: a prefix meaning *many* and derived from ancient Greek; it is appended to nouns and adjectives, as in "polyglot" and "polychrome"

pre: a Latinate prefix meaning *before*; it can be appended to nouns, verbs, and adjectives

pro: this morpheme also means *before*; this prefix is adopted from ancient Greek, as in "prognostication"

pro: derived this time from Latin, this prefix can also mean *forth* or *forward*, as in "projection" and "proceed"

pug: derived from Latin and meaning *to fight*, as in "pugilist," a boxer

ques: meaning *to seek*, it is derived equally from Anglo-Norman, French, and their linguistic predecessor, Latin; its simplest English relative is the nearly identical "quest"

qui: a Latin derivative meaning *quiet* or *rest*, as in "tranquil"

re: a prefix derived from Latin, meaning *again* or *back*, as in "return"

rog: a root derived from Latin and meaning *to ask*, as in "interrogate"

sci: this morpheme, meaning *to know*, is derived from Latin and forms such words as "science" and "conscious"

se: a Latinate prefix meaning *apart*, as in "select"

sent: derived from Latin and meaning *to feel or be aware*, as in "sentimental"

simil: another Latin derivative, meaning *resembling*, it is the root of "similarity," among other words

spec: a Latin derivative meaning *to look* or *to see*, as in "spectacles" and "inspect"

stru and **struct**: derived from Latin and meaning *to build*, as in "construct" and "structure"

sub: a Latin prefix meaning *below*, as in "submarine" and "subordinate"

super: the antonymic Latin prefix to "sub-"; this morpheme means *above*, as in "superior"

sym and **syn**: derived from ancient Greek and meaning *together* or *with*, as in "synthesize" and "symphony"

tent and **tenu**: these morphemes are Latin derivatives meaning *to stretch* or *to thin*, as in "tension"; a portable tent is actually named such because of the thinness of its material

tion: a variant of the Latinate suffix "-ion" meaning *the act or condition of*

tra: a root derived from Latin and meaning *to draw or pull*, as in "tractor" and "detract"

trans: a prefix derived from the Latin preposition meaning *across* or *beyond*; it is used to construct words such as "transmit" and "transparent"

tude: a suffix derived from Latin and meaning *the condition or quality of*, as in "attitude" and "finitude"

ul: a suffix meaning *tending or inclined to*, as in "articulate"

ute: a variant of the Latinate suffix "-ate," meaning *characterized by* or *resembling*; it is used in verbs such as "compute" and "execute"

val: a variant of "vol," meaning *to wish* or *to will*

ven and **vent**: derived from Latin and meaning *to come* or *to move forward*, as in "convene"

ver: another root derived from Latin meaning *truth*, as in "verify"

vi and **viv**: meaning *alive* or *life*, these morphemes are derived from the Latin word meaning *lively* or *vigorous*; they are morphologically common among all Romance languages and, in English, help to construct words such as "vivacious" and "vivid"

vid: another Latinate root and the other morphological half, alongside "vi," of the English word "vivid," it means *to see* and is clear in words such as "video" and "evident"

voc: derived from Latin and meaning *to call*, as in "vocation," "vocabulary," and "invoke"

vol: a root derived from Latin, meaning *to wish* or *to will*, as in "volunteer"

y: an adjectival suffix meaning *characterized by* or *inclined to*, as in "sticky" or "messy"

Chapter 7

Glossary of Grammatical Terms and Errors Found in This Book

active voice: The common name for syntactical structures in which subjects *do* things, rather than have things done to them, the active voice arises when a clause's object receives the action or effect of a verb, which is enacted by the subject. For example, "John ate cookies" is a sentence using the active voice, while "Cookies were eaten by John" uses the passive voice, which is weaker and less desirable.

adjective: Adjectives modify nouns, further describing or defining them. For example, the simple noun "dog" can be clarified or illuminated more fully with the addition of adjectives such as "hairy," "large," "brown," and "friendly."

adverb: Adverbs modify verbs, specifying particular ways in which actions are carried out. For example, the simple verb "ran" can be modified by adverbs such as "quickly," "fervently," and "sluggishly." Although it is untrue that all adverbs conclude with the suffix "-ly," that portrayal does serve as a useful, reliable rule of thumb.

antecedent: Morphologically, the word "antecedent" means "that which goes before," which describes perfectly what a grammatical antecedent is. Usually placed before modifiers such as pronouns, adverbs, and prepositional phrases, antecedents are the nouns to which pronouns, appositives, and the like refer. In the sentence "The voters, all of whom were more

269

than 40 years old, were told that they could not vote until noon," the noun "voters" serves as the antecedent of both the pronoun "they" and the appositive phrase describing the voters' age.

appositive: An appositive is a word or phrase that interrupts the flow of a clause for the sake of further explanation; as such, they are always off-set by commas. For example, in the sentence "Christopher Newport, an English mariner, captained the *Susan Constant* in 1607," the phrase "an English mariner" is an appositive, elaborating on the sentence's subject.

capitalization error: A capitalization error occurs either when letters that should be capitalized are not or when letters are capitalized that should not be, such as articles preceding proper nouns.

clauses, independent and dependent: Clauses differ from phrases in that a clause requires both a subject and a predicate (i.e., a noun and a verb). Independent clauses can effectively stand alone as sentences, while dependent clauses are grammatically incomplete, commonly identifiable as sentence fragments. A common, though not exclusive, identifier of a dependent clause is the presence of a conjunction standing at either its beginning or its end, signaling that more information must be attached to the clause in order to make it independent.

comma splice: The verb "splice" means "to cut," and a comma splice does just that: it cuts a sentence unnecessarily. This term is sometimes overused, however, as in situations where two independent clauses are joined solely with a comma; this conjuncture is not technically a comma splice because punctuation is required there, albeit a semicolon, rather than a comma.

compound adjective: A compound adjective is a collection of multiple words functioning as one adjectival phrase to modify a noun. For example, the phrase "honey-roasted peanuts" contains the compound adjective "honey-roasted," just as "soon-to-be-graduating students" contains its own adjectival phrase. Compound adjectives should always be hyphenated.

conjunction: A conjunction is a linking word or phrase; its grammatical purpose is to conjoin phrases, clauses, and smaller parts of speech. The acronym "F.A.N.B.O.Y.S." identifies the most common conjunctions, which are coordinating conjunctions: "for," "and," "nor," "but," "or," "yet," and "so." Subordinating conjunctions, such as "unless" and "because," strictly join clauses together and generally do not accompany commas.

contraction: The word "contract" morphologically means "to drag or pull together" (i.e., to squeeze), and a contraction does just that—squeezes words into smaller wholes. For example, the words "can" and "not" can be contracted into "can't," and the decade of the 1980s can be contracted into the abbreviated "'80s." The apostrophe in a contraction always replaces what is squeezed out, *per sé*.

correlative conjunction: These conjunctions are neither singular words nor composite phrases, but rather pairs of words that are placed separately but function together in a sentence; stated simply, correlative conjunctions are actually two conjunctions in one. Examples include "either/or," "not only/but also," and "both/and."

demonstrative pronoun: A demonstrative pronoun demonstrates or points at particular nouns (e.g., "this," "that," "those," and "these"). A demonstrative pronoun that does not point specifically at a noun in close proximity is technically a compositional error due to vagueness. See *unattributed pointing pronoun.*

dependent clause: See *clauses, independent and dependent.*

diction: One's diction is his or her choice of words, and a diction error thus involves the misuse of a word, probably mistaken for something similar to it. As I explain to my own students, a dictionary is named such because its purpose is to help a person to choose his or her words.

double negative: A double negative, such as "not nobody," functions as a positive statement, with the two negative words effectively contradicting and canceling out each other. This error is more common in informal speech than in writing.

e.g.: The acronym "e.g." comes from the Latin phrase *"exempli gratia"*; it is used instead of the phrase "for example" prior to offering a reader an actual example of whatever one's topic is.

extra information: This phrase is not a technical grammatical term, but an informal umbrella encompassing appositives, addresses, and other information unnecessary to the purpose and meaning of a clause. I use the phrase "extra information" as a catch-all in my own classes, explaining to students that any information that can be removed from a sentence without affecting its meaning or focus is technically extraneous and should thus be placed within commas. For example, in the sentence "New Jersey the Garden State is located adjacent to Pennsylvania," the phrase "the Garden State" is an appositive and can be removed from the sentence without altering its essential meaning; as such, it should be placed within commas.

faulty comparison: A faulty comparison occurs when a countable amount of something is compared in a sentence to some related but innumerable noun, rather than to another equivalently countable amount. For example, the clause "Chicago has more restaurants than Milwaukee" contains a faulty comparison, as the number of restaurants in Chicago is here compared to the city of Milwaukee itself, rather than to the number of restaurants in Milwaukee; this faulty comparison can be remedied by the inclusion of the concluding verb "contains" or "has," either of which functions as a *de facto* grammatical coda, establishing the contrast between the second number and the first. Faulty comparisons never arise, however, when forms of the infinitive "to be" are omitted; it is the one verb that is always implied and need not be used outright.

grammar error: The word "grammar" is commonly used, but somewhat misunderstood. Grammar can be thought of as an overall system of rules for language, syntactic and otherwise, or the study of those rules and linguistic relationships. In this way, grammar functions as an extremely large umbrella, under which fall the particularities of diction, syntax, punctuation, etymology, and the like. Errors labeled simply as grammatical errors in this book do not fit into and cannot be identified by smaller subsets of particular errors.

i.e.: The acronym "i.e." comes from the Latin phrase "*id est*," which means "that is." This acronym is used correctly in place of the phrase "in other words" prior to elaborating on or explaining further whatever one's topic is.

independent clause: See *clauses, independent and dependent*.

literary present tense: Events in literature are essentially frozen in time. As I explain it to my own students, even if they personally read *Romeo and Juliet* several years ago, were they to open the play once again to Act V, scene iii, Romeo would be right there on the page, committing suicide in the present tense before the reader's eyes, just as he will be when someone else reads the play in 10, 50, or 500 years. As such, all events occurring in literature should always be referred to in the present tense. However, a tricky situation develops regarding events that occurred prior to the actual inception of a story on page 1, such as the death of Prince Hamlet's father or the loss of Captain Ahab's leg, which should be referred to in the historical past tense, having occurred before the "actual time" when the plot begins.

misplaced modifier: A modifier is any word or phrase that elaborates upon, alters the meaning of, or . . . well, *modifies* another word or phrase. Adverbs, adjectives, prepositional phrases, and the like can all be classified as modifiers, which are misplaced when they modify parts of the sentence that they are not intended to describe. In the sentence "Hopefully, lunch will taste delicious," the adverb "Hopefully" is a misplaced modifier, as it here describes the way in which the lunch tastes, rather than the imaginings of the sentence's speaker, who hopes to eat well. Misplaced modifiers can be tricky to spot, but they nevertheless are common errors.

noun: Famously, a noun is a "person, place, or thing," as most students can tell you. Proper nouns are distinctive, often representing singularly identifiable things (e.g., "Bob Smith," "Canada," and "the White House"). Common nouns represent things that are not singularly distinctive, such as "grass" and "daughters."

parallel construction (a.k.a. parallel structure): Writers of lists must be careful that all elements, portions, items, or "things" in a list are formatted uniformly; it is always up to the writer just how those elements are set down, but they must *all* be nouns, *all* be verbs, *all* be adjectival phrases, *all* be gerunds, *all* be infinitives and start with the word "to," *all* begin with prepositions, or whatever else the writer decides. Such uniform construction of lists is labeled "parallel construction," and errors occur when structures of lists mix and match parts of speech or phrasal constructions.

passive voice: Syntactically weaker than the preferred active voice, passive voice arises when the subject of a clause, rather than its object, receives the action or effect of a verb. Passive voice basically inverts common syntax, essentially turning the object of a clause written in the active voice into the subject of a clause using passive voice. For example, the word "grades" is the object of the clause "Students earn grades," whereas the same word is the subject of the passively voiced "Grades are earned by students." Passive voice is weaker and thus less desirable than active voice because it is simply more effective syntactically to have subjects *do* things.

phrase: A phrase is, quite simply, a collection of words. It does not need to include both a noun and a verb, as a clause does. "Big house," "the Civil War," "under the radar," "under the bright stars shining," and "gray-eyed Athena" are all phrases.

pointing pronoun: See *demonstrative pronoun*.

possession error: A possession error occurs with the omission or unnecessary addition of either letters or apostrophes when attempting to make nouns possessive. The phrase "my cars four tires," for example, contains a possession error because it lacks a necessary apostrophe, while the phrase "Mr. Jones' classroom" also errs by its omission of an "s" following the apostrophe.

preposition: A preposition, simply stated, is a "relationship word," purposefully describing the relationship between parts of a sentence. Most teachers have and explain to students a trick or two for identifying prepositions (e.g., whatever one can do or wherever one can be in relation to a fence, a door, a barn, etc.). My personal favorite to use is the cloud, because one can go *through* a cloud, be *under* a cloud, move *about* a cloud, come *from* a cloud, travel *within* a cloud, go *to* a cloud, etc. As I also explain to my own students, the rule that sentences should never end in prepositions is not some arbitrary invention of difficult English teachers, but rather a sensible necessity; after all, if a preposition is a relationship word, then ending a sentence with one leaves an incomplete relationship, akin to beginning or ending a sentence with a conjunction.

pronoun: A pronoun's purpose is to replace or stand in for a noun. For example, one can say "it" rather than "the table," "her" rather than "Betsy Ross," and "they" rather than "the citizens of South Korea." Possessive pronouns, such as "his" and "my," have a self-explanatory classificatory name.

pronoun agreement: Pronoun agreement errors occur when pronouns are used incorrectly relative to other portions of sentences. For example, the sentence "A good student always does their homework" misuses the plural possessive pronoun "their" alongside the singular "good student"; in this case, the gender-neutral and singular "his or her" should be substituted for "their" in order to make the subject and predicate agree grammatically.

punctuation error: A punctuation error occurs when punctuation marks, from commas to colons to quotation marks, are misused. Although several specific errors (e.g., comma splices) can technically be classified as punctuation errors, this term is a large and rather unspecific umbrella that should be avoided if more particular names for errors exist; in other words, choose to label a comma splice as such, rather than as a general punctuation error.

redundancy: Redundancy is the stating or inclusion of things more times than necessary. The directive "quickly speed to the bank" and the phrase "close proximity" are redundant, as there surely is no other way to speed than quickly, so the adverb is unnecessary, and there is no proximity that is not, by definition, close.

seesaw conjunction: I personally prefer this self-explanatory term, which draws its commonsense name from playground equipment; nevertheless, see *correlative conjunction*.

split infinitive: An infinitive verb in any language is unconjugated. It is neither past tense nor present, neither singular nor plural, neither masculine nor feminine . . . it is simply the purest form of a verb. In English, infinitives take the form of the word "to" plus the verbal component (e.g., "to swim," "to languish," "to require," and "to be"). Although composed of two separate words, an infinitive is technically one complete verb, and it therefore should never be split down the middle by an adverb, which results in a split infinitive.

subject-verb agreement: Errors arise when subjects of sentences do not agree with their verbal predicates, often because of singular vs. plural issues. In the sentence "My father, along with my three brothers and I, are going fishing," the singular subject "father" disagrees with the plural verb "are," which should be singularized for correctness.

syntax: Syntax is the placement of words in a particular order to create meaning. Syntax can be orthodox (e.g., "put your weapon away, for I mean you no harm") or uncommon (e.g., "away your weapon put, for no harm I mean you"), but syntactical errors occur when accepted rules of common English syntax are violated, as with split infinitives.

unattributed pointing pronoun: Demonstrative (a.k.a. pointing) pronouns—"this," "that," "those," and "these"—always need to point *at* particular nouns, either immediately following or in proximity, for the sake of clarity. Such pronouns that do not precede nouns are vague, being unattributed to their objects, and thus qualify as grammatical errors.

unclear referent: This error concerns pronouns that are ambiguous (i.e., when sentences include pronouns that either refer to nothing in particular or refer unclearly to one of several other parts of the sentence, such as nouns). For example, in the sentence "Joey respected Michael Jordan because he loved basketball," the pronoun "he" can legitimately be interpreted as referring either to Joey or to Michael Jordan; this referent is therefore unclear.

verb: A verb is commonly understood and defined by students as an action, something that is done. Expansively, verbs are parts of speech that can express not only action, but also existence or occurrence, and their forms change when conjugated. "To be," "sit," "writes," "had," and "will swim" are examples of verbal forms.

Resources for
Further Study

Anderson, S. R. (1992). *A-morphous morphology*. Cambridge, England: Cambridge University Press.

Anttila, R. (1989). *Historical and comparative linguistics: Current issues in linguistric theory*. New York, NY: John Benjamins.

Bauer, L. (1983). *English word-formation*. Cambridge, England: Cambridge University Press.

Becker, B. (1990). Coaching for the Scholastic Aptitude Test: Further synthesis and appraisal. *Review of Educational Research, 60,* 373–417.

Becker, W. C. (1977). Teaching reading and language to the disadvantaged: What we have learned from field research. *Harvard Educational Review, 47,* 518–543.

Chomsky, N. (1965). *Aspects of the theory of syntax*. Cambridge, MA: MIT Press.

Davis, G. A., & Rimm, S. B. (1998). *Education of the gifted and talented* (4th ed.). Needham Heights, MA: Allyn & Bacon.

Flick, L. (1991). Where concepts meet percepts: Stimulating analogical thought in children. *Science Education, 75,* 215–230.

Fowler, T. W. (1975). *An investigation of the teacher behavior of wait-time during an inquiry science lesson*. Paper presented at the annual meeting of the National Association for Research in Science Teaching, Los Angeles, CA. (ERIC Document Reproduction Service No. ED108872)

Fromkin, V., & Rodman, R. (1998). *An introduction to language* (6th ed.). Orlando, FL: Harcourt Brace.

Gierl, M. J., Tan, X., & Wang, C. (2005). *Identifying content and cognitive dimensions on the SAT*. College Board Research Report No. 2005-11. New York, NY: College Board.

Gove, P. B. (Ed.). (1993). *Webster's third new international dictionary of the English language, unabridged*. Springfield, MA: Merriam-Webster.

Horrocks, G. (1987). *Generative grammar*. New York, NY: Longman.

Jensen, J. T. (1990). *Morphology: Word structure in generative grammar*. Philadelphia, PA: John Benjamins.

Lawrence, I. M., Rigol, G. W., Van Essen, T., & Jackson, C. A. (2003). *A historical perspective on the content of the SAT*. College Board Research Report No. 2003-3. New York, NY: College Board.

Mason, L. (1994). Cognitive and metacognitive aspects in conceptual change by analogy. *Instructional Science, 22,* 157–187.

Matthews, P. H. (1974). *Morphology: An introduction to the theory of word-structure*. Cambridge, England: Cambridge University Press.

McKeown, M. G., & Curtis, M. E. (Eds.). (1987). *The nature of vocabulary acquisition*. Hillsdale, NJ: Lawrence Erlbaum.

Morgan, R. (1989). *An examination of the relationships of academic coursework with admissions test performance*. College Board Report No. 89-6. New York, NY: College Board.

Paul, R. (1992). *Critical thinking: What every person needs to survive in a rapidly changing world*. Rohnert Park, CA: Foundation for Critical Thinking.

Pinker, S. (1994). *The language instinct: How the mind creates language*. New York, NY: HarperPerennial.

Powers, D. E. (1982). *Estimating the effects of various methods of preparing for the SAT*. College Board Report No. 82-2. New York, NY: College Board.

Powers, D. E. (1986). Relations of test item characteristics to test preparation/test practice effects: A quantitative summary. *Psychological Bulletin, 100,* 67–77.

Powers, D. E., & Alderman, D. L. (1983). Effects of test familiarization on SAT performance. *Journal of Educational Measurement, 20,* 71–79.

Pyles, T., & Algeo, J. (1993). *The origins and development of the English language* (4th ed.). New York, NY: Harcourt Brace.

Ross, B. H. (1984). Remindings and their effects in learning a cognitive skill. *Cognitive Psychology, 16,* 371–416.

Sathy, V., Barbuti, S., & Mattern, K. (2006). *The new SAT and trends in test performance*. Retrieved from http://professionals.collegeboard.com/data-reports-research/cb/new-sat-trends-performance

Schrader, W. B. (1984). *Three studies of SAT-verbal item types.* College Board Report No. 84-7. New York, NY: College Board.

Spencer, A. (1991). *Morphological theory: An introduction to word structure in generative grammar*. Oxford, England: Basil Blackwell.

Stahl, S. A., & Fairbanks, M. M. (1986). The effects of vocabulary instruction: A model-based meta-analysis. *Review of Educational Research, 56,* 72–110.

VanTassel-Baska, J. (1986). Effective curriculum and instructional models for talented students. *Gifted Child Quarterly, 30,* 164–169.

References

Alexander, P. A. (1984). Training analogical reasoning skills in the gifted. *Roeper Review, 6,* 191–193.

Armbruster, B. B., Anderson, T. H., & Meyer, J. L. (1991). Improving content-area reading using instructional graphics. *Reading Research Quarterly, 26,* 393–416.

Bruno, L. (2006). *More universities are going SAT-optional.* Retrieved from http://www.usatoday.com/news/education/2006-04-04-standardized-tests_x.htm

Chen, Z. (1996). Children's analogical problem solving: The effects of superficial, structural, and procedural similarity. *Journal of Experimental Child Psychology, 62,* 410–431.

Dagher, Z. R. (1994). Does the use of analogies contribute to conceptual change? *Science Education, 78,* 601–614.

Gajilan, A. C. (2009). *Chew on this: Gum may be good for body, mind.* Retrieved from http://www.cnn.com/2009/HEALTH/04/22/chewing.gum.benefits/index.html

Landau, E. (2008). *More colleges move toward optional SATs.* Retrieved from http://www.cnn.com/2008/US/05/30/test.drop/index.html

Macklin, M. C. (1996). Preschoolers' learning of brand names from visual cues. *Journal of Consumer Research, 23,* 251–261.

Marzano, R. J., Pickering, D. J., & Pollock, J. E. (2001). *Classroom instruction that works: Research-based strategies for increasing student achievement.* Alexandria, VA: Association for Supervision and Curriculum Development.

Mayer, R. E. (1989). Models for understanding. *Review of Educational Research, 59,* 43–64.

Newby, T. J., Ertmer, P. A., & Stepich, D. A. (1995). Instructional analogies and the learning of concepts. *Educational Technology Research and Development, 43,* 5–18.

Newton, D. P. (1994). Pictorial support for discourse comprehension. *British Journal of Educational Psychology, 64,* 221–229.

Powell, G. (1980). *A meta-analysis of the effects of "imposed" and "induced" imagery upon word recall.* Paper presented at the annual meeting of the National Reading Conference, San Diego, CA. (ERIC Document Reproduction Service No. ED199644)

Powers, D. E., & Rock, D. A. (1998). *Effects of coaching on SAT I: Reasoning test scores.* College Board Report No. 98-6. New York, NY: College Board.

Pruitt, N. (1993). *Using graphics in content area subjects.* Master's thesis, Kean College of New Jersey. (ERIC Document Reproduction Service No. ED355483)

Roan, S. (2009). *Chewing gum raises kids' math scores.* Retrieved from http://latimesblogs.latimes.com/booster_shots/2009/04/chewing-gum-raises-kids-math-scores.html

Rowe, M. (1974). Wait-time and rewards as instructional variables, their influence on language, logic, and fate control. Part one: Wait-time. *Journal of Research in Science Teaching, 11,* 81–94.

Swift, J. N., & Gooding, C. T. (1983). Interaction of wait time feedback and questioning instruction on middle school science teaching. *Journal of Research in Science Teaching, 20,* 721–730.

Tobin, K. (1987). The role of wait time in higher cognitive level learning. *Review of Educational Research, 57,* 69–95.

About the Author

R. Brigham Lampert is dual-certified in English and gifted education, and is one of fewer than 50 Teachers as Leaders endorsed by the Virginia Department of Education. A National Board Certified Teacher, Lampert has been nominated by students and parents alike for several national commendations, including a 2006 Disney Teacher Award and a 2008 Claes Nobel Educator of Distinction selection by the National Society of High School Scholars. He is the author of *Advanced Placement Classroom: Romeo and Juliet*, also available from Prufrock Press, of original poems in national publications such as *Möbius* and the *Parnassus Literary Journal*, and of numerous curricula published in conjunction with the Center for Gifted Education at the College of William and Mary, including six Shakespearean *Navigator* titles and three updated editions of the Center's award-winning literature units for gifted learners.

Lampert is currently pursuing his Ed.D. in curriculum leadership at the College of William and Mary, where he both earned his M.Ed. and was awarded a scholarship for Excellence in Gifted Education. He received his B.A. in English from Haverford College. Additionally trained as a building administrator, Lampert has chosen to remain a classroom teacher at Jamestown High School in Williamsburg, VA, where he chairs the English department, serving as its curriculum leader. He and his family reside in Williamsburg.

Common Core State Standards Alignment

Grade Level	Common Core State Standards
Grade 7 ELA-Literacy	L.7.2 Demonstrate command of the conventions of standard English capitalization, punctuation, and spelling when writing.
	L.7.4 Determine or clarify the meaning of unknown and multiple-meaning words and phrases based on grade 7 reading and content, choosing flexibly from a range of strategies.
	L.7.5 Demonstrate understanding of figurative language, word relationships, and nuances in word meanings.
Grade 8 ELA-Literacy	L.8.1 Demonstrate command of the conventions of standard English grammar and usage when writing or speaking.
	L.8.2 Demonstrate command of the conventions of standard English capitalization, punctuation, and spelling when writing.
	L.8.4 Determine or clarify the meaning of unknown and multiple-meaning words or phrases based on grade 8 reading and content, choosing flexibly from a range of strategies.
	L.8.5 Demonstrate understanding of figurative language, word relationships, and nuances in word meanings.
Grade 9-10 ELA-Literacy	L.9-10.4 Determine or clarify the meaning of unknown and multiple-meaning words and phrases based on grades 9–10 reading and content, choosing flexibly from a range of strategies.
	L.9-10.5 Demonstrate understanding of figurative language, word relationships, and nuances in word meanings.

Grade Level	Common Core State Standards
Grade 9-10 ELA-Literacy, *continued*	L.9-10.6 Acquire and use accurately general academic and domain-specific words and phrases, sufficient for reading, writing, speaking, and listening at the college and career readiness level; demonstrate independence in gathering vocabulary knowledge when considering a word or phrase important to comprehension or expression.
Grade 11-12 ELA-Literacy	L.11-12.2 Demonstrate command of the conventions of standard English capitalization, punctuation, and spelling when writing.
	L.11-12.4 Determine or clarify the meaning of unknown and multiple-meaning words and phrases based on grades 11–12 reading and content, choosing flexibly from a range of strategies.
	L.11-12.6 Acquire and use accurately general academic and domain-specific words and phrases, sufficient for reading, writing, speaking, and listening at the college and career readiness level; demonstrate independence in gathering vocabulary knowledge when considering a word or phrase important to comprehension or expression.

Printed in the United States
by Baker & Taylor Publisher Services

Printed in the United States
by Baker & Taylor Publisher Services